ROUTLEDGE LIBRARY EDITIONS: DEMOGRAPHY

I0131233

Volume 5

WEST EUROPEAN POPULATION CHANGE

WEST EUROPEAN POPULATION CHANGE

Edited by
ALLAN FINDLAY
AND
PAUL WHITE

Routledge
Taylor & Francis Group
LONDON AND NEW YORK

First published in 1986 by Croom Helm Ltd

This edition first published in 2024
by Routledge
4 Park Square, Milton Park, Abingdon, Oxon OX14 4RN

and by Routledge
605 Third Avenue, New York, NY 10158

Routledge is an imprint of the Taylor & Francis Group, an informa business

British Library Cataloguing in Publication Data
A catalogue record for this book is available from the British Library

ISBN: 978-1-032-53819-8 (Set)
ISBN: 978-1-032-55020-6 (Volume 5) (hbk)
ISBN: 978-1-032-55025-1 (Volume 5) (pbk)
ISBN: 978-1-003-42861-9 (Volume 5) (ebk)

DOI: 10.4324/9781003428619

Publisher's Note
The publisher has gone to great lengths to ensure the quality of this reprint but points out that some imperfections in the original copies may be apparent.

Disclaimer
The publisher has made every effort to trace copyright holders and would welcome correspondence from those they have been unable to trace.

WEST EUROPEAN POPULATION CHANGE

Edited by ALLAN FINDLAY and PAUL WHITE

CROOM HELM
London • Sydney • Dover, New Hampshire

© 1986 Allan Findlay and Paul White
Croom Helm Ltd, Provident House, Burrell Row,
Beckenham, Kent BR3 1AT
Croom Helm Australia Pty Ltd, Suite 4, 6th Floor,
64-76 Kippax Street, NSW 2010 Australia

British Library Cataloguing in Publication Data

West European population change.
1. Europe—Population—History
I. Findlay, Allan M.   II. White, Paul,
1950-
    304.6′094   HB3581
    ISBN 0-7099-3667-2

Croom Helm, 51 Washington Street, Dover, New Hampshire 03820, USA

Library of Congress Cataloging-in-Publication Data

West European population change.

    Includes index.
    1. Europe—population.   2. Europe—census.   3. Europe
—statistical services.   I. Findlay, Allan M.
II. White, Paul D. Phil.
HB3581.W47   1986   304.6′094   86-8823
ISBN 0-7099-3667-2

Typeset in 10pt Times Roman by Leaper & Gard Ltd, Bristol, England
Printed and bound in Great Britain
by Billing & Sons Limited, Worcester.

CONTENTS

List of Figures   vii

List of Tables   x

Preface   xiii

Part 1

1. The 1980–1982 European Census Round:
    An Evaluation of the Census as a Data Source
    Allan Findlay   1

2. Household Trends Within Western Europe
    1970–1980 *Ray Hall*   18

3. Counterurbanisation in Western Europe
    Anthony Fielding   35

4. International Migration in the 1970s: Revolution
    or Evolution? *Paul White*   50

Part 2

5. Denmark *Yvonne Court*   81

6. Eire *John Coward*   102

7. France *Philip Ogden and Hilary Winchester*   119

8. The Federal Republic of Germany *Jürgen Bähr
    and Paul Gans*   142

9. Italy *Russell King*   163

10. Portugal *John Dewdney and Paul White*   187

11. Great Britain *Anthony Champion*   208

Part 3

12. The Course of Future Change in European
    Populations *Allan Findlay and Paul White*   233

Notes on Contributors   248

Index   249

FIGURES

2.1 Female activity rates in the countries of the European Community 1970–83   31

3.1 Migration and settlement size 1950s to 1980s: A possible sequence   36

3.2 The relationship between migration and settlement size: France 1954–82   38

3.3 Summary of evidence on counterurbanisation in Western Europe during the 1970s   41

4.1 Unemployment rates 1970–83, selected countries   55

4.2 Gross migration flows 1970–83, selected countries   68

5.1 Denmark: Population growth per annum 1930–82   82

5.2 Denmark: Total number of live births per annum 1960–82   83

5.3 Denmark: Age-specific fertility rates 1971–81   84

5.4 Denmark: Immigration and emigration 1970–82   87

5.5 Denmark: Foreign nationals resident in Denmark 1974–84   89

5.6 Denmark: Net migration by county 1970–82   91

5.7 Denmark: Percentage population change by municipality 1970–83   92

5.8 Denmark: Population change by component 1970–81   93

5.9 Denmark: Economically active population by sector 1955-81   99

6.1 Eire: Scales of data collection and the Irish counties and county boroughs   103

6.2 Eire: Age structure of the population 1961 and 1981   106

6.3 Eire: Variations in natural change, net migration and population change 1971–81   108

7.1 France: Total population by age and sex, 4 March 1982   122

7.2 France: Activity rates for women by age group 1962–82   124

7.3 France: Regional patterns of population change 1975–82   131

7.4   France: Evolution of population growth rates of
       rural and urban *communes* 1962–82   132
7.5   France: Sex ratios amongst foreign population in
       1982 compared with total population   137
7.6   France: Regional importance of foreigners as a
       percentage of total population 1982   138
8.1   Federal Republic of Germany: Population
       development 1971–84   143
8.2   Federal Republic of Germany: Natural population
       change 1815–1983   144
8.3   Federal Republic of Germany: Population change
       by *Länder* and *Regierungsbezirke* 1970–83   155
8.4   Federal Republic of Germany: Principal net
       migration streams between *Länder* 1980–82   157
8.5   Federal Republic of Germany: Migration to and
       from other European states (including Turkey)
       1960–83   158
9.1   Italy: Inter-censal population change by province
       1951–61   171
9.2   Italy: Inter-censal population change by province,
       1961–71   172
9.3   Italy: Inter-censal population change by province
       1971–81   173
9.4   Italy: Natural increase by province 1971–81   175
9.5   Italy: Net migration by province 1971–81   177
9.6   Italy: Annual emigration and return migration
       1946–82   183
10.1   Portugal: Administrative districts (*distritos*)   189
10.2   Portugal: Population density 1981   190
10.3   Portugal: Regional population change 1970–81   191
10.4   Portugal: Population trends by *distrito*, 1940–81   193
10.5   Portugal: Some regional indicators   195
10.6   Portugal: Patterns of emigration 1960–82   200
11.1   Great Britain: Annual population change, mid-1961
       to mid-1983   210
11.2   Great Britain: Population and migration;
       inter-censal changes 1971–81 and shifts 1961–81
       by counties and regions   216
11.3   Great Britain: Population change 1971–81 (by
       Local Labour Market areas) grouped by urban
       status   218

11.4 Great Britain: Age structure 1971 and 1981   220

11.5 Great Britain: Dependants per hundred persons of working age 1981   221

11.6 Great Britain: Residence-based unemployment rates 1981   224

11.7 Great Britain: New Commonwealth and Pakistan immigrants 1981   229

TABLES

1.1 Date of Census-taking in Western Europe   3
1.2 *De jure* and *de facto* populations in Italy 1951–1981   4
1.3 Availability of census data on sensitive issues in Western Europe   7
1.4 Availability of employment data by economic sectors and scale in West European censuses   11
1.5 Census data on internal migration in Western European censuses   13
2.1 Percentage change of population and households 1970–1980   22
2.2 Trends in household size 1960–1980   22
2.3 Size distribution of households c.1970 and c.1980   23
2.4 Percentage of households with children c.1970 and c.1980   26
2.5 Percentage of households which are families   26
2.6 Single-person households c.1980 and percentage of total households which are elderly one-person households   27
2.7 Age structure of one-person households c.1980   27
2.8 Percentage of elderly living alone: Great Britain and Italy 1980/81   28
4.1 Annual growth rates of Gross Domestic Product in real terms in Western Europe   53
4.2 Average annual growth rates of Gross Domestic Product in real terms, core and periphery Europe   54
4.3 Gross Domestic Product and industrial production increases 1970–83   57
4.4 The Netherlands: Migrant characteristics   70
4.5 Sweden: Net migration 1970–80   72
4.6 West Germany: Net migration 1970–80   73
4.7 Selected migrant flows 1970 and 1980   74
4.8 Foreign residents, selected countries 1970 and 1980   76
5.1 Denmark: Abortions and sterilisations 1973–82   85
5.2 Denmark: Life expectancy at birth 1931/5–1980/1   87
5.3 Denmark: Percentage of population living in urban areas of different population sizes   94

5.4   Denmark: Household size 1980 and 1984   95
5.5   Denmark: Relative distribution of family type by
      households 1980 and 1983   96
5.6   Denmark: Number of persons of working age and in
      the labour force 1971–81   96
5.7   Denmark: Female activity rates by age 1970–81   97
5.8   Denmark: Employed women as a percentage of the
      total number employed in each sector   99
6.1   Eire: Population change 1926–84   104
6.2   Eire: Population change by type of district 1971–81   113
7.1   France: Components of population increase   120
7.2   France: Unemployment   125
7.3   France: Population by household type 1982   127
7.4   France: Persons per household   128
7.5   France: Number of children per family   128
7.6   France: Dimensions and components of urban
      decline   133
7.7   France: Rural population change by type of
      commune 1975–82   134
7.8   France: Population composition by nationality 1982   135
7.9   France: Selected social indicators for households
      with a head of foreign nationality 1982   136
8.1   Federal Republic of Germany: Population
      projection estimates by age groups 1982–2030   147
8.2   Federal Republic of Germany: Population, labour
      force and employment 1961–83   148
8.3   Federal Republic of Germany: Gainfully employed
      persons by economic sectors   150
8.4   Federal Republic of Germany: Gainfully employed
      persons by employment status   151
8.5   Federal Republic of Germany: Private household
      structures 1961–82   151
8.6   Federal Republic of Germany: Foreign population
      by nationality   160
8.7   Federal Republic of Germany: Demographic
      structure and length of residence of the foreign
      population 1973 and 1983   160
9.1   Italy: Population characteristics from the 1981
      census   167
9.2   Italy: Employment structures 1951–81   169
9.3   Italy: Population of major cities 1951–81   179

9.4   Italy: Population of selected peri-urban *comuni*
      1951–81   180
9.5   Italy: Distribution of population amongst size classes
      of *comuni* 1971 and 1981   181
10.1 Portugal: Sectoral breakdown of Portuguese
      employment 1960–81   197
10.2 Portugal: Destinations of Portuguese legal emigrants
      1960–82   201
10.3 Portugal: Place of residence in 1973 by place of
      residence in 1981   205
11.1 Great Britain: Components of population change   212
11.2 Great Britain: Population change by region
      1961–81   214
11.3 Great Britain: Population distribution and change
      by type of functional region 1971 and 1981   219
11.4 Great Britain: Labour-force characteristics 1971
      and 1981   223
11.5 Great Britain: Usually resident population 1981 by
      country of birth   227
12.1 Projected West European populations 2000   237

PREFACE

The 1980–82 West European census round resulted in the creation of a vast data bank of valuable demographic, social and economic information about one of the world's major population groups. Collection of the data by a large number of independent nation-states has meant that the earliest analysis of these censuses has been at the level of individual states. The purpose of this volume is to attempt an international comparative analysis of trends in Western Europe in order to identify the macro-economic and demographic forces moulding the shape and distribution of Europe's population. This ambitious task was initially proposed by the Population Study Group of the Institute of British Geographers, and led to a workshop held at the University of Sheffield in March 1985 at which census experts on different West European countries met to analyse the common and divergent trends revealed by the recent census round. This book represents the development of the ideas which emerged at the initial workshop.

Emphasis is given to the geographical dimension of population trends often ignored in demographic studies. Analysis of the 1980--82 census round reveals that although similar national trends in household size, fertility levels and mobility patterns are shared by most European countries (Chapters 2, 3 and 4), regional patterns within and across national boundaries are also of significance. At a macro-scale it is also true that the location of nations relative to the economic core of Europe is a very important determinant of demographic trends.

It is hoped that the census results interpreted in this volume will be of particular interest to students of population geography as well as those concerned with the emergent character of West European economies. Those wishing only to examine census patterns in specific countries in the West European 'core' will find detailed analysis in Chapters 7, 8, 9 and 11, while representative case-studies of more 'peripheral' countries are also included (Chapters 5, 6 and 10). Throughout the book international comparison is encouraged by the conscious effort on the part of the contributors to consider common themes. Comparison between

the national case-studies is possible in terms of the following seven
topics: recent natural population change, changes in labour-force
characteristics, modifications in household composition, regional
differentials in population growth and decline, counterurbanisation
and population redistribution, international migration and the evolution of minority populations. The book avoids giving a long
historical perspective — this aspect of European populations being
more than adequately covered by other texts — and focuses
instead on the most recent census interval. It is the trends of the
1970s and early 1980s which are of the greatest importance to the
policy-maker.

The results of the 1980–82 census round identify the demographic characteristics of Western Europe's younger age-cohorts
who by the year 2000 will be seeking employment in the ever-
shrinking labour market. Equally relevant to the planner are the
trends revealed by the most recent census round in the demographic and socio-economic characteristics of Europe's immigrant
populations, with all the implications that these have for the
welfare of the large urban conurbations in which they live. More
difficult to define but also evident from the European census
round are the problems associated with the increasing numbers of
elderly persons in Western Europe. The final chapter seeks to
develop analysis of these and other trends which are likely to be
important aspects of Europe's future population structure. If in
drawing attention to the emergent characteristics of Western
Europe's population this book can in any way contribute to forward planning to the benefit of the Europeans of the year 2000 it
will have proved a most worthwhile task. Its broader aim remains
the propagation of a better understanding of 'Pan-European'
trends in population patterns and processes of the 1970s and early
1980s.

In preparing this volume the editors are particularly grateful to
the large number of demographers, population geographers and
census experts who provided information about European
censuses. Chapter 1 was made possible only by the co-operation of
many people across Europe who assisted the editors in undertaking a 'census' of censuses and alternative data sources. These
included Gordon Anderson, Jürgen Bähr, Tony Champion, Bosse
Chytraeus, Elizabeth Clutton, Yvonne Court, John Coward, John
Dewdney, Paul Gans, Herman Van der Haegen, Russell King,
Dietlinde Mühlgassner, Philip Ogden, Hans Solerød and Hilary

Winchester. Paul White translated Chapter 8 from German to English, while Barbara Bolt and Penny Shamma tackled the much harder translation of the editors' often illegible manuscript into an excellent typescript. The departments of Geography at the Universities of Glasgow and Sheffield provided considerable cartographic and photographic assistance in the production of this volume. Finally, we would like to thank the individual contributors without whose considerable co-operation this work would have been impossible.

Allan Findlay and Paul White

1 THE 1980–1982 EUROPEAN CENSUS ROUND: AN EVALUATION OF THE CENSUS AS A DATA SOURCE

Allan Findlay

Introduction

Europe is the home of modern census-taking. The earliest modern censuses are claimed by Iceland, Norway and Sweden in the eighteenth century, and most West European countries have been covered by detailed censuses since the early nineteenth. An appreciation of the value of census statistics, offering as they do a complete coverage of national populations, grew during the first half of the present century, so that across Europe censuses became longer and more comprehensive as census-takers sought to discover more of the characteristics of the populations under study. In the 1980s for the first time this trend has apparently been reversed, partly because of the increased availability of alternative data sources, which reduces the need for detailed and lengthy census investigation, and partly because of increasing public opposition to in-depth investigation of household and personal characteristics involving the use of census methods. This has led to divergent experiences across Europe in the quantity and quality of data published from the 1980–82 census round. In the early 1980s, West Germany and the Netherlands took no official censuses. The abandonment of the census in both countries resulted largely from public disquiet, although both also had very good registration data. In Denmark, the census of January 1981 was not a 'normal' enumeration, all the census-type information being derived from the country's system of continuous population registration. In the United Kingdom, the census was shorter than at any time since 1951, with fewer questions to be answered by individual respondents; while inversely in Spain the length of the census and the detailed scale at which data were published was still increasing relative to previous censuses.

The purpose of this chapter is to compare the quantity and quality of census data across the nations of Western Europe in the 1980s, and to evaluate the consequences of the divergent trends in

1

census-taking which have been outlined above. The data presented in tabulated form in this chapter was collected from a 'census of censuses', carried out in January 1985. Census-users from each of the West European countries were invited to complete a short questionnaire concerning the utility of census data in 'their' country. The micro-states of Andorra, Gibraltar, Liechtenstein and San Marino were excluded from the survey. It is difficult to summarise census data availability for so many countries in standardised tables, and although Tables 1.1 to 1.5 provide an overview of certain aspects of the availability of European census data, readers should consult the chapters of this book giving details on individual countries for more precise discussion of specific census questions.

Census Timing and Definitions

Despite the long history of European census-taking there have been few attempts to harmonise national censuses to permit international comparisons. Definitions, questions and even census timings have eluded most attempts at standardisation. For the 1980s, a European Community Directive (73/403/EEC) required that all member states of the European Community undertake a general population count between 1 March and 31 May 1981, yet as Table 1.1 indicates only half of the EEC member states complied with this proposal. Italy held its census in October 1981, while France was given permission to postpone its census until 1982 in order to maintain consistency in its unusual recent census interval of seven years. Amongst non-EEC members four held their national censuses in 1980, with the net result that the timing of the European census round was spread over a period of almost two years. Nevertheless this was an improvement from the situation in 1970–71, when France was completely deviant, holding one census in 1968 and another in 1975.

At a national level, comparison of census results through time is perhaps easier than across space. Table 1.1 indicates that in many states comparisons over a ten- or eleven-year period are possible, while in most of the Scandinavian countries a more frequent census interval permits even closer temporal monitoring of demographic and socio-economic change. Most countries succeeded in holding their censuses in the same month as the previous census;

but in Belgium, Denmark, Luxembourg, Portugal and Spain there was a slippage of three months or more, making comparisons between censuses very difficult. Even small changes in the timing of censuses have been shown to be critical in influencing demographic and economic patterns. In Greece, for example, the 1981 census was delayed by three weeks from the planned date (exactly ten years to the day from the date of the 1971 census) because of an earthquake. As a result of this delay the seasonal influx of tourists to the Aegean islands had commenced, inflating the population totals relative to the position in 1971. Kolodny (1983) also suggests that the delay in holding the 1981 census was responsible for the 'repopulation' of many pastoralist villages in the Peloponnese mountains, which in 1971 had been deserted.

A fundamental issue on which European census-takers have not yet reached agreement is the definition of which population should

Table 1.1: Date of Census-taking in Western Europe

	1970s (last census)	1980s	Census interval (years, months)
EEC Member states			
Belgium	31 Dec. 1970	1 Mar. 1981	10.3
Denmark[b,c]	1 July 1976	1 Jan. 1981	4.6
Eire[a]	5 April 1971	5 April 1981	10.0
France	20 Feb. 1975	4 Mar. 1982	7.0
W. Germany	27 May 1970	No census	—
Greece	14 Mar. 1971	5 April 1981	10.1
Italy	25 Oct. 1971	25 Oct. 1981	10.0
Luxembourg	31 Dec. 1970	31 Mar. 1981	10.3
Netherlands	28 Feb. 1971	No census	—
United Kingdom	26 Apr 1971	5 April 1981	10.0
Non-member states			
Austria	12 May 1971	12 May 1981	10.0
Finland	1 Jan. 1976	1 Nov. 1980	4.10
Norway[b]	1 Nov. 1970	1 Nov. 1980	10.0
Portugal	15 Dec. 1970	16 Mar. 1981	10.3
Spain	31 Dec. 1970	1 Mar. 1981	10.3
Sweden[b]	1 Nov. 1975	15 Sept. 1980	4.10
Switzerland	1 Dec. 1970	2 Dec. 1980	10.0

Notes: a. Eire also held a mini-census on 1 April 1979

b. Denmark, Finland and Sweden all held censuses in the early 1970s as well as the mid-70s

c. The last 'normal' Danish census was in 1971, with both the 1976 and 1981 censuses being based on register data

be enumerated. Census-users are mainly interested in the distribution of population by location of usual residence. This *de jure* definition is not easy to achieve, however, since it involves redistributing population from their location on the night of the census to their *de jure* address. Not surprisingly, some censuses produce population statistics only for the *de facto* distribution (actual distribution on census night). Finland, Greece and Switzerland publish data only on a *de facto* basis, while Austria, Belgium, Denmark, Norway and Sweden provide only *de jure* statistics. The remaining countries in Table 1.1 produce population tabulations on both definitions at a national level, while the majority choose a *de jure* basis for regionally disaggregated data. Britain, in switching from a *de facto* enumeration in 1971 to a *de jure* basis in 1981, has therefore come into line with the general practice of European census-taking, but in so doing has created problems of temporal comparability between the 1971 and 1981 detailed regional population counts. The *de jure/ de facto* definitional split is only one of many. In Britain, for example, the 1981 census published no less than four different figures for the population of each area (Glennie, 1985, p.6).

The statistical differences which emerge in population totals because of differences in definition can be shown to be very significant in those European countries producing data on both a *de jure* and *de facto* basis. Table 1.2 shows the differences in the population counts of the last four Italian censuses. Traditionally, Italy has had fewer people present at the census (*de facto*) than are normally resident (*de jure*) because of temporary emigration, but in 1981 the situation was reversed with a net inflow of temporary workers from abroad (see Chapter 9). Differences between *de jure*

Table 1.2: *De jure* and *de facto* Populations in Italy 1951–1981 (thousands)

Census	A *de jure* Total	B *de facto* Total	Difference (A-B)
4.11.51	47,516	47,159	+357
15.10.61	50,624	49,904	+720
25.10.71	54,137	53,745	+392
25.10.81	56,244	56,336	− 92

Source: Istat, 12° Censimento Generale della Popolazione, 25 October 1981, vol. 1

and *de facto* population totals become of even greater significance at a regional scale, where they reflect temporary population movements within a nation. For example, in the 1981 Spanish census the province of Madrid recorded 4,727,000 persons as present on census night compared with a population of 4,687,000 registered as normally resident there. Conversely, rural provinces such as Albacete had large deficits of population due to the temporary absence of persons on census night.

The Shape of European Censuses: Data Collection Constraints

The quality and quantity of European census data are influenced by the feasibility and accuracy of data collection under different systems of enumeration. Equally important in shaping European censuses are the costs of data collection and processing, and the relative efficiency with which data-users' needs can be met by census information compared with alternative data sources (Denham and Rhind, 1983, p. 19).

In the 1980s the majority of European censuses used enumerators to identify households but relied on the population to complete the census forms. In most countries self-enumeration was carried out by the head of household, but in France the concept of a 'reference person' was introduced (see Chapter 7). The quality of any census depends firstly on the ability of the national census organisation to identify effectively all living accommodation in an enumeration district and to define adequately the number of households living in a building; and secondly on the willingness and ability of the population being enumerated to complete the census forms. Even in countries with a long tradition of census-taking under-enumeration remains a problem. A post-enumeration survey in England and Wales suggests that as many as 296,000 people may have been overlooked by the 1981 census, with omissions being most severe in inner city areas (see Chapter 11). For example, the population of Inner London is estimated to be 2.5 per cent greater than that enumerated by the census.

The system of self-enumeration by heads of household depends on the literacy of the respondents and their willingness to complete the questionnaire. The presence of large immigrant minority populations in many of the north European countries presented a considerable problem in this respect. In England and Wales it was necessary to print the census forms in nine different languages and provide interpreters to ensure adequate coverage of immigrant groups (Dewdney, 1985). Immigrant workers are often eager to avoid enumeration because of uncertainty over their residence status and fear of repatriation. Ogden (1985) has shown, for example, that the French census of 1982 only identified 3.7 million foreign nationals, while the estimate produced by the French Ministry of the Interior in the same year placed the foreign population at a figure 0.7 million persons higher than that given by the census. King (1984) has identified similar discrepancies between the level of emigration recorded from Portugal, Spain and Italy and the volume of immigration from these countries reported by the French; but perhaps the greatest discrepancies in immigrant registration occur amongst France's North African population (Talha, 1983), which includes many second- and third-generation immigrants. The only European census specifically to ask a question about second-generation immigrants was in Switzerland, where coverage of immigrant issues by the census was particularly good compared with most other countries. Even although census coverage of foreign populations is less reliable than of most other issues, it is nevertheless critical that European censuses continue to seek to enumerate minority populations with the greatest possible care, since census data may often form the only complete survey of immigrant groups. For example, the EEC statistical organisation Eurostat was still making use of the Eire census of 1971 as recently as 1983, because this remained the single most reliable source for estimating the size of the foreign population living in the Republic of Ireland.

A severe problem in census-taking is the acceptability both of the census as an institution and of individual questions within the census. In Northern Ireland, for example, the political context at the time of the 1981 census led to a campaign of deliberate non-co-operation. In 1971 a poor response rate was recorded in Northern Ireland to the question on religious persuasion. By 1981 the non-response to this question had doubled, and, more seriously, enumerators were unable to visit approximately 10 per cent of households (Compton, 1985). As a result a special programme had to be mounted to persuade the estimated 48,000 households for which no census form was initially returned to participate in the census. The intense follow-up exercise reduced the level of under-enumeration to under 20,000 households by the end of 1981; and in 1982, after a further round of letters to non-respondents, only an estimated 6,000 households continued to refuse to complete the census. Although the final coverage of Northern Ireland by the census was very satisfactory given the circumstances, the very fact that there was initial resistance to the census remains a problem for census-users since it is difficult to be confident about the precise size of the population on census day as a result of the late return of so many census forms.

With the exception of Northern Ireland, the level of public co-operation in completing the British census was considerable, and compared with the 1971 census there was less support for groups such as the National Council for Civil Liberties who believe that a legally compulsory census questionnaire should be restricted to details of name, date of birth, sex and usual place of residence. This contrasts strongly with the situation in West Germany, where the opposition of similar civil rights groups led to the abandonment of the planned 1980 census altogether. Very considerable national variations exist within Europe concerning which census questions are considered sensitive and likely to arouse public opposition. Obvious issues on which national censuses differ are questions on income, religion and nationality. Table 1.3 summarises the shape of European censuses on these key topics. Only the Danish,

Table 1.3: Availability of Census Data on Sensitive Issues in Western Europe

	Income	Religion	Nationality/citizenship
Austria	No	Yes	Nationality
Belgium	No	No	Nationality
Denmark	Yes	No	No
Eire	No	Yes	Birthplace
Finland	Yes	No	Nationality
France	No	No	Nationality
Great Britain (England, Scotland and Wales)	No	No	Birthplace
Greece	No	No	—
Italy	No	No	Birthplace
Northern Ireland	No	Yes	Birthplace
Norway	Yes	Yes	Nationality
Portugal	No	Yes	Birthplace
Spain	No	No	Birthplace
Sweden	No	No	Nationality
Switzerland	No	Yes	Nationality

Finnish and Norwegian censuses offered information on personal household income, generally derived (as in the Finnish case) from adding tax register data to the census results for a given area. A number of countries make this information available in non-census publications. It is ironic that an absence of census questions on religion and nationality reflects two very different extremes: one in which population homogeneity nullifies the point in data collection and the second in which a sensitive split in the composition of the population makes precise enumeration of the characteristic unacceptable. This was the case, for example, with the abandonment of a language question from the Belgian census after 1946. No European censuses attempt to define population on a rigidly ethnic basis with questions about racial origin of the type included in Australian, South African and United States censuses (Saunders, 1978). Although the Office of Population Censuses and Surveys in Britain considered introducing an ethnic question in 1981, and strong arguments were presented to support the collection of this information, a pre-census test amongst the immigrant communities of Haringey showed that the question would probably encounter opposition and prejudice the success of the census. Approximately half of the European censuses inquired about nationality or citizenship, and the remainder were satisfied with birthplace information. Nationality data is likely to become of increasing importance: for example, in 1981 a third of the population of Luxembourg were non-nationals, the majority of immigrants coming from other EEC states (Eurostat, 1983). Birthplace information is clearly less valuable than nationality data since it fails to distinguish between nationals of a country who have been born abroad and foreign citizens who have subsequently migrated to the country. The distinction is important in the many European countries which during the 1970s experienced substantial return migration of 'colonists' from abroad, such as the Portuguese *retornados*. A further highly significant problem lies in using the available data to identify the second generation of migrant communities in countries where only birthplace data exist. In general it must be accepted that censuses are at their weakest as data bases for studies of minority populations; nevertheless they are often the only information sources that do exist.

Comparison of the data presented in Table 1.3, with information collated by Blake and Donovan (1971) for the 1960 European census round suggests that there has been little change in the pattern of census questions on income, religion and nationality over the last two decades. If any trend does exist it is towards greater caution on the part of the census-takers and greater sensitivity on the part of the populations being enumerated. The 1984 address to the Directors-General of the National Statistical Institutes of the European Community by the Director of the US Bureau of Census astutely expressed the census-taker's problem: 'Its Orwellian overtones and the menacing implications of technology require that we increase our efforts to convince individuals that they cannot be harmed by answering our census ...' (reported by Glennie, 1985, p. 6).

The majority of census topics are of course completely non-controversial, but many constraints other than public opinion operate to shape census design and coverage. The expense of census-taking limits the number of questions asked (because of the cost of processing extra information) and was one of the major factors encouraging the reduction in length of the British census in 1981 to only 16 questions for each individual person enumerated. This made the British census shorter than that of neighbouring states, such as Eire with its 22 questions. It is not simply the total cost of census-taking which is important (less than £1 a head in the United Kingdom in 1981), but the cost-effectiveness of the census relative to other forms of data collection (Ballard and Norris, 1983). The availability of even more detailed registration data in many European countries has somewhat undermined census-taking and has, indeed, led to its being discontinued in West Germany, Denmark and the Netherlands.

Census Coverage

Not surprisingly, all the census-taking countries publish data for the age, sex and marital status of their populations. This is available at national and regional levels, with slight variations occurring in the way the variables are cross-classified in provincial volumes of the census. There are even minor variations in how different countries set out to define age cohorts (Eurostat, 1983). One of the great strengths of censuses over other data sources is that they make available cross-tabulations of demographic and other variables at regional and often parish levels. Cross-tabulations of age, sex and marital status are published right down to parish

levels in Austria, Italy, Norway and Sweden, and the systems existing in many countries for producing census data disaggregated at a
fine spatial resolution through computer-readable small-area
statistics make the census a very useful information source for
regional studies. Also of value is the fact that many European censuses tabulate data in special volumes for urban agglomerations or
municipalities, such as Denmark, Eire, France, Great Britain,
Greece, Norway, Portugal, Spain, Sweden and Switzerland. These
tabulations are particularly useful when they extend to include data
on the labour force and housing conditions.

Table 1.4 attempts to analyse the scales at which employment
data are available in European census volumes. Employment
statistics are produced in many different forms: professional status,
occupation groupings, socio-economic categories and by type of
economic activity. Table 1.4 chooses the last of these measures and
indicates, with the exception of Portugal, that data on employment
by economic sectors is published at a county level (*département,
province*) across Europe. At more detailed levels coverage is
patchy, with the Nordic and Alpine countries apparently offering
the best employment data at parish level. Most countries also
cross-tabulated employment data on other variables such as age,
education level and marital status; and in Finland it is cross-
tabulated against income levels. It should be noted that employment data was one clear area where the shape of European
censuses reflected the presence or absence of other national
surveys. Those countries without other independent detailed manpower surveys often investigated employment issues in more
depth. Certain other countries, such as Italy, despite holding independent labour-force surveys, chose to enumerate employment
characteristics in detail in the census in order to check on the
accuracy of alternative sources.

All European censuses with the exception of Denmark's gave
information on household size categories. Considerable differences
existed, however, in the way the term 'household' was defined and
in the way family structure was analysed. These issues are not
discussed in detail here, since they are taken up in Chapter 2. In
general it would be fair to say that census information concerning
social structures was strongest in northern Europe; conversely, the
Mediterranean countries paid more attention to agricultural issues
such as land-holding.

No issue is examined in as many different ways as internal

Table 1.4: Availability of Employment Data by Economic Sectors and Scale in West European Censuses

Country	National	Regional (e.g. UK Standard Regions)	County	Urban agglomerations	Parish	Cross-tabulations of employment and other variables at country level
Austria	Yes	No	Yes	No	Yes	Yes
Belgium[a]	Yes	Yes	Yes	No	Yes	—
Denmark	Yes	No	Yes	Yes	Yes	Yes
Eire	Yes	Yes	Yes	Yes	No	Yes
England, Wales, Scotland	Yes	No	Yes	Yes	No	Yes
Finland	Yes	Yes	Yes	No	Yes	Yes
France	Yes	Yes	Yes	Yes	No	Yes
Greece[a]	Yes	Yes	Yes	Yes	No	Yes
Italy	Yes	Yes	Yes	No	Yes	Yes
Norway	Yes	No	Yes	No	No	No[b]
Northern Ireland	Yes	Yes	Yes	No	No	No
Portugal	Yes	Yes	No	No	No	No
Spain	Yes	Yes	Yes	Yes	Yes	Yes
Switzerland[a]	Yes	No	Yes	No	Yes	Yes
Sweden	Yes	No	Yes	Yes	Yes	Yes

Notes: a. Census volumes were not available at all scales at the time of writing. Results are based on the previous census
b. Cross-tabulation with sex, but without other non-employment variables

migration. As a result, comparability across Europe is extremely difficult. This is true not only because of the different definitions of internal migration used in different censuses, but also because migration statistics are highly sensitive to the size and shape of the administrative areas within which they are recorded (White, 1985). Table 1.5 shows that one of the most popular (and perhaps the least useful!) definitions of 'migrants' is as persons born outside their area of present residence. Just over half the European censuses inquired about the region or county of birth of the population. A migration measure of declining popularity is place of residence at the time of the previous census. This information was provided by a handful of countries, and in the case of Austria was the only measure of migration. Questions on migration from place of residence one and five years ago are of greater value to planners and academics, but these questions suffer from the problem of imprecise recall by respondents when asked about behaviour over abstract time periods. Inevitably, comparative analysis of European inter-regional migration matrices becomes very difficult with such a diverse range of definitions, but the fragmentary information which does exist is not to be spurned.

Census versus Registration and Survey Data

The absence of any censuses in West Germany and the Netherlands is a major problem for those undertaking comparative population analysis across Europe. Both countries have mandatory systems of registration for births, deaths, marriages, migration and several other issues but the type of data generated by these registration systems is different in quality and quantity from census data. In West Germany and the Netherlands, a wide range of demographic data are published annually in national yearbooks. West Germany produces this information at quite detailed geographical scales in its statistical yearbook (*Statistiches Jahrbuch Deutscher Gemeinden*). While the frequency with which such data can be made available is a clear advantage, the accuracy of registration systems is generally lower than that of censuses. Errors arise for a number of reasons, such as the problem of double counting which occurs when persons change residence more than once within the registration period. In Italy, the 1981 census showed that the registration statistics were grossly inflated due to

Table 1.5: Census Data on Internal Migration in West European Censuses

	Place of birth	Residence at previous census	Residence 5 years ago	Residence 1 year ago	Inter-regional matrices	Crosstab. with socioeconomic data
Austria	No	Yes	No	No	No	No
Belgium[a]	Yes	No	Yes	Yes	Yes	No
Denmark[b]	No	No	No	No	No	No
Eire	Yes	Yes	No	Yes	Yes	Yes
England, Wales and Scotland	No	No	No	Yes	Yes	Yes
Finland	No	No	No	No	No	No
France	Yes	Yes	No	No	Yes	Yes
Greece[a]	No	No	Yes	No	Yes	Yes
Italy	Yes	No	Yes	No	No	Yes
N. Ireland	Yes	Yes	Yes	Yes	Yes	Yes
Norway	No	No	No	No	No	No
Portugal[c]	No	No	Yes (8)	Yes (2)	No	Yes
Spain	Yes	Yes	No	No	Yes	Yes
Sweden	No	No	No	No	No	No
Switzerland	Yes	No	Yes	No	No	No

Notes: a. Data not yet published: table based on previous census
b. Register sources give data on a quarterly and annual basis
c. Figures in brackets refer to years

the failure of many migrants to deregister on departure from their place of previous residence (Eurostat, 1985). For this reason the census population totals given in Table 1.2 are at least one million persons less than the published registry figures for 1981 (Frey, 1983, p. 227), and the Italian government has required registry offices to revise their records in the light of the census results.

One considerable problem over the exclusive use of registration data concerns the limited range of cross-tabulations that may be available and, in particular, the difficulties of matching demographic data with other variables. Thus, for example, German researchers are finding that the impossibility of obtaining detailed information linking demographic and housing measures is a considerable drawback.

Nevertheless registration data can be of tremendous potential, and it is quite possible that more countries will in future follow the examples of Denmark and the Netherlands by dispensing with an enumerated census and relying instead on their registration records supplemented with occasional sample surveys or 'microcensuses'. The British General Household Survey is a variant of this type of sample census. This survey is interviewer-administered and consequently has been used to provide information on apparent ethnicity that cannot be obtained from the normal census (Peach, 1985).

The most significant use of registration data is as a replacement for census questions on recent migration. Thus certain countries in Table 1.5 which produce no census data on migration have no need of it because of the exceptional quality of their continuous registration data on this topic. Finland produces perhaps the best migration data, even publishing annual data on moves within administrative parishes so that the usual definition of migration as moves across administrative borders is further refined. Other countries with high-quality information on internal movement from registration data include Sweden, Norway, Belgium, Denmark, West Germany and the Netherlands. Italy, on the other hand, has a registration system of doubtful accuracy (see Chapter 9). France has no such data source, whilst in Britain the only available information is that obtained from the National Health Service Central Register (Stillwell, 1985).

Carefully controlled sample surveys will always be able to produce more detailed information on a restricted topic area, and they will be able to do so more quickly and more cheaply than the census. Increasingly academics and planners require this information to supplement the census results, and to update their information bases. Sample surveys should, however, be seen as complementary to rather than competitive with the census. By definition a sample covers only part of the population, and if the sample is to be useful it must relate to a reliable sampling-frame of the type provided by the census, with its complete coverage of the population. To the geographer the census is of particular value since it offers information at very detailed geographical scales giving insights which can seldom be gleaned from national sample surveys. Examples of work at these scales include Visvalingam's (1976) study of regional variations in sex ratios and Coulter's (1978) study of the population characteristics of inner city areas. To the planner, geographically disaggregated data will always be essential. Locational decisions, whether they be for hospitals, schools or superstores, require comparative data at appropriate levels of spatial disaggregation.

Inevitably, the census provides only a temporal snapshot of population and labour 'stocks' at one point in time. Surveys during the inter-censal period are necessary to provide 'flow' information about demographic and socio-economic processes. The more diverse, both structurally and geographically, a population is the more difficult it is to carry out reliable sample surveys (as has been shown recently with regard to British political opinion polls relative to national voting patterns). When this problem is extended to the continental scale the problem of establishing adequate sampling-frames increases, especially given the lack of standardisation in census definitions and procedures. The sampling problem at the European scale therefore strengthens the case for producing reliable census data. Such data are required firstly because of the increased need for reliable census 'snapshots' in the absence of Pan-European sample surveys and secondly as a mechanism permitting improvements in European survey methods. Herein lies a paradox, since the better the census coverage the better the sampling-frame and consequently the less immediate the need for a further census round!

In addition to the completeness of coverage offered by censuses, several other advantages exist which should ensure the continuation of censuses into the twenty-first century. The relative continuity of census questions from decade to decade give censuses an immense value in monitoring long-term changes. Census-takers constantly face a tension in census design between modifying census procedures so as to monitor contemporary processes more precisely and maintaining census definitions and questions (and enumeration boundaries) so as to permit inter-censal comparisons. Censuses offer a unique opportunity to examine interrelationships between a wide range of socio-economic and demographic variables at geographically disaggregated scales, in a way that is not possible from comparing independent specialist sample surveys. While sample surveys are of great value to their designers, they are generally of much less value to other information-users than is a multi-purpose census data base. The information gaps and comparability problems which have arisen in non-census-taking countries are considerable, and it is interesting to note that West Germany has now rescheduled its census to occur in 1986.

It is possible to argue that census-taking in the future will become a more rather than less attractive method of data collection. The possibility of linking census data to other geo-graphical information systems makes the utility of census data greater than ever before, while technical advances in processing census information make it likely that census results will become available much more quickly in future. If these advances in census-taking are to be realised they will have to be matched by similar progress in making censuses acceptable to the public. Public dis-quiet over the possible negative consequences of data-rich geo-graphical information systems must be reduced through the efforts of census-users in publicising the benefits which arise from census data, through the improved capacities which result for equitable and efficient resource allocation by government and private bodies.

This chapter has argued that, despite difficulties in comparing census data compiled in different European countries, meaningful comparisons are possible on a wide range of variables for many of the European states. Although much work remains to be done in harmonising the data quality and quantity of European censuses, the 1980–82 census round provides evidence that some progress is possible towards standardising definitions and census method-ologies. The task now falls to census-users to demonstrate the unique value of recent European censuses in making international comparisons of demographic, social and economic trends.

Acknowledgements

The author would like to thank John Coward, Anthony Champion and Paul White for helpful comments on an earlier version of this chapter.

References

Ballard, B. and Norris, P. (1983) 'User's needs: an overview' in D. Rhind (ed.) *A Census User's Handbook*, pp. 89–113 Methuen, London, Blake, J. and Donovan, J. (1971) *West European Censuses, 1960*, University of California Press, Berkeley

Compton, P. (1985) 'The 1981 Northern Ireland Census of Population — estimates of non-enumerated population', *Stormont Policy Planning and Research Unit Social Division, Occasional Paper, 9*, 24–45

Coulter, J. (1978) 'Grid square census data as a source for the study of deprivation in British conurbations', *Census Research Unit Working Paper, 13*, Department of Geography, University of Durham

Denham, J. and Rhind, D. (1983) 'The 1981 census and its results' in D. Rhind (ed.), *A Census User's Handbook*, Methuen, London, 17–87

Dewdney, J. (1985) *The UK Census of 1981* (Catmog Series, 43), Geobooks, Norwich

Eurostat (1983) *Demographic Statistics 1981*, Eurostat, Luxembourg

Eurostat (1985) *Demographic Statistics 1983*, Eurostat, Luxembourg

Frey, L. (1983) 'Census development and labour market analysis', *Review of Economic Conditions in Italy, 83(2)*, 223–48

Glennie, C. (1985) 'Shaping the next census', *Population Trends, 39*, 5–7

King, R. (1984) 'Population mobility: emigration, return migration and internal migration', in A. Williams (ed.), *Southern Europe Transformed*, Harper & Row, London, pp. 145–78

Kolodny, E. (1983) 'Evolution récente et répartition spatiale de la population en Grèce (1951–1981)', *Méditerranée, 50*, 43–50

Ogden, P. (1985) 'France: recession, politics and migration policy', *Geography, 70*, 24–35

Peach, C. (1985) 'Immigrants and the 1981 urban riots in Britain' in G.A. Van der Knaap and P. White (eds.), *Contemporary Studies in Migration*, Geobooks, Norwich, 143-54

Saunders, C. (1978) *Census 1981 — Question on Racial and Ethnic Origin*, Runnymede Trust, London

Stillwell, J. (1985) 'Migration between metropolitan and non-metropolitan regions in the UK' in G.A. Van der Knaap and P. White (eds.), *Contemporary Studies of Migration*, Geobooks, Norwich, 7-26

Talha, L. (ed.) (1983) *Maghrébins en France*, CNRS, Paris

Van der Haegen, H. (1983) *Atlas Statistique du Recensement de la Population et des Logements 1981*, INS, Brussels

Visvalingam, M. (1976) 'Chi-square as an alternative to ratios for statistical mapping and analysis', *Census Research Unit Working Paper, 8*, Department of Geography, University of Durham

White, P. (1985) 'Levels of intra-urban migration in West European cities', *Espace, Populations, Sociétés, 1*, 161–9

2 HOUSEHOLD TRENDS WITHIN WESTERN EUROPE 1970-1980

Ray Hall

Introduction

In comparison with that of other world regions the European household has shown distinctive and diverse characteristics from an early date, the historical evolution of which has been increasingly investigated (Hajnal, 1965; Laslett, 1972; Anderson, 1980; Mitterauer and Sieder, 1982; Goody, 1983). The past two decades in particular have seen an acceleration of trends leading to a convergence of household patterns over a wide area, away from the heterogeneity that was evident as recently as the 1960s.

Two distinct family household models were identified as existing in Europe in the 1970s, characterised by smaller and by larger average household sizes respectively (Eurostat, 1982). Smaller households result from the trends leading to fewer children, mononuclear and single-person households. These are characteristic of countries with more developed economies. Conversely, larger average household sizes are characteristic of newly industrialising or still basically agricultural countries. The two models can be seen as successive phases in household development as predominantly agricultural economies give way to industrialised economies and as traditional cultures break down (Eurostat, 1982).

The modern European household is therefore rapidly assuming common characteristics which can be readily appreciated by analysis of 1980s census data. At the same time transformations are taking place within the household so that, for example, the head of the household can no longer be regarded as the representative of the social, economic and occupational status of the household. Increasingly, all members have a degree of social and economic independence.

The main points to be considered in this chapter are: data and definitions; trends in average household size and the size distributions of households; and some consideration of the processes involved in these changes especially with reference to the family household and one-person household.

Data and Definitions

The study of households, along with nuptiality, is one of the least developed in demography, and to a large extent this is a function of lack of data. As the introductory chapter of this volume shows, census data vary in quality and quantity, and international data are even more limited. Within Europe, population censuses with a reasonable range of data on households include those of Great Britain, Finland, France, Italy, Sweden and Switzerland, but 1980 census data were not collected in West Germany, Denmark and the Netherlands.

The limitations of censuses are well recognised and national sample surveys are becoming important for a wide range of population data, especially household-type information. More questions can be asked in depth and at more frequent intervals, such as in Britain's General Household Survey (GHS), which from 1971 has sampled private households to provide a range of published and unpublished household and other social data. The sample size of 14,564 households in 1981 was reduced to 12,480 in 1982 as part of the economies in the Government's Statistical Service (GHS, 1984, p. 1). The Netherlands held the *Woningbehoeftenonderzoek* (Dwelling Needs Inquiry) in 1981 to compensate for the lack of data normally provided by the census. A volume on households was part of this survey.

Within the member-states of the European Community, a household survey has to be held every two years (from 1973) in conjunction with the labour force sample survey. With the exception of Denmark, results from the mid-1970s surveys (along with the 1970 censuses) appeared in 1982 in a Eurostat publication which acknowledged that 'the need for statistics on families is becoming more and more urgent' (Eurostat, 1982).

Even using survey data, it is not possible to study easily the dynamics of the household and especially the nuclear family within the household, in the way that births, marriages and deaths can be studied (Murphy, 1983, pp. 50–70). Surveys tend to concentrate on one member of the household, usually defined as the 'head', who is of decreasing relevance when it comes to defining the characteristics of contemporary households. Indeed the household itself is often inadequately defined, and there is little evidence of harmonisation of definitions within the European Community. For example, the definition of the household used in the censuses of

Britain, France, Switzerland and Finland changed in 1980/2 from that of 1970/5. Within Great Britain, household definitions varied as between the Labour Force Survey (LFS), the General Household Survey and the census. In 1981 a new common definition was adopted, the effect of which was to reduce the number of households recorded, possibly by 100,000 households, in the grossed LFS results.

A family — related by kinship — is different from the household — connected by place of residence, and while in most censuses it is possible to differentiate the family from the household, this is not always so. And some, such as the Italian census, using the word *famiglie* (families) define the household in terms of the family. In general, where the family is separately defined it cannot span more than two generations. In the British census, for example, parents living in a household with their married children and their offspring would not be counted as family members.

Traditionally in household analysis, most emphasis has been put on the head of household, which means that households are often classified by the characteristics of the head. But 'head of household' is a term undergoing considerable change at present. In general, the head of household is defined as the person making the major economic contribution to the household. In Belgium, for example, the head was defined (in 1970) as the person who exercises the greatest authority; some other countries' censuses state that it is the person designated as such, although in the case of a married couple living together it is the husband who is chosen (e.g. Switzerland; the Netherlands in 1971). The British census differentiates between the head of household, who is the person entered in the first column of the census form, provided he or she is over 16 and the head of family, who in the case of a couple is assumed to be the husband. The General Household Survey (1982, p. 255) defines the head of household in order of preference as 'the husband of the person, or the person who: owns the household accommodation, or is legally responsible for the rent of the accommodation...'

But new terminology is emerging, as is apparent from the 1980 census round. The 1980 Swedish census dispensed with the term 'head of household', along with the idea of defining household members in relation to the head of household, in favour of the term 'reference person', which could refer to the cohabiting couple or other individuals where applicable. Remaining household members were classified respectively as 'children', 'other members of the household' and 'unknown'. Finland's 1980 census also used the term 'reference person' as interchangeable with 'head of household', who was still the person mainly responsible for providing the earnings of the household.

In France, *personne de référence de ménage* replaced the term *chef de ménage*. But in order to make results comparable with earlier censuses, the eldest occupied person was selected in households with no families; and in families, the adult male was chosen. The rest of the household members were then classified according to their relationship with the reference person. Terminology changed in West Germany in 1984, when the statistical yearbook (*Statistiches Jahrbuch Deutscher Gemeinden*) used the term *Bezugsperson* (reference person) to replace *Haushaltsvorstandes* (head of household).

It seems then, that while the terms may be changing, in general the reference person is still defined in ways that mean that the majority will continue to be men in mixed sex adult households.

Similarly, attitudes and therefore data, on cohabiting couples vary. In Sweden cohabiting couples are included with married couples. Elsewhere in Scandinavia, cohabiting couples with children are included with married couples. The Finnish census (1975) noted that 'the head of household and the spouse were not necessarily married to each other.' France noted the problem of defining marital status for certain people where only three responses were possible: single, married or divorced.

Even the meaning of the term 'child' varies among censuses. In some it is all unmarried children living in the parental home whatever their age, as in Italy; in some there is an age limit (under 25 in the case of France), and in Britain amongst others, dependent children are separated out from independent children. Classifications of households also vary among censuses as shown by Appendix 2.1.

Trends in Household Size and Size Distribution

As Table 2.1 shows, there has been a much more rapid percentage increase in the numbers of households between 1970 and 1980 than of total population numbers. At one extreme, in Switzerland the increase in the number of households was twelve times greater than for the population as a whole; whereas in Ireland the ratio approached parity. This more rapid increase in household numbers is reflected in the decline of average household size throughout Western Europe between 1970 and 1980. Most countries experienced a decline of between 0.3 and 0.5 persons; the largest decline was in Greece, followed by the Netherlands and Finland, and (apart from Spain, 0.02) the smallest declines were in Great Britain, followed by Ireland and Belgium. So of the 14 countries shown in Table 2.2 eight had an average household size

Table 2.1: Percentage Change of Population and Households 1970–80

	Population	Households
Finland (70–80)	4.1	17.3
France (68–82)	9.2	24.3
Great Britain(71–81)	0.8	7.0
Ireland (71–81)	16.6	23.0
Italy (71–81)	4.4	16.4
Netherlands (71–81)	10.7	28.1
Portugal (70–80)	14.9	28.4
Sweden (70–80)	3.0	14.7
Switzerland (70–80)	1.5	19.2

Source: National censuses

Table 2.2: Trends in Household Size 1960–80

	Average household size			Absolute change 60–70	Absolute change 70–80
	c. 1960	*c.* 1970	*c.* 1980		
Belgium	2.99	2.95	2.69	−0.04	−0.26
Denmark[a]	2.96	2.74	2.39	−0.22	−0.32
Finland (60, 70, 80)	3.50	3.10	2.60	−0.40	−0.50
France (62, 68, 82)	3.10	3.06	2.70	−0.04	−0.36
Great Britain (61, 71, 81)	3.09	2.91	2.71	−0.18	−0.20
Greece[a]	-	3.31	2.73	-	−0.58
Ireland (71, 81)	3.97	3.94	3.68	−0.03	−0.26
Italy (71, 81)	3.59	3.30	3.00	−0.29	−0.30
Netherlands (71, 81)	3.56	3.21	2.70	−0.38	−0.51
Portugal (81)	-	3.66	3.27	-	−0.39
Sweden (70,80)	-	2.59	2.32	-	−0.27
Switzerland (70, 80)	3.26	2.93	2.51	−0.33	−0.42
West Germany[a]	2.87	2.74	2.43	−0.13	−0.31

Note: a. Non-census sources

of three or more in around 1970 — with Ireland at the top of the list — compared with only four in around 1980. Spain now headed the list, closely followed by Ireland, and Sweden was still bottom as in 1970.

The reason for the decline in average household size is apparent from Table 2.3 showing the changing size distribution of households. The number of small households, and particularly one-person households, had increased dramatically; while that of larger households, particularly those comprising six or more, had declined equally dramatically. In Ireland alone, large households were still very numerous.

Table 2.3: Size Distribution of Households *c.*1970 and *c.*1980

| | | Total households | \multicolumn{6}{c}{Percentage distribution by house size} |
			1	2	3	4	5	6
Denmark	b	2,062,148	29.1	31.2	15.8	16.1	5.7	2.1
Finland	a	1,518,819	23.7	22.1	19.2	16.8	9.3	8.7
	b	1,781,771	27.1	25.7	19.4	17.6	6.7	3.6
	c		+33.0	+36.4	+18.5	+22.9	−15.5	−51.5
France	a	15,762,508	20.3	26.9	18.6	15.0	9.2	10.0
	b	19,590,400	24.6	28.5	18.8	16.1	7.4	4.6
	c		+50.7	+31.8	+25.4	+33.6	−0.6	−42.8
Great Britain	a	18,745,000	18	32	19	17	8	6
	b	19,492,428	22	32	17	18	7	4
	c		+22.8	+7.8	−3.8	+12.2	−5.2	−33.7
Ireland	a	726,400	14.2	20.6	15.9	14.1	11.6	23.7
	b	894,400	16.9	20.2	14.9	15.4	13.0	19.6
	c		+47.2	+20.6	+15.1	+34.8	+38.2	+2.1
Italy	a	15,981,172	12.9	22.0	22.4	21.2	11.8	9.7
	b	18,605,100	17.9	23.8	22.0	21.4	9.5	5.4
	c		+61.1	+26.0	+14.5	+17.7	−6.3	−35.4
Netherlands	a	3,990,000	17.1	25.3	18.1	19.1	10.5	9.7
	b	5,111,000	22.1	29.9	15.6	20.7	7.8	3.9
	c		+65.2	+51.2	+10.7	+39.2	−4.8	−50.0
Sweden	a	3,050,354	25.3	29.6	19.4	16.3	6.5	3.0
	b	3,497,801	32.8	31.1	15.0	14.7	4.8	1.4
	c		+48.9	+20.7	−11.1	+3.6	−14.5	−44.9
Switzerland	a	2,051,592	19.6	28.5	19.3	16.9	8.8	6.7
	b	2,449,784	29.0	29.7	15.8	16.4	6.2	2.9
	c		+76.3	+24.5	−2.2	+15.9	−16.2	−49.2
West Germany	a	21,991,000	25.1	27.1	19.6	15.2	\multicolumn{2}{l}{(5 and over 12.9)}
	b	25,336,000	31.3	28.7	17.7	14.3	\multicolumn{2}{l}{(5 and over 8.0)}
	c		+43.4	+22.2	+3.7	+8.5	\multicolumn{2}{l}{(5 and over −29.0)}

Note: a. 1970s census round. Year of census is shown in Table 2.2
　　　b. 1980s census round
　　　c. % change in size categories between 1970 and 1980

Table 2.3 shows that single-person households had increased in number from 1970 by 28 per cent in Great Britain, to over 60 per cent in Italy, 65 per cent in the Netherlands and 76 per cent in Switzerland. Two-person households had also increased in number, most countries having an increase of between 20 and 30 per cent; Great Britain showed an increase of only 8 per cent, while the Netherlands showed an increase of over 50 per cent. Three-person households showed much smaller increases, and declined in numbers in several countries — by over 11 per cent in Sweden. France showed the largest increase in this category: by over 25 per cent. Four-person households increased everywhere, by under 4 per cent in Sweden to 39 per cent in the Netherlands. Households with five people declined everywhere (apart from in Ireland), by over 16 per cent in Switzerland but by less than 1 per cent in France. The number of six-person households declined by even greater amounts: from −34 per cent in Great Britain, reaching −50 per cent in the Netherlands and Finland.

Reasons for Changes in Household Size

Common factors, especially the decline in the birth rate and increasing life expectancy, explain the downward movement of household sizes. In Britain, fertility reduction may account for half the drop in household size between 1970 and 1980 (Eversley, 1983). The increasing numbers of older age groups in Western Europe — a function both of lowered mortality and the large numbers born immediately after the First World War — partly accounts for the increase in one- and two-person households. Declining marriage rates and rising divorce rates are also relevant, together with the increasing tendency for younger age groups as well as older groups to live alone. Rising real incomes and the growth of the housing stock are also important in explaining declining household size.

These factors have not, of course, operated uniformly throughout Western Europe. The decline in the birth rate experienced throughout Western Europe (apart from Ireland) from the mid to late 1960s, which reached very low levels in the mid-1970s, explains the reduction in the numbers of households with children and the overall decline in family size, and also in average household size (see Table 2.3).

Ireland, where there has been no decline in the birth rate, has shown the least decline in average household size and the continuing existence of many large households. In Italy, the decline in the birth rate came later, so that even in 1980 nearly 15 per cent of households consisted of five persons or more. (Such a figure masks significant regional variations: in the north, 10.7 per cent of households consist of five or more, but in the Mezzogiorno the figure rises to 22.2 per cent.) In the Netherlands, where in the late 1960s the birth rate was even higher than in Italy, the proportion of large households was virtually halved between 1970 and 1980.

The decline of fertility has been less pronounced in France, reaching 13.6 per thousand in 1976 but recovering to 14.9 by 1980, and here the number of five-person households has remained almost unchanged between 1968 and 1982. Three-person households in particular increased rapidly in number. By contrast, in West Germany, where the birth rate has reached very low levels (9.4 per thousand in 1978, 10.1 per thousand in 1982) the proportion of households consisting of five or more persons was already small in 1970 (13 per cent) and had declined even further — to 8 per cent — by 1980.

Changing Household Composition

Family Households

Data for seven countries around 1980 and five around 1970 are used to illustrate changes in the numbers of households with children (see Table 2.4). In 1970, the proportions of households with children ranged from 58 per cent in Finland (45 per cent for children under 18) and 50 per cent in Switzerland, to 37 per cent in Sweden (children under 18). In Switzerland nearly 30 per cent of households had two or more children, while in France only 23 per cent and in Sweden 20 per cent had two or more.

By 1980, typically only a third of households had children, ranging from nearly 60 per cent in Italy (but no upper age limit on children) and 46 per cent in Ireland (children aged under 15) to 29 per cent in Sweden. In West Germany and Sweden, only about 15 per cent of households had two or more children.

The typical European household still comprises a married couple with or without children, or an adult with one or more children (Table 2.5). Italy has the largest proportion of such

Table 2.4: Percentage of Households with Children *c.*1970 and *c.*1980

	Definition	*c.*1970	*c.*1980	% of all households which are single-parent *c.*1980
Finland	All children[a]	57.6	51.0	10.2 (all children)
	under 18	44.6	38.7	5.6 (dependents)
France	Children 0–16	39.6	35.7	8.8
	2 and more children	23.0	19.3	
Great Britain	Dependent children	38	36	8.3 (all children E&W)
	youngest 0–4	18	13	4.7 (dependent E&W)
Ireland			45.9	
Italy	All children[a]		59.2	4.0 (all children)
	youngest 0–5	17.9		
Netherlands	under 18		49.9	6.0
Sweden	under 18	36.5	28.9 (under 16)	
	2 and more	19.8	15.4	
Switzerland	All children	49.7		
	2 and more	29.7		
West Germany	under 18		32.1	5.1 (all children)
	2 and more		15.5	2.5 (dependents)
	under 6		10.8	

Note: a. Includes all unmarried children

Table 2.5: Percentage of Households which are Families[a]

	% Households which are families		% Household couples without children	
	*c.*1970	*c.*1980	*c.*1970	*c.*1980
Finland	74.7	68.0	17.2	17.0
France	76.5	72.1	36.8	36.4
Great Britain	65	62	27	26
Italy	-	78.5	-	19.3
Netherlands	-	72.3	-	22.7
Sweden	66.3	62.1	29.8	33.1
Switzerland	78.2	—	28.5	—

Note: a. Defined as couples with or without children and one-parent households with a child/children. All figures exclude cohabiting couples without children except for Sweden (1981)

households — nearly 80 per cent — and Sweden and Great Britain the lowest, each with 62 per cent.

One-Person Households

The decline of the birth rate along with the rise in life expectancy has contributed to the growing proportion of older age groups in Europe. Although the increase in the numbers of older people helps to explain the rapid growth of one-person households, this in itself is not a sufficient explanation (Table 2.6); for along with the growth in numbers there has been an increasing tendency for the elderly to live alone rather than with their children or relatives as was especially common in rural societies and southern countries. This 'isolation of the elderly' is a relatively recent phenomenon, especially in more traditional and until recently, peasant societies, such as much of Italy. The Italian census (1982, p. xxi) commented on 'the decomposition of the extended family with the phenomenon of the isolation of the elderly'. Typically, the one-person household is a widowed female past retirement age. In France, for example, 65 per cent of all one-person householders are women, and 38 per cent are women aged 65 and over.

Census data from seven countries (Table 2.7) show a variation in the age composition of single-person households, ranging from 65 per cent over retirement age in Great Britain to only 38 per cent in Finland, where numbers aged under 45 are proportionally

Table 2.6: Single-person Households *c.*1980 and Percentage of Total Households which are Elderly One-Person Households

	Total % one-person households	% of total households which are elderly one-person households
Finland	27.1	10.4
France	24.6	11.6
Great Britain	21.8	14.2
Ireland	16.9	7.2
Italy	17.9	11.5
Netherlands	22.1	9.0
West Germany	31.8	14.3

Table 2.7: Age Structure of One-person Households *c.*1980

	% aged 60/65 or retirement age and over	% aged under 45
Finland (65)	38.2	33.7
France (65)	49.4 (38.0 F)	29.2
Great Britain (retirement age)	65.2	—
Ireland (65)	42.8	—
Italy	64.1	—
Netherlands (65)	41.0	38.2
West Germany	45.8 (39.1 F)	32.3

large. Indeed, Finland (25 per cent) along with the Netherlands (31 per cent) and France (22 per cent) have large numbers of single householders aged under 35. So at the other end of the age spectrum too, increasing numbers are setting up home independently. Indeed, the explanation given for the increase of single-person households in Greece, for example, was the increasing tendency for young people to live alone; although it was also noted that this was less widespread than elsewhere in the EEC (Katsanevas and Papaspiliopoulos, 1981, p.36). In Spain, the small number of single-person households (8.6 per cent) are dominated by the non-active sectors of the population: students, the retired and elderly (Tirado, 1982, p.126).

Although there is an increasing tendency for both young and old to live alone, there are contrasts between countries. For example, both Italy and Great Britain have large proportions of elderly single-person households (Table 2.7); but whereas in Great Britain nearly a third of the retired population live alone, in Italy only 12.6 per cent of those aged 60 and over live alone (Table 2.8). These contrasts can be explained by the social differences between the two countries: the extended household may be breaking up in Italy, but the process is still far from complete.

The distribution of one-person households within countries shows similarities, especially their concentration in large towns. This is the case in Belgium, and in Brussels many communes have a third or more single-person households (the figure of 56 per cent is reached in Ixelles). Overall the distribution of one-person households in Belgium is one of the few demographic maps which shows only a small difference between Wallonia and Flanders.

In France, too, the concentration is notably urban: 30 per cent

Table 2.8: Percentage of Elderly Living Alone: Great Britain and Italy 1980/81

Great Britain:		% living alone (GHS 1980/81)		
	Age group	65-74	75-84	85 and over
Males		14	24	37
Females		38	56	54
Italy:	Age group	60 and over		75 and over
North		14.0		16.0
Centre		9.9		11.1
Mezzogiorno		12.5		17.4
Italy		12.6		15.3

of households in the Ile-de-France are one-person, rising to 48 per cent in the Ville de Paris. On the other hand, rural communes near to towns have the smallest proportion of one-person households.

In Britain, a particular concentration in coastal resorts is evident. Along the Sussex coast the proportion of one-person households rises to over 30 per cent, reaching 36 per cent in Hove, where 25 per cent of households comprise pensioners living alone. Inner London, too, has high rates of one-person households — 32 per cent — but only 16 per cent of pensioner households. In the Netherlands, nearly 26 per cent of households in urban West Netherlands are one-person, rising to 39 per cent in Amsterdam.

The extent to which one-person households will continue to increase in number will depend not only on further changes in the age structure, but also the continuing development of other social trends, such as young people leaving home before marriage, as well as divorce and separation early in marriage. It will also depend on changing standards of living as well as the growth of the housing stock.

The Significance of Other Social and Economic Factors

Changing social habits directly affect the number of households Divorce is a particularly obvious example as during the 1970s divorce rates doubled in Belgium, Denmark, France and Norway, trebled in the Netherlands and Sweden, and quintupled in England and Wales (Roussel and Festy, 1979).

Eversley (1983) has suggested that each divorce is likely to lead in the medium term to the formation of 1.5 new households for each one that is dissolved. Since present divorce trends in England and Wales, if continued, suggest that ultimately one in three marriages will be dissolved, then this alone is likely to have a profound impact on future household structures. As present trends also suggest that only one in five of all spouses eventually remarries after a divorce, a further growth in one-parent households seems certain (Haskey, 1983).

Marriage rates also declined during the 1970s, and marriage age increased. To some extent this has been offset by an increase in cohabitation, but, apart from in Scandinavia, data on this subject are scarce. The General Household Survey included a question on cohabitation from 1979.

Economic factors have also contributed to declining houehold size. On the one hand, a general improvement in standards of living, coupled with an increasing housing stock, has led to the formation of new households. Fewer young married couples live with their parents, which largely explains the reduction in number of two-family households in Britain (Ramprakash, 1983, p. 24).

At the same time, a decline in traditional economies, particularly peasant agriculture and artisan industry, has led to a reduction in the number of extended families. In Italy especially, a rapid decline in the agricultural labour force — from 16.9 per cent in 1970 to 11.2 per cent in 1980 — has been accompanied by an overall decline in household size. In the north, where agriculture employs only 7.3 per cent of the labour force, average household size is 2.8; while in the Mezzogiorno, where 20.4 per cent are employed in agriculture, average household size is 3.3. In Ireland, where large households are still numerous, 22.4 per cent of all households with six or more members have a head employed in agriculture; while 21.7 per cent have a head who is a skilled manual worker.

Likewise the widespread increase in female activity rates, seen especially in northern Europe, can be viewed as one of the social trends leading to a decline in household size. It has had implications for fertility in particular, as women in paid employment generally have lower fertility rates than do the rest and hence smaller families. Women's greater economic independence may also have contributed to the increased numbers of them living alone, whether unmarried, separated or divorced. Moreover, rising female activity rates mean that an increased number of households have more than one economically active member.

The numbers of women gainfully employed increased everywhere during the 1970s, as illustrated by the EEC data in Figure 2.1. In France, for example, the number of women in paid employment rose from 7.1 million to 9.6 million between 1968 and 1982. The numbers of married women in paid employment, including those with dependent children, have also increased. In Britain 50 per cent of women with dependent children are currently in full- or part-time employment, and in Sweden 85 per cent of mothers with children under 17 are gainfully employed. Finland too has seen an increase in the numbers of married women in employment. From a half in 1960, the proportion of married women in gainful employment had risen to two-thirds by 1980. Overall in Finland during

Figure. 2.1: Female Activity Rates in the Countries of the European Community 1970–83

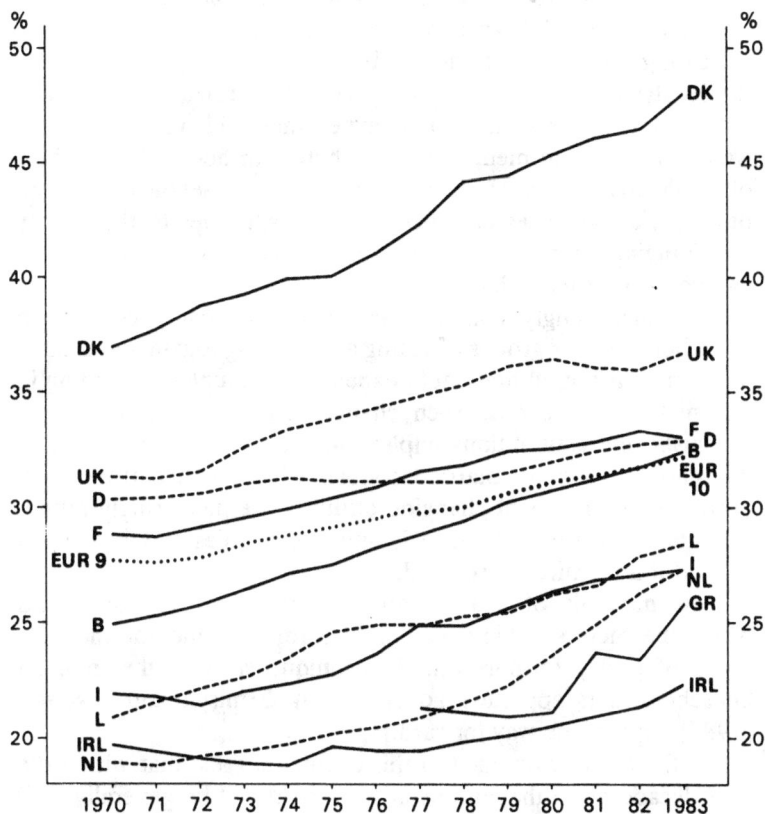

the last two decades, the female participation rate has increased from 35 to 42 per cent, while that of men has declined from 57 to 51 per cent. An increased number of women in the work-force not only implies smaller families — a trend that seems unlikely to be reversed — but is also likely to have repercussions for the care of the elderly.

Conclusion

There are both demographic and social dimensions to the processes behind the reduction in household size and the increase in numbers of households. The increasingly uniform low fertility evident everywhere in Western Europe has resulted in a rapid reduction in the number of large households. Similarly, the compression of the childbearing period into fewer years, along with the increasing propensity of young adult children to move away from the family home, is hastening a reduction in the size of households. At the same time increases in life expectancy, which have favoured women rather than men, have contributed further to the numbers of small households, especially one-person households, although other social processes are also involved. Attitudes to the elderly are changing: increasingly, the elderly expect to live alone and be independent of their children.

Also increasingly common are more informally constituted households: either groups of young adults living together and sharing some but not all household expenses, or couples cohabiting in informal sexual unions. Such changes render increasingly anachronistic the assumptions implicit in such concepts as 'head of household'. Amongst married couples where both partners may have paid employment changing attitudes are increasingly found, such that rigid views about male and female roles may have been blurred if not entirely discarded.

New methods of analysis are required, both to understand better the factors behind household formation and for the purposes of policy formulation. A technique such as the minimal household unit approach advocated by Ermisch and Overton (1985) implies one way forward.

All the trends examined in this chapter suggest that within the next decade or so the European household will be generally — if not uniformly — small, mononuclear and increasingly made up of one person, with two as the most common household size. For analytical purposes, despite the continued existence of a north-south divide, with Ireland in the latter division, the most interesting variations in household size and composition are likely to exist as much within national states as between them. For policy-making purposes, however, there will be continuing concern across nation-states about the raising of taxes from, or more especially in support of, elderly single-person households and the once-common large family households.

References

Anderson, M. (1980) *Approaches to the History of the Western Family*, Macmillan, London

Ermisch, J. and Overton, E. (1985) 'Minimal household units: a new approach to the analysis of household formation', *Population Studies, 39*, 33–54.

Eurostat (1982) *Economic and Social Features of Households in the Member States of the European Community*, Eurostat, Rome

Eversley, D. (1983) 'The family and housing policy' in *The Family: OPCS Occasional Paper, 31*, 82–95

Finnish Census (1975) *Households and Families*, 111

French Census (1982) Recensement Général de la Population, *Principaux Résultats: Sondage au 1/20, France Métropolitaine*

General Household Survey (GHS) (1984), OPCS, London

Goody, J. (1983) *The Development of the Family and Marriage in Europe*, Cambridge University Press, Cambridge

Hajnal, J. (1965) 'European Marriage Patterns in Perspective' in Glass, D.V. and Eversley, D. (eds.) *Population in History*, Edward Arnold, London, pp. 101–43

Haskey, J. (1983) 'Marital status before marriage and age at marriage', *Population Trends, 32*, 4–24

Italian Census (1981) *Dati sulle caratteristiche strutturali della popolazione e delle abitazioni*

Katsanevas, T. and Papaspiliopoulos, S. (1981) *Evolution of Social Policy in Greece*, Report for the Commission of the European Communities, Athens

Laslett, P. (1972) *Household and Family in Past Time*, Cambridge University Press, Cambridge

Mitterauer, M. and Sieder, R. (1982) *The European Family*, Blackwell, Oxford

Murphy, M. (1983) 'The life course of individuals in the family' in *The Family: OPCS Occasional Paper, 31*, 50–70

Ramprakash, D. (ed.) (1983) *Social Trends, 13*

Roussel, L. and Festy, P. (1979) *Recent Trends in Attitudes and Behaviour Affecting the Family in Council of Europe Member States*, Council of Europe, Strasbourg

Tirado, A. (1982) *L'Emploi des Femmes en Espagne*, Commission des Communautés Européennes, Luxembourg

Appendix 2.1: Classification of Households in Different European Censuses

France: Single person; other households without a 'family'; households in which the principal family is a single parent; households in which the principal family is a couple (with or without a child).

Italy: In 1961 and 1971 the four types were single person; married couple; married couple and children; extended family. The typology was refined in 1981 to differentiate between married and unmarried children, and lone parents.

Finland: The Finnish census has six types of household dwelling unit: one person; non-family household dwelling unit (at least two people); one family; one family and others; two families; three or more families.

Great Britain: The nine census types are: household with no family: one person; no family: two persons or more; household with one family: married couple, no children, without others; married couple, no children, with others; married couple with children, without others; married couple with children, with others; one parent family, without others; one parent family, with others; two or more families.

Eurostat, 1982:   The four types were single member; single nucleus with or without other members; two or more nuclei; no nuclei (nucleus being a married couple with or without children, or one parent and children).

3 COUNTERURBANISATION IN WESTERN EUROPE

Anthony Fielding

Introduction

In 1950, the pattern of net migration in the countries of Western Europe was almost without exception that of gains being positively correlated with settlement size: the smaller settlements experienced the highest rates of net loss and the largest settlements experienced the highest rates of net gain (Figure 3.1). It is this positive association between net migration and settlement size that constitutes the concept of 'urbanisation' used by Berry (1970) in his work on population redistribution in the United States, and it is the one that is used in this chapter. 'Urbanisation' is thus confined to its 'geographical' meaning, that is to the process of spatial agglomeration.

Those seeking to show that there has been 'a clean break with the past' (Vining and Pallone, 1982) claim that by the late 1970s the dominant net migration pattern was one that was inversely correlated with settlement size: the largest settlements were experiencing net migration loss and the rates of gain were highest among small and medium-sized settlements. Figure 3.1 shows the inverse relationship said to exist for the late 1970s together with a possible transition path from the 'urbanisation dominant' position to that of the 'counterurbanisation dominant' position.

This chapter brings up to date the empirical results of a paper published in 1982 under the same title (Fielding, 1982). To achieve this end three questions will need to be answered: (i) is the descriptive model of the transition from urbanisation to counterurbanisation developed in that paper (Fielding, 1982, pp. 8–13) and based upon census data for France supported or undermined by the results of the 1982 census conducted shortly after the paper was published?; (ii) in what ways, if any, should the generalisations made about counterurbanisation trends in the early 1970s (Fielding, 1982, p. 14) be changed in the light of the publication of the 1980–82 round of population censuses?; and (iii) should the picture of population redistribution in Western Europe in the

Figure. 3.1: Migration and Settlement Size 1950s to 1980s: A Possible Sequence

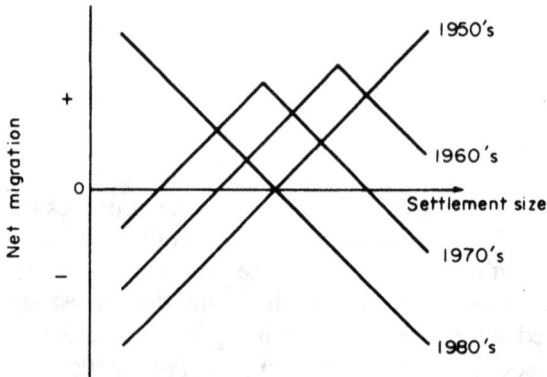

recent period be modified as a result of the publication of data for the years since 1980 based upon population registers available for eight major countries in Western Europe?

The Changing Relationship between Net Migration and Settlement Size: France 1954–82

Evidence favouring the claim that there had indeed been a major change in the pattern of population redistribution in Western European countries sometime around 1970 was presented in my 1982 paper. In the case of seven countries it was possible to assert that counterurbanisation had replaced urbanisation as the dominant trend. In a further five countries there was evidence of a trend towards counterurbanisation without that inverse relationship between net migration and settlement size actually coming about. The case of France was examined in detail because the data seemed to be in a form that was particularly appropriate to an analysis of these trends. The problems involved in analysing the French data on net migration and settlement size have been discussed elsewhere (Fielding, 1982 p.33). A graph of the relationship between net migration and settlement size for the inter-censal periods 1954–62, 1962–68 and 1968–75 showed that a major change in that relationship had taken place and that there were similarities between the manner in which the change had occurred and the descriptive model presented above (Figure 3.1).

In Figure 3.2 this graph has been updated to include the data from the 1982 census. The graph has been drawn in such a way as to show both the absolute gains and losses by settlement size category for the period 1975–82 (the shaded areas) and the rates of gain and loss (linked together to form the curves). The graph seems to reinforce the evidence for the model: net migration gains were confined to the smallest urban agglomerations and to the larger rural *communes*, while losses characterised the larger towns and cities, and Paris in particular. This indeed is how the data was interpreted by the two French demographers (Boudoul and Faur, 1982) at the national statistical office, when they wrote:

> The check to urbanisation is the most striking phenomenon revealed by the census results ... During the period 1975–82, the growth of the rural *communes* is, on average, faster than that of the towns. Only towns of less than 20,000 inhabitants have a rate of growth higher than that for the whole of France. In over a century, this is the first time that such a phenomenon has been observed. It has its origins in the sharp reversal in the migration flows in favour of the rural *communes* ...

The picture of urban and regional population redistribution emerging from the 1982 census is thus conformable with the notion that counterurbanisation has replaced urbanisation as the dominant trend. There is, however, reason to be sceptical about the suitability of the data used in Figure 3.2 for an accurate description of the turnaround. The method used to define agglomerations (*unités urbaines*) (which involves firstly defining the continuously built-up areas and then assigning all *communes* to the agglomeration that had any part of their areas within the built-up area so defined) served fairly well in the 1950s and 1960s to delimit the *de facto* towns and cities of France. But by 1982 this was no longer the case. 'Peri-urban' growth in small settlements was now taking place in *communes* that were further away from the centre of the settlement than those that contained within their boundaries parts of the continuously built-up areas of those settlements. For this reason we can be certain that the 1975–82 curve in Figure 3.2 exaggerates the importance of the rural *communes* and understates the importance of the settlements with populations of between 10,000 and 100,000.

Figure. 3.2: The Relationship Between Migration and Settlement
Size: France, 1954–82

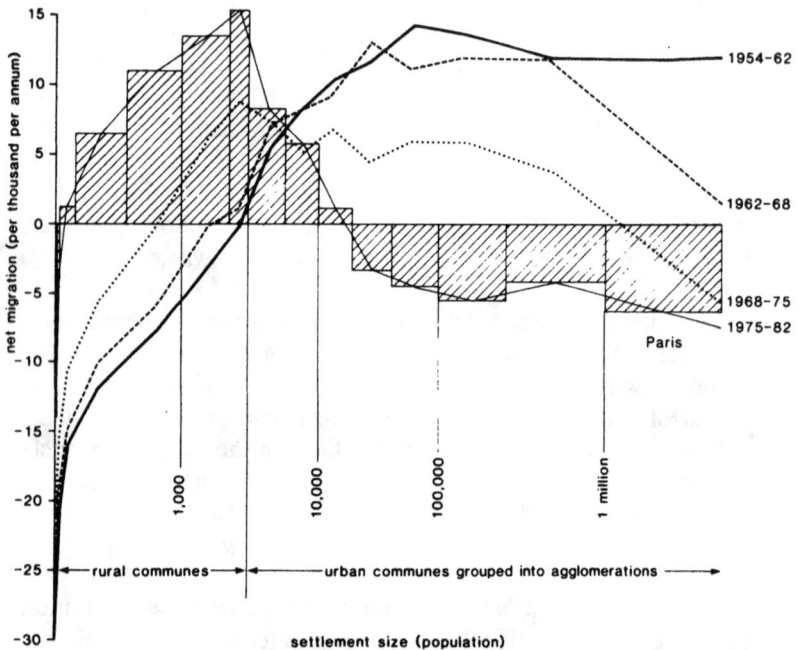

Other data from the 1982 census for the nation's urban agglomerations and urban regions suggest, however, that any change to
Figure 3.2 to allow for this bias would not be enough to alter the
basic shape of the curve. This assertion is founded upon data on
net internal migration at the planning region level. The two most
densely populated regions, Ile-de-France (the Paris region) and
Nord-Pas-de-Calais (the industrial region centred on Lille), were
the two regions that experienced major losses of population
through net internal migration (−443,000 and −129,000 respectively). The 'problem' agricultural regions of western and south-
western France, on the other hand, gained population through net
internal migration: each of the five regions stretching from
Brittany in the north-west to Midi-Pyrénées (Toulouse) in the
centre-south made net migration gains and the sum of their gains
amounted to a quarter of a million people.

Our conclusion, therefore, is that the descriptive model of the transition from urbanisation to counterurbanisation as outlined in Figure 3.1 is largely supported by the facts of French urban development over the period 1954–82.

Evidence on the Net Migration/Settlement Size Relationship for the 1970s from Other West European Censuses 1980–81

Of the 14 countries of Western Europe studied by Fielding (1982), seven had fairly reliable to very reliable population redistribution data based upon a population register. The remainder depended upon the census results for this data, and since the research for the 1982 paper was carried out in the first few months of 1980 it was not possible to know for these countries what had been happening during the 1970s. The case of France has already been discussed, and Switzerland has, since 1981, joined the list of countries with a registration system, so it will be counted under both headings. This means that in this section six countries need to be examined: Austria, Ireland, Portugal, Spain, Switzerland and the United Kingdom.

In the cases of Ireland, Portugal and Spain, the rates of rural depopulation during the 1960s had been very high as had been the rates of net migration gain in the major cities. In the 1970s, the rates of rural depopulation decreased markedly but net migration losses in rural areas in Portugal and Spain did not disappear entirely. Similarly, net migration gains continued to occur in the major urban areas, but these gains were smaller both in terms of rates and in terms of the absolute numbers of people involved. From the figures contained in the appendix to this chapter it can be seen that it was only in the case of Spain that a significant positive relationship between net migration and population density was maintained into the 1970s; in Ireland and Portugal, the relationship was weakly positive but the shift away from urbanisation towards counterurbanisation was also very marked. The case of Ireland is particularly interesting because net migration gains were made in all planning regions — even the most rural — during the 1971–81 period, and because the relationship between net migration and population density actually becomes negative in the latter part of the inter-censal period (1979–81). (Ireland had an extra census in 1979.)

The 1981 census results for Austria have been analysed at three spatial scales. At two of the three levels there was a slight tendency towards counterurbanisation when comparing the 1970s figures with those of the 1960s, but the relationship between net migration and population density remained weakly positive at all three levels during the 1970s. In the case of Switzerland, the figures used in the calculations are for population change rather than net migration. They show that an urbanisation relationship for net migration and population density in the 1960s had been replaced in the 1970s by a weakly negative relationship between population change and population density. The results of the United Kingdom 1981 census have already been used on several occasions to show that counterurbanisation was the dominant trend during the 1970s (Robert and Randolph, 1983). A major concern in the analysis of these results has been whether or not the definitions of the statistical areas used has been effective in separating counter-urbanisation from intra-labour-market area redistribution in the form of extended suburbanisation. To ensure that it was inter-labour-market area redistribution that was being measured, the population change rates were calculated for the 20 city-regions used in an earlier study of inter-regional migration in England and Wales (Fielding, 1971). The results were quite striking. A very significant negative relationship between population change and population density was found to exist for the 1970s, and the trend between the 1960s and the 1970s was also towards counter-urbanisation, although here the relationship was much weaker.

Combining these results with those published in the earlier paper produces Figure 3.3. We can say that in six countries of Western Europe — Austria, Ireland, Italy, Norway, Portugal and Switzerland — there was no significant relationship in the 1970s between net migration and population density, in other words urbanisation had come to an end; in one country —Spain — the relationship was still positive, that it to say urbanisation remained dominant; but in seven cases (Belgium, Denmark, France, the Netherlands, Sweden, the United Kingdom and West Germany) the relationship had become negative, which means that for these countries the counterurbanisation form had, sometime around 1970, come to replace the urbanisation form of the relationship.

Figure. 3.3: Summary of Evidence on Counterurbanisation in Western Europe During the 1970s
(Non-significant relationships are shown in lower case)

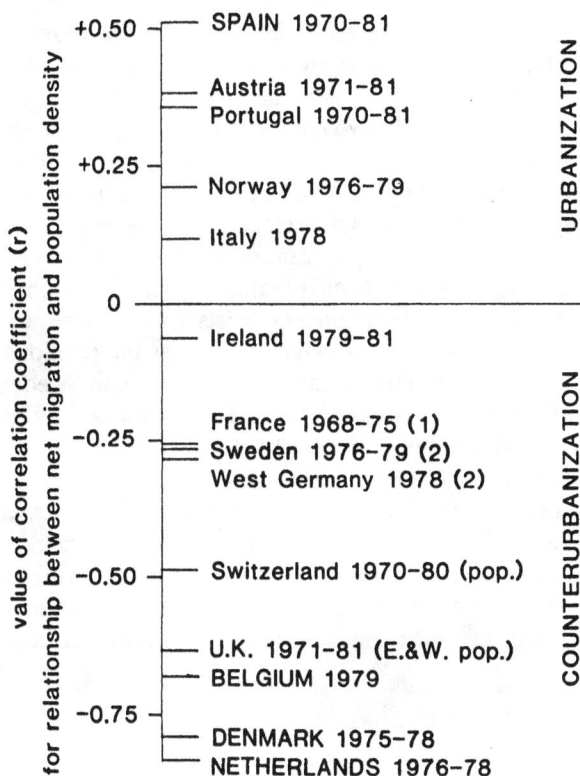

Notes: (i) see Figure 3.2 for 1975–82   (ii) see Fielding (1982, pp.47 and 51)

Evidence on the Net Migration/Settlement Size Relationship for the Early 1980s from Population Register Data

Eight of the 14 main countries of Western Europe have developed registration procedures that give rise to migration data on a year-by-year basis. In six of these countries analysis of the relationship between net migration and population density in the late 1970s had shown that a counterurbanisation form of this relationship had come into being, replacing the urbanisation of the 1950s and early

1960s. The picture for the early 1980s is, however, rather more complicated than this.

In each of the eight countries the net migration rates for the period 1981–83 were regressed against population density. In the case of the most populous countries, Italy and West Germany, the analyses were carried out at two spatial scales: (i) at the level of regions of 20,000 to 25,000 km², and (ii) at the level of regions of about 5,000 km². In only two countries do the results show a clear-cut counterurbanisation form, the first being at the level of the smaller regions in Italy and the second at both levels in West Germany. In all other cases the relationship was weak, too weak to have proved statistically significant at the 5 per cent level had the values on the variables been obtained from a random sample. However, an interesting regularity exists within these weak relationships; in the three Scandinavian countries the relationship was weakly positive, which in the cases of Denmark and Sweden represents a reversal of the situation that existed in the late 1970s; while for Belgium, the Netherlands, Switzerland (and Italy at the level of the larger regions) the relationship was weakly negative.

Thus registration data on urbanisation and counterurbanisation for the early 1980s suggests that in the minority of cases, where a clear redistribution pattern exists, it is one of counterurbanisation, but that elsewhere the definite counterurbanisation experienced in the late 1970s has either been reduced or mildly reversed.

References

Berry, B.J.L. (ed.) (1976) 'Urbanisation and counterurbanisation', *Urban Affairs Annual Review, 11*

Boudoul, J. and Faur, J.P. (1982) 'Renaissance des communes rurales ou nouvelle forme d'urbanisation?', *Economie et Statistique, 149*, I–XVI

Fielding, A.J. (1971) *Internal Migration in England and Wales*, Centre for Environmental Studies, UWP14, London

Fielding, A.J. (1982) 'Counterurbanisation in Western Europe', *Progress in Planning, 17*, 1–52

Robert, S, and Randolph, W.G. (1983) 'Beyond decentralisation: the evolution of population redistribution in England and Wales 1961–81', *Geoforum, 14*, 75–102.

Van der Haegen, H. and Pattyn, M. (1982) 'The Belgian city regions 1970' in H. Van der Haegen (ed.) *West European Settlement Systems*, Acta Geographica Lovaniensia, Brussels, pp. 251–364

Vining, D.R. and Pallone, R. (1982) 'Population dispersal from major metropolitan regions: a description and tentative explanation of the patterns in twenty-two countries, *Geoforum, 13*, 339–410

Appendix 3.1

Austria

The country was divided into 4 × 20,000 km² regions, 7 × 10,000 km² regions, and 16 × 5,000 km² regions. In each case the regions were made as compact and as nodal in their internal structure as was feasible. Net migration rates (per cent) for the inter-censal periods 1951–61, 1961–71 and 1971–81, were then regressed on population density at the starting date. This produced the results tabulated below. (U = Urbanisation; C = Counterurbanisation; N = No significant relationship; Nu = Insignificant relationship but with a trend towards urbanisation; Nc = Insignificant relationship but with a trend towards counterurbanisation.)

Region size	1951–61	1961–71	1971–81	Shift 1971–81
20,000 km²	Nu	Nu	Nu	Nu
10,000 km²	U	Nu	Nu	Nc
5,000 km²	U	Nu	Nu	Nc

The equations for the 1970s were:

$$20,000 \text{ km}^2 \quad Y = 1.00 + 0.0183X; \quad r = +0.525; \quad T = 0.87$$
$$10,000 \text{ km}^2 \quad Y = -0.97 + 0.0160X; \quad r = +0.530; \quad T = 1.40$$
$$5,000 \text{ km}^2 \quad Y = -0.99 + 0.0127X; \quad r = +0.378; \quad T = 1.53$$

Belgium

The analyses have been carried out at the level of the nine provinces, that is using regions that average 3,500 km² in size, with radii of 30–35 km. Three variables were regressed on the appropriate values for population density:

(i) net migration rate 1971–81:
$$Y = 2.32 - 0.00296X; \quad r = -0.358; \quad T = 1.01$$
This shows a weak counterurbanisation form for the 1970s.
(ii) shift in net migration rates 1960s to 1970s:
$$Y = 4.32 - 0.0122X; \quad r = -0.869; \quad T = 4.65$$
This is a clear indication of a shift towards counterurbanisation.
(iii) net migration rate 1981–83:
$$Y = 0.28 - 0.00107X; \quad r = -0.407; \quad T = 1.18$$
Once again this is a weak counterurbanisation form of the relationship.

An indication of population redistribution trends is provided by figures for the most densely populated province (Brabant, centring on Brussels) and the least densely populated province (Luxembourg, in the Ardennes):

	Net migration rate		
	%	%	per thousand
	1961–71	1971–81	1981–83
Brabant	+7.22	+2.07	−2.28
Luxembourg	−2.89	+1.18	+4.47

It is fair to say, however, that there is some degree of statistical underbounding affecting the Brabant figures. Indeed, cross-commuting between towns and provinces in Belgium, although largely confined to flows within the language regions, is significant (van der Haegen and Pattyn, 1982).

Denmark

Urbanisation and counterurbanisation in Denmark have been studied in detail by Yvonne Court (Portsmouth Polytechnic) in her doctoral research. The only statistical analysis included here is the calculation of the net migration/population density relationship at the level of the counties, where the counties of the Copenhagen area have been grouped together to avoid statistical under-bounding, and Bornholm has been linked with Storstroms. This results in eleven regions. The regression equation is:

$Y = -0.13 + 0.000424X$; $r = +0.164$; $T = 0.50$

The relationship is very weak, but it is interesting that the value of the coefficient is positive indicating a slight tendency towards urbanisation.

This is in marked contrast with results for the mid-1970s.

Eire

When the 1982 paper was written, Ireland was the one country in Western Europe for which there was evidence of a significantly positive relationship between net migration and population density during the 1970s. This result was based upon data from the 1979 census at the level of the nine planning regions. Using the same areas but basing the results on the 1981 census, a rather different picture emerges. Three variables were regressed against population density:

(i) net migration rate 1971–81:
$Y = 1.83 + 0.0206X$; $r = +0.430$; $T = 1.26$
This shows that, for the 1970s as a whole, a weak urbanisation form of the relationship prevailed.

(ii) net migration rate 1979–81:
$Y = -0.22 - 0.000476X$; $r = -0.074$; $T = 0.20$
There is almost no relationship between the variables; what there is takes the counterurbanisation form.

(iii) shift in net migration rate 1971–79 to 1979–81:
$Y = -3.44 - 0.0241X$; $r = -0.848$; $T = 4.23$
This is a very significant relationship and shows a strong trend towards counterurbanisation.

Italy

Analysis of the migration data from the Italian registration system for the years 1981–83 have been carried out at two levels:

(i) at the level of 13 large regions. Each of these areas is comprised of one or more administrative region(s) and the average size of the areas is about $20,000 \, km^2$. The regression of net migration rate 1981–83 on population density in 1981 produces the following equation:
$Y = 5.71 - 0.00421X$; $r = -0.080$; $T = 0.27$
Thus the relationship, though very weak, is of a counterurbanisation form.

(ii) at the level of 69 small regions. Each of these areas is about $4,000 \, km^2$. Regressing the same variables produces the following equation:
$Y = 8.20 - 0.00768X$; $r = -0.246$; $T = -2.07$
This relationship is also of a counterurbanisation form but is much stronger.

Another way of viewing this data is to divide Italy into just four regions and look at the net migration balances for these regions:

	net migration 1981–83
Golden Triangle (Piedmont, Lombardia, Liguria)	+ 8,000

Rest of northern Italy	+110,000
Rome (Roma, Umbria)	+ 57,000
Rest of southern Italy	+ 95,000

This suggests that, at a time of net immigration nationally, the industrial north-west is failing to compete for migrants (a) with the 'third Italy' of north-east and north central Italy, (b) with the capital region, and (c) with the Mezzogiorno.

Netherlands

The net migration rate 1981–83 was regressed on population density 1981 for the 11 provinces of the Netherlands to produce the following result:

$$Y = 1.48 - 0.00185X; \quad r = -0.124; \quad T = 0.38$$

This shows that the relationship between the variables was very weak but took on a counterurbanisation form.

Norway

As with the Netherlands the population register data was used to regress net migration rate 1981–83 on population density in 1981. The eight regions used were composed of counties or groups of counties, where the latter were formed to avoid statistical underbounding of urban areas. The results were:

$$Y = -4.24 + 0.280X; \quad r = +0.534; \quad T = 1.55$$

This relationship, though weak, shows an urbanisation form.

Portugal

Mainland Portugal is divided into 18 administrative districts which average about $5,000 \, km^2$ in size. Regions of this size have a radius of $40 \, km$ and are suitable for inter-urban analysis in countries other than those with extremely spatially extensive city-regions (such as the United Kingdom). In the case of Portugal, however, the capital region is split into two districts. These have been combined in the following calculations, which are therefore based upon 17 statistical regions. Two variables were regressed against population density:

(i) net migration 1970–81:
$$Y = -2.14 + 0.0226X; \quad r = +0.357; \quad T = 1.48$$
This shows that a weak urbanisation form of the relationship continued into the 1970s.
(ii) net internal migration 1979–81:
$$Y = -5.47 + 0.0190X; \quad r = +0.531; \quad T = 2.43$$
This shows that, for internal migration only, rural depopulation and urban growth still characterised Portuguese population redistribution at the end of the 1970s.

Spain

Mainland Spain is divided into 48 provinces which average about 10,000 km² in size. For the purposes of this exercise the three small provinces of the Basque region (Alava, Guipuzcoa, Vizcaya) were combined thus reducing the 48 provinces to 46 statistical regions. The regression of net migration 1970–81 on population density in 1970 produces the following result:

$$Y = -7.52 + 0.0467X; \quad r = +0.513; \quad T = 3.96$$
The relationship takes the urbanisation form and remains significant despite a marked decline in the rates of gain of the major cities and rates of loss of the rural areas compared with the 1960s.

Sweden

Swedish counties have been grouped together to form twelve statistical regions, the average size of each being about 20,000 km² (except those in the far north). The net migration rate 1981–83 was regressed on population density in 1981 to produce the following equation:

$$Y = -3.21 + 0.0773X; \quad r = +0.370; \quad T = 1.26$$
This can be interpreted to mean that a weak urbanisation relationship exists in the early 1980s. As with Denmark, this represents a marked contrast with the situation in the late 1970s.

Switzerland

The Swiss cantons are virtually useless as statistical areas, and the analysis reported below is based upon eleven regions each composed of a group of districts, where each region is compact, nodal in internal structure and approximately 3,500 km² in area. Two variables were regressed against population density:

(i)   population change rate 1970–80:
$$Y = 3.34 - 0.0141X; \quad r = -0.492; \quad T = 1.70$$
This calculation is based upon the 1980 census results and shows that a weak form of the counterurbanisation relationship had developed by the 1970s.

(ii)   net migration rate 1981–83:
$$Y = 27.9 - 0.0738X; \quad r = -0.506 \quad T = 1.76$$
This calculation shows a weak form of the counterurbanisation relationship.

It is based upon the population register data available in a suitable form since 1981. The weakness of the relationship arises in part from the continued attractiveness to migrants of Lausanne–Geneva (and, to a lesser extent, Berne), which counteracts the net losses of Basel and the lack of attractiveness to migrants of Zürich.

United Kingdom

Only two rather limited exercises have been carried out on UK data. The first involves the regression of the rate of population change 1971–81 on population density in 1971, using data for city-regions in England and Wales where these have been defined in journey-to-work terms:

$$Y = 5.51 - 0.0113X; \quad r = -0.653; \quad T = 3.66$$
This equation reveals a strong inverse relationship, which means that counterurbanisation dominated population redistribution in England and Wales during the 1970s.

The second exercise uses the same areas and regresses the shift in population change rates between the 1960s and the 1970s on population density:

$$Y = 1.24 - 0.00187X; \quad r = -0.136; \quad T = 0.58$$
This shows that there was, at this level, a very slight trend towards counterurbanisation between the 1960s and the 1970s.

West Germany

The country (excluding West Berlin) was divided into $12 \times 20,000\,km^2$ regions, and $50 \times 5,000\,km^2$ regions. In each case the regions were made as compact, and as nodal in internal structure as was feasible. Net migration rates based on registration data for the years 1981–83 were regressed on population density in 1981. This produced the following results:

(i) 20,000 km^2 regions:
   $Y = 5.15 - 0.0181X$; $r = -0.633$; $T = 2.59$
(ii) 5,000 km^2 regions:
   $Y = 5.97 - 0.0169X$; $r = -0.449$; $T = 3.48$
   These equations can be interpreted as confirming that a counterurbanisation form of the relationship existed in the early 1980s.

This negative relationship was obtained despite the net migration gains of certain major cities such as Munich, and the net migration losses of certain rural/small town regions such as those in north-eastern Bavaria.

4 INTERNATIONAL MIGRATION IN THE 1970s: REVOLUTION OR EVOLUTION?

Paul White

Introduction

The 1970s witnessed extremely important changes in international migration affecting the countries of Western Europe. A whole series of developments transformed the patterns of flow. Single male labour migrants gave way to family reunification. Emigration became return migration. The demand for unskilled industrial labour halted. High-level manpower movements increased. And new governmental action was taken in many countries to control migration. Most attention has been paid to the changes that occurred in low-level migration whereby temporary migrants became settled ethnic minority communities of migrant origin (Castles, 1984; Salt, 1985a; White and Woods, 1983). This chapter will deal with the broader contextual situation of migration within and to Western Europe, and will present interpretations of the resulting flows. It is the overall thesis here that the common ascription of the causal mechanism for change to the economic events following the oil-price rise of late 1973 is far too much of an over-simplification and that the influences altering the migration scene in the 1970s were far more varied and complex.

It must be stated at the outset, however, that the study of international migration flows is a far from easy task: there are great difficulties of definition and data availability, especially in any comparative study. As has been made clear in chapter 1, data on migration are inadequately covered in censuses, and similar problems often also apply to data on the resultant minority communities. The most satisfactory data on international flows come from those countries that have continuous population registers, such as Denmark, Norway, Belgium or West Germany. Amongst other countries, data problems are often severe: certain countries (Greece, for example) tabulate information only on movements of their own nationals, whilst others (such as Spain) only produce data on those who emigrate with assistance from state labour agencies (SOPEMI, 1984). The result of these problems is that any data produced on migration flows, especially where such flows may be temporary or ephemeral, must be treated solely as best estimates rather than as accurate statements; even data on flows between a single pair of countries may show a totally different picture depending on which country's figures are believed. To attempt to produce an international migration matrix of all flows in a single year is a herculean task and one that shows up the unreliability or non-existence of some of the data (Poulain and Wattelar, 1983). Particular difficulties occur with flows operating under free conditions, such as within the European Community or between metropolitan and overseas departments (as, for example, in the case of movements between France and her overseas *départements*).

The Context of Migration in the 1970s

Economic factors

The accepted interpretation of international migration in Western Europe up to the early 1970s has been cogently stated by Böhning (1972, pp.54–71). The expanding economies of countries moving towards a phase of post-industrial society and faced with a shortage of labour because of relatively low fertility levels produced upward social mobility, which drew nationals away from the less desirable occupational sectors and led to these vacancies being filled by migrants. Although obviously highly simplified here, this interpretation is in accordance with those of other commentators (Castles and Kosack, 1973; Giner and Salcedo, 1978; Paine, 1977).

However, this 'academic' interpretation has been at variance in some respects with 'official' or governmental views of international flows. Academic analysts have stressed the structural need for migrant labour, a need which is further consolidated as certain occupations or niches in society become associated with the migrants. The official view, on the other hand, was generally that migrants would not be needed permanently and were required only as a temporary expedient during a short-term labour shortage (Kreuzaler, 1977); indeed, migrants could be used as a buffer against the unemployment of the indigenous work-force if recession occurred (Kuhn, 1978) or — interpreted in Marxian terms — as part of an 'industrial reserve army' (Carney, 1976).

However, as Salt (1985a) has suggested, such ideas relied too heavily on a very crude vision of a direct causal mechanism linking labour-market change with migration; in the long term, the structural theories of the academic analysts have proved more accurate.

In any thesis that it was the oil crises of late 1973 which brought labour migration to a halt in Western Europe, it might be expected that certain economic indicators would provide convincing correlations with migration changes. The most significant indicator would almost certainly be economic growth. If labour was needed to fuel economic growth, and if growth stopped in the mid 1970s, then migration of labour should also stop. Table 4.1 shows the annual rates of increase of Gross Domestic Product for the 17 major states of Western Europe from 1970 to 1983, these rates of increase in all cases being calculated on a basis of constant prices.

The information in Table 4.1 can be considered from a variety of perspectives, and certain general points are of significance here. Firstly, it is true that there was a major crisis of economic growth soon after the oil-price shock: the continent saw its highest average economic growth rate in 1973 and its greatest average decline two years later, in 1975. However, by 1976 economic growth was, on average, back above its 1971 level and growth continued, albeit in more modest terms, right up to the second recessionary crisis of 1981.

The 1973–5 period cut economic growth drastically in certain major labour-importing countries. However, in several of these countries recovery was rapid so that by 1976 in West Germany, the Netherlands, France and Austria growth was back to its level of 1972–3. Indeed, it was only in the years 1980–3 that economic growth rates consistently fell below 2 per cent per annum for periods of three or more years in West Germany, the Netherlands, Belgium, Luxembourg, the United Kingdom, Eire, France, Switzerland, Greece, Italy and Spain. The recession of 1975 may have seemed severe at the time, but in practice it was short-lived; only at the very end of the decade did a longer period of economic crisis set in.

A further interesting feature of the details in Table 4.1 can be more clearly seen by dividing the countries listed into two groups: ten countries of 'core' Europe, and five of 'periphery' Europe (see Table 4.2). Norway and Italy are omitted from this classification because they are, arguably, transitional cases. In every year except 1974 and 1976 peripheral Europe had higher economic growth

Table 4.1: Annual Growth Rates of Gross Domestic Product in Real Terms in Western Europe

	1970	1971	1972	1973	1974	1975	1976	1977	1978	1979	1980	1981	1982	1983	Average
Finland	8.3	2.4	7.0	6.5	4.3	0.6	0.3	0.4	2.3	7.6	6.0	1.5	2.5	3.8	3.8
Sweden	5.3	−0.2	1.6	3.4	4.1	0.7	1.2	−2.5	2.3	4.3	1.9	−0.6	0.5	2.3	1.7
Norway	3.5	4.7	5.0	4.0	5.3	3.3	6.8	3.6	4.5	5.1	4.2	0.9	1.0	3.2	3.9
Denmark	2.7	3.7	4.3	2.9	−0.7	−1.0	6.9	1.9	1.8	3.7	−0.4	−0.9	3.4	2.5	2.2
West Germany	3.5	3.7	3.2	4.9	0.5	−2.6	5.6	2.6	3.1	4.5	1.8	−0.2	−1.1	1.3	2.2
Netherlands	6.4	5.0	2.9	6.5	3.1	−1.0	5.0	2.9	2.8	1.8	0.9	−0.8	−1.6	1.3	2.5
Belgium	6.3	4.0	5.5	6.4	4.5	−1.8	5.3	5.2	3.1	2.1	3.3	−1.2	1.1	0.4	3.2
Luxembourg	2.3	2.4	4.4	7.0	4.4	−5.1	1.8	0.8	4.5	4.2	2.0	−1.1	−1.3	−1.4	1.8
United Kingdom	2.0	2.5	1.3	7.6	−0.7	−0.8	3.9	1.1	2.7	1.9	−1.8	−0.9	1.4	3.4	1.7
Eire	1.6	4.1	5.7	4.6	4.2	2.0	2.2	6.8	5.8	3.4	3.7	1.6	1.2	1.0	3.4
France	5.8	5.3	5.6	5.7	3.9	0.2	5.2	3.0	3.7	3.5	1.2	0.3	1.6	0.5	3.3
Switzerland	6.4	4.1	3.2	3.0	1.5	−7.3	−1.4	2.4	0.4	2.5	4.6	1.5	−1.1	0.7	1.5
Austria	8.1	5.5	6.4	5.8	4.1	−2.0	6.2	3.7	0.5	4.8	3.0	−0.1	1.0	2.1	3.5
Greece	8.3	8.0	9.1	8.3	−1.8	5.1	6.1	2.9	6.4	3.6	1.9	−0.2	0.2	0.2	4.2
Italy	4.9	1.7	3.1	5.9	4.2	−3.5	5.7	1.7	2.7	4.9	3.9	0.2	−0.4	−1.2	2.4
Spain	6.0	4.4	8.2	8.0	5.3	0.7	3.0	3.3	2.7	0.2	1.5	0.2	1.2	2.0	3.3
Portugal	8.7	5.7	8.1	10.9	0.7	−3.7	6.9	5.6	3.4	6.6	4.1	0.5	3.5	0.1	4.4
Average (17 countries)	5.3	3.9	5.0	6.0	2.8	−1.0	4.2	2.7	3.1	3.8	2.5	0	0.8	1.3	2.9

Sources: Calculated from data given in: OECD Economic Surveys, various countries, various dates
OECD Main Economic Indicators, December 1984
United Nations statistical yearbook 1975 and 1981

Table 4.2: Average Annual Growth Rates of Gross Domestic Product in Real Terms, Core and Periphery Europe

	Core[a]	Periphery[b]
1970	4.9	6.6
1971	3.5	4.9
1972	3.9	7.6
1973	5.4	7.7
1974	2.6	2.5
1975	−1.3	0.9
1976	4.0	3.7
1977	2.2	3.8
1978	2.5	4.1
1979	3.3	4.3
1980	1.7	3.4
1981	−0.5	0.7
1982	0.5	1.7
1983	1.3	1.4
Average 1970–83	2.4	3.8

Notes: a. Core — Sweden, Denmark, West Germany, Germany, the Netherlands, Belgium, Luxembourg, United Kingdom, France, Switzerland, Austria
     b. Periphery — Finland, Eire, Greece, Spain, Portugal
Source: as Table 4.1

than core Europe: in some years (1972, 1973, 1975) peripheral growth was over 2 per cent faster than in the core. Three of the five periphery countries (Finland, Eire and Spain — all traditional labour-exporting countries before the 1970s) never showed year-on-year economic decline during the period. The only core country in the same position was France (Table 4.1). Of the three countries with the fastest overall long-period growth two were peripheral (Portugal and Greece — again, both traditional labour-exporters) whilst the third, Norway, was unclassified in the analysis for Table 4.2. Of the three countries with the lowest overall economic growth rates, all were core countries (Switzerland, Sweden and the United Kingdom — the first two being traditionally labour recruitment countries before the 1970s).

Economic growth is not, however, the only indicator that might have a close relationship with migration. In particular, given the official view of the reason for international labour moves, there should be a strong link with unemployment. In 'buffer' theory, migrants should be laid off and sent home to avoid the unemployed of indigenous workers; yet in practice that rarely happened in the 1970s. Figure 4.1 shows unemployment levels in 14 of the

Figure 4.1: Unemployment Rates 1970–83, Selected Countries

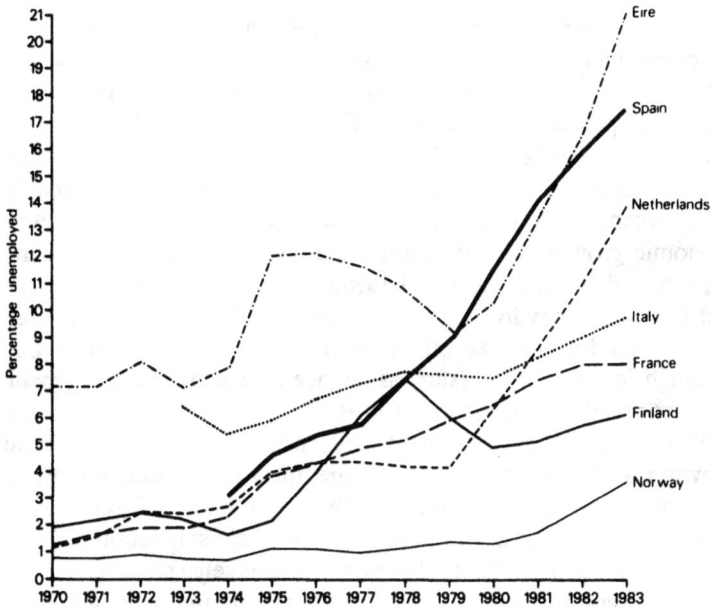

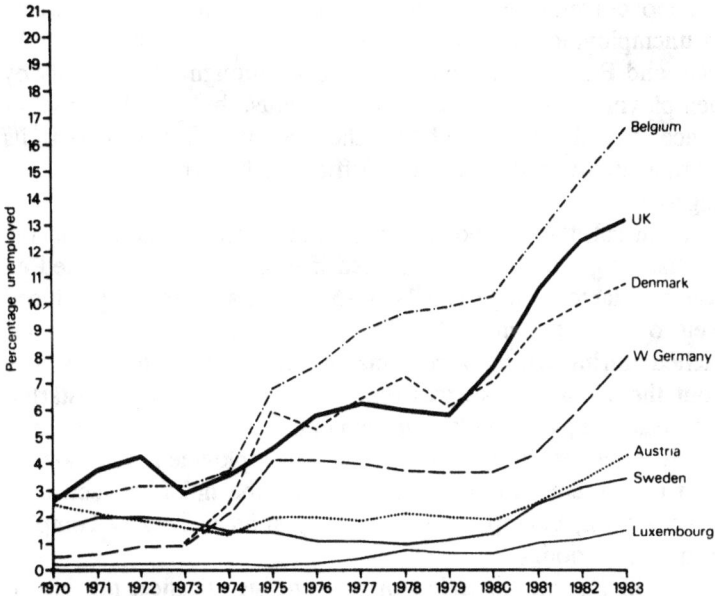

Source: as Table 4.1

17 countries considered in Table 4.1. No satisfactory data exist for Greece and Portugal, whilst the unemployment rate in Switzerland was close to zero for much of the period; there are also problems concerning data from Denmark, Spain and Italy, for each of which definitions of the labour force or of unemployment were revised during the period. Comparison of Figure 4.1 with Table 4.1 shows that there are few close links between economic growth rates and unemployment levels. Certainly the crisis year of 1975 resulted in higher unemployment everywhere except in Sweden, but although economic growth recurred during the later 1970s unemployment rates stayed up and increased further — only in West Germany and Eire were they lower in 1979 than in 1976. In most countries there was a further take-off of unemployment in 1979 or 1980, although in a few cases (such as France or Spain) unemployment rose continually from the mid 1970s.

It is interesting to note that certain countries with low economic growth also had very low rates of unemployment. Undoubtedly in Luxembourg and in Switzerland (White, 1985a), migrants were successfully used as a buffer so that economic stagnation did not generate indigenous unemployment. Conversely, some countries with high economic growth (such as Finland, France or Spain — all with above-average long-period growth) suffered high and increasing unemployment levels through the latter half of the 1970s. In Spain and Finland these could have been brought about partly by unemployment among returning migrants, but in the case of France it could be argued that the country failed to export its unemployment in the way that 'official' labour migration theory suggested.

In general, though, unemployment rates did not behave in the way that might have been expected if migration was activated by economic factors only. The 1974–5 oil crisis recession produced levels of unemployment that were little higher than the levels reached during earlier recessions of the 1960s. What was new about the 1974–5 crisis was that as economic growth re-started there was no upsurge in labour demand. It was not, however, until the recession of 1980 onwards that unemployment took off to reach its present extreme levels. In total the links between economic growth, unemployment and migration were very complex during this period.

One final economic indicator of some significance, not just in economic terms but because of its social implications, concerns the nature of growth. Table 4.3 compares overall national rates of GDP growth from 1970 to 1983 with rates of increase of industrial output. Where industrial output rose faster than GDP, it can be argued that industry was the mainspring of economic growth; where industrial output rose slower than GDP, it was those sectors other than industry that were creating growth and the country could be said to be undergoing a relative degree of de-industrialisation. On this basis, eleven of the 17 West European economies of Table 4.3 were de-industrialising, although at least two of these (Italy and Austria) only moved into this condition during the period under consideration. It was generally the peripheral countries which were industrialising: all of these, plus Norway (but excluding Spain) had higher GDP growth than occurred in any of the de-industrialising economies.

In total, the economic context of international migration in the 1970s was therefore highly complex: far removed from a simple process of blocked economic growth after 1973 with a massive rise in unemployment leading to a halting of all new movement and increased forced return migration. Instead, the years 1970–83 can

Table 4.3: Gross Domestic Product and Industrial Production Increases 1970–83

	Percent increase in GDP 1970–83 in real terms (1)	Percent increase in industrial production 1970–83 (2)	Difference (2)-(1)
Portugal	65.7	99.6	33.9
Greece	61.9	84.8	22.9
Spain	48.7	65.5	16.8
Eire	57.3	71.7	14.4
Norway	65.6	79.0	13.4
Finland	55.4	66.0	10.6
Italy	32.5	30.7	− 1.8
Austria	49.1	46.3	− 2.8
Denmark	31.6	28.6	− 3.0
Netherlands	32.5	28.0	− 4.5
Sweden	20.4	15.0	− 5.4
Switzerland	14.3	5.2	− 9.1
West Germany	30.6	16.0	−14.6
United Kingdom	23.4	8.2	−15.2
France	47.5	30.0	−17.5
Belgium	44.7	24.0	−20.7
Luxembourg	24.3	−10.1	−34.4

Sources: As Table 4.1, plus OECD, Indicators of Industrial Activity, 1984, II

be divided into four periods. The years 1970–3 were growth years of low unemployment, but it is significant that much faster economic growth was occurring in peripheral parts of the continent — notably Finland, Greece and Portugal — which traditionally had been suppliers to the labour markets of the core economies. The years of rapid economic growth in these core countries were already passing at the start of the decade.

The second period, 1974–5, saw the crisis occasioned by the oil-price shock, retarding economic growth and increasing unemployment throughout the continent. The following years, 1976–80, saw renewed economic growth, although at lower levels than earlier in the decade. From 1977 onwards the differential between core and periphery economies was re-established, with the latter once again having faster growth. But despite renewed economic growth, unemployment levels remained relatively high or worsened. The fourth period began in 1981, with a more prolonged recession than that of 1974–5, and saw rapid increases in unemployment rates everywhere. The economic background to international migration during the 1970s was therefore one of some complexity.

External Political Factors

Influences on international migration that can be grouped under this heading include political events that were not directly concerned with migration but which had important indirect effects, along with migration-provoking factors operating outside Western Europe. These influences played a considerable role in migration flows to the continent during the 1970s.

Amongst the more significant migration flows were those of refugees. The decade opened with considerable populations of Czech refugees from the events of 1968 housed in Austria and Switzerland, and with the United Kingdom having recently absorbed 15,000 Kenyan Asians between March 1968 and January 1970. The year 1972 saw the expulsion of non-Ugandan passport holders from that country, resulting in a flow of 27,200 into the United Kingdom over a period of four months with settlement of a further 3,600 in other European countries. Later in the decade the fall of Saigon in 1975 and the continued troubles in South-East Asia led to a massive outflow of refugees, principally from Vietnam but also from Kampuchea and Laos. France, with her old colonial connections with the area, had taken 82,000 Indo-

Chinese refugees by May 1982, with significant numbers also settled in West Germany and the United Kingdom. Certain countries, notably France, Switzerland and West Germany, have pursued more liberal policies on refugees than others: indeed, one of the Swiss government's objections to repeated referendum proposals to limit the numbers of foreigners in the country was that this would jeopardise her liberal refugee policy. A further important influx was experienced by West Germany during the later 1970s: a stream of approximately 50,000 per annum of people of German ethnicity repatriated from Eastern European countries, the biggest contingents coming from Upper Silesia in Poland (15–20,000 per annum) and Transylvania in Romania (10–12,000 per annum). International treaties to facilitate these population transfers — a reminder of historical patterns of population distribution in Eastern Europe — were signed by the Federal Republic with Poland in 1970 and 1975 and with Romania in 1978.

Two further major population flows into Western Europe during the 1970s occurred as a result of decolonisation. The Portuguese *coup* of 1974 was immediately followed by the announcement of independence for Angola and Mozambique, in both of which the Portuguese had been involved in colonial wars. Mozambique achieved independence in June 1975, whilst the continuing civil war in Angola delayed independence there until November of that year. By May 1976 the total number of refugee returnees from Angola and Mozambique arriving in Portugal had reached about 650,000 (see Chapter 10).

The other 'decolonising' flow into Western Europe was that of Surinamers to the Netherlands at the time of Surinam's independence in November 1975. Under the act granting independence all Surinamers who were in the Netherlands by Independence Day were to retain Dutch citizenship, whilst a transitional period of a further five years provided for further entry rights to the Netherlands. These arrangements resulted in two peaks of movement: one in independence year, when movement from Surinam accounted for almost one-third of all movement into the Netherlands, and another in 1979–80 towards the end of the transitional period. Migrants in the first peak came in order to retain Dutch citizenship; those in the second peak had already lost it but wished to capitalise on the still remaining opportunity to move to the Netherlands before controls came down. In total the

Netherlands received a net inflow of 125,799 from Surinam during the period 1970–82.

The total result of the operation of external political factors was an inflow into Western Europe during the period 1970–82 of something approaching 1.5 million people from a variety of sources.

Social Factors

In the early 1970s there was a growing governmental recognition in many countries that the social costs of international migration were beginning to mount up (OECD, 1978, p. 7). Social costs and social factors do not, however, just affect host populations and governments; they also concern the migrants themselves. They must therefore be dealt with in two sub-groups.

It is undeniable that throughout the 1970s a great deal of social pressure and public opinion built up against large-scale immigration into many countries of north-west Europe. Such pressures were not consequent upon economic crisis but, in most cases, preceded the slowing-down of economic growth. It was not simply a case, as was sometimes argued (OECD, 1978, p. 21), of social tensions arising from competition for limited resources in a period of slow growth and scarcity.

The Swiss people were already concerned about *Überfremdung* (foreign dominance) well before the start of the decade, and the issue of tighter controls was put to referenda in 1970, 1974, 1977, 1981 and 1982. Although in the first three of these, proposals put by groups such as the *Nationale Aktion Gegen die Überfremdung von Volk und Heimat* (National Action Against Foreign Domination of People and Homeland) were defeated (Johnston and White, 1977; Johnston, 1980), the climate of public opinion had to be taken into account by government (Tribalat, 1984).

In France, increased racial tension between French nationals and immigrants, particularly Algerians, culminated in violent incidents and deaths in Marseille and other southern French cities from 1973 onwards, and in continued troubles in other areas of immigrant concentration. Immigration became a major political issue, arising significantly in the campaigning of Georges Marchais, the Communist candidate in the 1981 presidential election, and becoming a major manifesto item in the policies of Jean-Marie Le Pen's National Front, which scored considerable electoral successes in 1984 and 1985 (Ogden, in press).

In the United Kingdom, despite the imposition of strict controls on Commonwealth immigration through parliamentary acts of 1962 and 1971, immigration remained a sensitive matter throughout the following period, the most delicate issue of all being the entry of dependants (Smith, 1981). In Sweden, the 1982 general election campaign witnessed racial tension between young Swedes and Turks. Racist attacks, in some cases on refugees, also occurred in Denmark in July 1985.

Certainly some of the agitation against immigration is attributable to supposed links between the presence of foreigners and high levels of unemployment. Such was the case in Sweden in 1982, despite the fact that Swedish unemployment in that year was amongst the lowest in Western Europe (Figure 4.1); it has also been the case in the campaigning of the National Front in France, and in the 1985 unrest in Denmark. However, it is important to note that anti-immigrant feelings date back to before the onset of economic crisis.

Added to public concern about immigration *per se* there have also been anti-immigrant feelings, sometimes brought to the fore by events or episodes of lawlessness in the 'host' countries. Thus the urban riots of 1981 in the United Kingdom were quickly labelled in the popular press as race-related, although such a description is, in practice, far too simple (Peach, 1985). Dutch society has occasionally been alarmed at terrorist incidents involving its South Moluccan (Ambonese) community, most notably in 1970, 1975 and 1977. In October 1979 the Federal German government estimated that 145 extremist organisations existed amongst foreigners in West Germany; and in that country, Belgium and France there have periodically been political disturbances between rival groups amongst the migrant communities (for example, between different Iranian factions in West Germany, Algerians in France, or Yugoslavs in Belgium).

The 1970s were thus marked by a hardening of public opinion against international movements of population and the minority communities thus created. Therefore, to take only one example, it is unsurprising that in the autumn of 1974, 77 per cent of French people were, according to an opinion poll, in favour of stopping all new immigration (Girard, 1977).

It must, in addition, be remembered that the sending countries themselves have not always looked favourably on emigration. Algeria, for example, has always talked of the reintegration of the emigrants to France as a matter of national priority. And the new government of Surinam was less than delighted at seeing one-third of the country's population migrate to the Netherlands during the period 1975–80.

Whilst it is acceptable to categorise the social attitudes of the host countries as being generally negative to immigration throughout the 1970s, the attitudes of the migrants themselves were probably somewhat more complex. It is also unfortunate to note that relatively little useful research has been done on this topic.

It has now been shown (King, 1984) that a high, and increasing, level of return migration from northern Europe was occurring in the early 1970s and was not, therefore, causally dependent on the 1974–5 economic crisis. It is likely that a significant proportion of the earlier post-war migrants had by then come to the end of their expected stays abroad and were returning home by choice, largely uninfluenced by macro-scale economic considerations (King, 1977). Return migration of Italians and Spaniards from the countries of north-west Europe ran at a high level throughout the decade, and it may be suggested that this was to a large extent inevitable and operated in response to social and familial influences on decision-making at a micro-scale level.

However, evidence has also been produced of more recent migrants (from the 1960s) maintaining long-term ambitions of staying away from home: ambitions which often turn from economic considerations of saving to social ambitions of upward mobility for children. The long-term prospect may be return, but the time horizon of such an intention may be very vague, as Dahya (1973) has shown amongst Pakistanis in the United Kingdom, and it may not affect the increasing population of adults in the second generation. There is evidence that in the rapidly growing return migration of Turks from West Germany of 1984–5, adolescents born and brought up in the Federal Republic are doing everything they can to stay on rather than go back with their parents to a land they scarcely know.

Working from intensive interviews with Portuguese women in the Paris agglomeration, Lévi (1977) has shown how the experience of life in France has socialised many of the women to new norms, and that they progressively hold fewer active ambitions to return to Portugal. And although Lichtenberger (1984) in her important study of immigrants in Vienna refers to them throughout as temporary migrants, she also notes that only 31 per cent of her respondents could actually be classed as likely returnees in the near future, against 41 per cent who were ambivalent, 19 per cent who were now effectively rootless and 7 per cent who were potential permanent settlers in the city.

So, whilst the host countries' attitudes to immigration were generally negative during the 1970s, the attitudes of the immigrants themselves were rather more equivocal. Undoubtedly many migrants retained fatalistic attitudes towards their situation, but others made specific decisions to return home or to stay, even in the face of otherwise adverse influences. That the negative attitudes of host populations had an effect, however, is seen in the development of policy during the period.

Immigration Policies

The 1970s saw a series of restrictions introduced on international movements. Generally, these could be brought in overnight: only in the United Kingdom was an act of Parliament, with the inevitable long-drawn-out debate, needed before new immigration rules could be introduced in the form of the 1971 Immigration Act.

It should, however, be noted that Western Europe contains two major areas of free labour movement: that of the Nordic countries (Norway, Sweden, Denmark and Finland) and that of the European Community (six countries until 1973, nine until 1981, then ten). (Denmark is the only member of both.) Even before both countries joined the European Community, there was no restriction on movement from Eire to the United Kingdom. Certain overseas territories also had access to Europe during the decade: France's *départements d'outre-mer*, for example. Varying degrees of control exist on all other international flows, with the tightest controls operating on entry to the micro-states. (Liechtenstein even took steps to control the immigration of Swiss in 1981.)

It is instructive to consider certain examples of the stepping-up of controls during the 1970s. In the summer of 1973 — before the oil crisis but after the international exchange crisis of February of that year — West Germany acted to stabilise her stock of foreign workers by sharply increasing the recruitment tax on such employees. Then, in November, came a ban on new labour recruitment followed by attempts to limit the proportion of foreigners resident in particular regions of the country (OECD, 1978, p. 20).

However, a serious repatriation grant scheme was not introduced until 1983 (Salt, 1985b; see also Chapter 8).

Norway instituted a one-year ban on most categories of labour immigration in February 1975 and later extended it indefinitely; the ban did not, however, apply to refugees, building workers on specific contracts, 'intellectuals' or those from the Nordic free-labour area. Norway's reason for the ban was to give it breathing space to deal with the housing and social problems of the immigrants already in the country.

Switzerland adopted a stabilisation policy on foreigners in 1970, although even within this overall objective regulations on Italian immigrants were relaxed somewhat in 1972 in response to pressure from the Italian government. The Swiss stabilisation policy has operated by manipulating the lengths of qualifying periods required for transition between different categories of labour permit and by rigidly adhering to the quotas set for each category — in 1975 even introducing a quota on foreign au pairs. The policy was undoubtedly a response to public opinion, and the Swiss government interpreted the rejection of the various draconian referendum proposals as an endorsement of its own policies: the 1974 referendum, if passed, would have led to a halving of the country's foreign population in five years, resulting in the expulsion of 80,000 migrants who had 'established' status in the country as well as of all those on annual permits. The government argued that certain economic sectors — the food industry especially — would be very badly affected because of their dependence on foreign workers, whilst changes in occupation and social status would be inevitable for many Swiss workers. In addition Swiss international relations with the sending countries, particularly Italy, would be severely strained and retaliatory action could be expected. With these arguments the Swiss government hammered a nail in the coffin, holding the view (which they themselves had previously held) that immigration was a temporary expedient that could be eliminated if need be.

Similar arguments were used elsewhere as governmental responses to calls for large-scale immigrant repatriation; they were used, for example, by the West German government in its reaction to von Thadden's NPD (National Democratic Party) in the early 1970s. Nevertheless repatriation schemes have featured in some governments' measures, although often playing only a marginal role.

The case of France is of considerable interest. The first ban on migration to France was imposed not from Paris but by the Algerian government, who in September 1973 acted to suspend all movement to France in response to growing racialist attacks on Algerians in that country. In 1972 the French had moved to reduce illegal immigration by tightening the link between residence and work permits, but this had not applied to Algerians because of their special status under agreements made in 1962, 1964, 1968 and 1971. The ban on all immigration of foreign workers (which did not, of course, apply to citizens of EEC countries) imposed in July 1974 was part of the new Giscard government's package of measures designed, as later in Norway, both to cut the numbers of new entries and also to improve the circumstances of those already in the country. A year later, as part of the latter objective, France stated that all existing immigrants would be allowed to bring in their families, providing suitable conditions for them existed. A real policy on repatriation was not introduced, however, until 1980 when, under an agreement with Algeria, the repatriation grant was related to an applicant's wage level (SOPEMI, 1984, p. 13), with Algeria offering special tax concessions and training programmes for those returning from France. By then France's avowed objective was to ease unemployment. However, the level of the grant was insufficient to encourage return moves over and above those that would probably have occurred anyway. Thus in practice, despite the existence of a series of control policies, annual net out-flows from France to Algeria were generally relatively limited throughout the 1970s, and in some years (1970, 1973, 1974 and 1981) net inflow actually occurred (Verhaeren, 1983). It is only since the Peugeot–Talbot–Citroën strike of 1983–4 that applications for repatriation have increased significantly (*La Semaine*, 1 May 1985).

Certain general conclusions can be drawn from these examples of policy measures on immigration during the 1970s. (Other countries tightening their immigration controls included Denmark, the Netherlands, Sweden and the United Kingdom.) Firstly, restrictions on immigration were generally a response to social concerns rather than to economic decline, unemployment or crisis (Salt, 1985a). Measures to control and limit international flows date from the early 1970s and precede the economic crisis of 1974–5, if only by a few months in some cases (Anon, 1981). The exception is Norway, where restriction occurred only in 1975; but

Norway was the country with the highest economic growth rate in Europe over the years 1974–6 and was little affected by the recession. Elsewhere, although controls may have been tightened still further because of unemployment (as in Switzerland, where the total number of unemployed rose from 74 in August 1974 to 10,114 a year later, provoking a reduction in entry quotas) the initial reasons for bans lay in social concerns and public opinion rather than in economic influences.

A second conclusion is that although governments took steps to either control immigration or ban it entirely, they did not go so far as to operate large-scale repatriation. Certainly short-term entry permits were not renewed during the oil crisis years, but governments found it impolitic compulsorily to repatriate large numbers of those who had established rights of residence, for the reasons given above by the Swiss government.

A final general point is that immigration bans and restrictions operated on labour migrants. In most cases they did not apply to the dependents of such migrants, who were eligible for entry as long as certain residence requirements had been met by the initial mover and as long as suitable accommodation was available. These rights of family reunification were sometimes negotiated further by the sending countries (as, for example, Italy in the case of Switzerland or Algeria in that of France) and were also seen as appeasing the increasingly active immigrant organisations within the destination countries.

The policies of governments in north-west Europe during the 1970s, therefore, were to a large extent determined by considerations of social cost. In moving to cut down labour migration they cut out the remaining rotational elements in movement, produced conditions where many migrants decided to stay on if they could possibly do so, and encouraged desires for family reunification. Just as in the United Kingdom in the early 1960s, the imposition of control in the rest of Western Europe in the early 1970s can be interpreted as an important influence creating ethnic minority communities out of migrant groups (White and Woods, 1983; Castles, 1984). Only in Switzerland and Austria did the old concept of the 'guest-worker' system still apply by the start of the 1980s, and even in these countries the concept was much less relevant than it had been ten years previously (White, 1985a).

Migration Flows

In 1978 an OECD report spoke of 'the nearly total interruption of migratory flows in Europe since the beginning of the current recession' (OECD, 1978, p. 13). Such an erroneous statement has its origin in the practice of looking only at labour movement and not at total migration. In practice, in many instances the scale of migratory flow into and within Western Europe remained relatively constant during the 1970s, but it was the components of flow that changed significantly.

Figure 4.2 shows the gross annual migration flows to and from six of the 17 countries of Western Europe (similar graphs for Denmark and West Germany can be found as Figures 5.4 and 8.5). Consideration of individual countries is instructive. Luxembourg saw peak immigration flows from 1971 to 1974, and then stability: emigration remained relatively constant throughout. Luxembourg used migrants as a buffer against unemployment (Figure 4.1) and did this by cutting back on immigration in 1975–6 rather than by increasing the number of returnees, forced or otherwise.

In Norway's case, after 1970 gross migration flows were remarkably constant despite the 1975 ban on new labour recruitment. Sweden shows a more complex pattern, with massive net inflow in 1970 (when 53 per cent of arrivals were Finnish) followed by net outflow in 1972 and 1973. The oil crisis years actually saw net migration influx, and it was only in the early 1980s that a net migration balance approaching zero was reached.

Belgium saw immigration peak in 1974 and 1975, with a slow but steady decline thereafter towards a position of balance in 1982. However, this evidence, derived from one set of Belgian government figures, is at variance with data from an alternative official source which shows net emigration in 1978 and from 1980 onwards. The Dutch pattern is profoundly affected by the movement from Surinam (see above).

In contrast with the other countries in Figure 4.2, the United Kingdom is the only one with traditional net out-movement. This was at its greatest in 1974 and 1981, but there is little overall trend in the annual figures. However, there is some evidence that new destinations for movement, such as the Middle East, may be of increasing importance (Findlay and Godden, 1985).

Finally there is the case of West Germany (see Figure 8.5), the

Figure 4.2: Gross Migration Flows 1970–83, Selected Countries

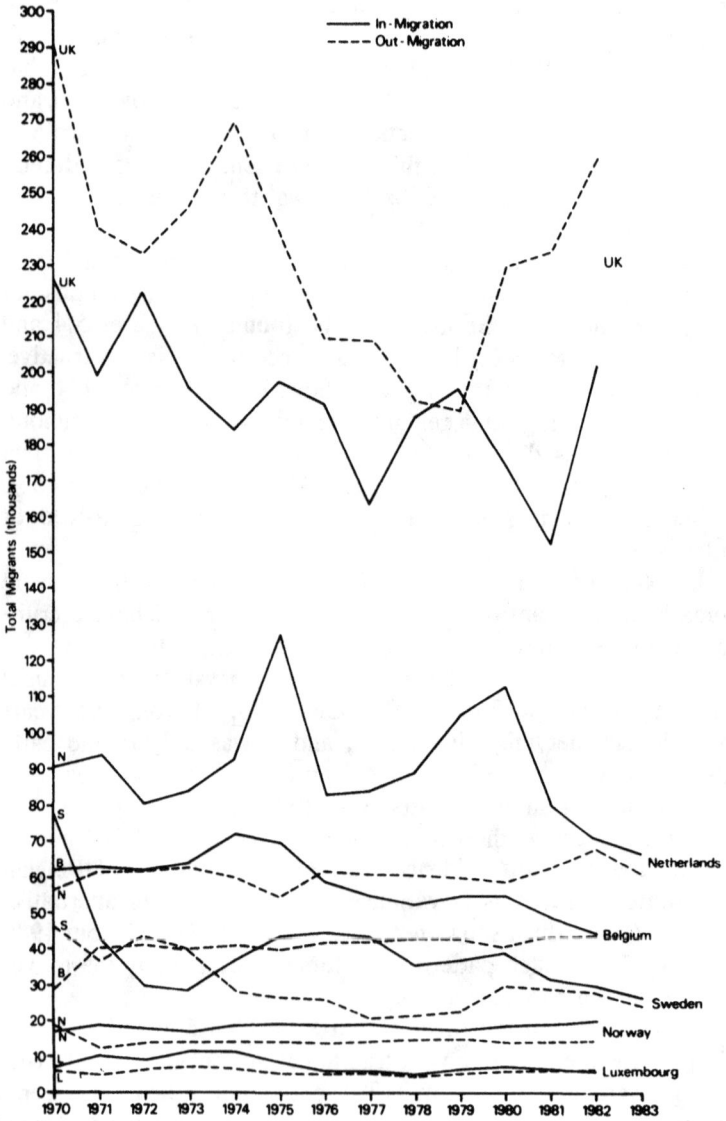

Source: National statistical yearbooks; OPCS Monitor

giant on the basis of which too many sweeping generalisations have in the past been made about the evolution of migration trends. After 1973 the immigrant flow into West Germany was cut back by about 50 per cent whilst at the same time there was an increase, up to 1976, in emigration. Much of this was almost certainly spontaneous return migration of the earliest arrivals. But after 1975 West Germany once again experienced increasing numbers of immigrants each year, and a decrease in emigration up to 1979–80, since when the trend has been towards balance at a low level of movement. Even in West Germany, then, net immigration occurred throughout the later 1970s at a time when unemployment stood at four times its rate of 1971–72 (see Figure 4.1).

It is not possible to present similar data on gross flows for other countries because of non-collection of data or difficulties over definitions. The most curious case is France, where official sources have steadfastly maintained that in every year since the mid-1970s the country's net migration balance has been precisely zero, a figure that cannot be believed.

Figures collated by the Council of Europe (1983) and by the European Community (Eurostat, 1984), and largely calculated by the residual method after known natural change is accounted for, suggest that there was net in-migration to Greece from 1975 onwards and that net in-movement also replaced net outflow in Spain from 1975 onwards with the exception of 1979 (net inflow had also occurred in 1971). In the case of Italy, there was net in-movement in the years 1972, 1973 and 1978–80 (see also Chapter 9). In Portugal, only the years of the *retornados* (1974 and 1975) saw net inflow: otherwise, that country lost migrants on a net basis in every other year of the period. Eire saw net inflow from 1971 to 1978 inclusive: an unprecedented event in Irish demographic history (see Chapter 6). The effect of Swiss control measures was to produce a net outflow of migrants between 1970 and 1978, although after that year net influx started again. The Austrian pattern was much more complex, with year-to-year variations in the direction of the net flows.

The total picture of gross and net flows that emerges from this discussion is thus not a simple one. It certainly does not show a straightforward reversal of net migration flows in the mid-1970s, nor does it suggest a drastic curtailment of movement. Admittedly it has been calculated that total departures from the seven principal countries of migrant origin (Finland, Portugal, Spain, Italy,

Yugoslavia, Greece and Turkey) fell from 500,000 in 1973 to only 140,000 in 1975 (Anon, 1981, p. 2), but movement quickly picked up again after the latter date. Only at the very end of the period under consideration is there some evidence of reduced general levels of movement, as has happened also with other forms of mobility such as inter-regional (Courgeau and Pumain, 1984) or intra-urban (White, 1985b).

What certainly did change during the 1970s were the directions and types of movement involved: the origins and destinations and the characteristics of the movers. Once again, brief case-studies of specific countries can provide insights into some of these developments.

Table 4.4 shows the characteristics of migrants into and out of the Netherlands in three specific years, avoiding those most affected by movement from Surinam. The first observation is that over the period covered the sex balance of immigration became more normal after what had been a disproportion in favour of males. A further extremely important feature is that the proportion of immigrants who were economically active dropped markedly, especially amongst those from the Mediterranean basin. After the early 1970s the number of labour migrants was much reduced and family reunification became the dominant motive for migration; indeed, the annual figures show that labour movement was already

Table 4.4: The Netherlands: Migrant Characteristics

	1970		1976		1981	
Immigrants	Total	%	Total	%	Total	%
Total	90,829		82,853		80,183	
Male		61.0		50.8		51.6
Female		39.0		49.2		48.4
Economically active		53.3		30.6		27.2
Economically active of those from Mediterranean basin		82.8		22.5		10.8
Emigrants						
Total	57,375		61,530		63,195	
Male		54.7		53.3		54.0
Female		45.3		46.7		46.0
Economically active		38.9		41.0		36.9
Economically active of those to Mediterranean basin		83.7		45.9		24.8

Source: Statistical yearbook of the Netherlands 1977 and 1982

declining and being replaced by family movement right from the start of the decade. There was a certain time-lag before return flows of families to the south, but the final row of Table 4.4 indicates a similar fall-off after 1970 in the proportion of emigrants in employment then leaving for Mediterranean countries, although this occurred at a slower rate.

The extent of continued — and, indeed, increased — family movement after the bans on labour migration of the mid-1970s was not, at first, realised by commentators scrutinising data solely on worker flows. Lebon and Falchi (1980), for example, make no mention of family flow. These flows were of immense importance in many countries, such as West Germany, Switzerland, Austria and Belgium, but they were not universally present. For example, Sweden, with its liberal policies on dependants' movement since the 1960s, did not show a change-over to family migration in the 1970s for movement was already fairly well balanced: demographically, the only real trend during the decade was for movement towards sex balance in emigration from an earlier position of male dominance, especially among young adults.

However, Sweden can be used to illustrate a further point of some importance concerning exchanges with the Mediterranean countries. Throughout the decade migratory flows between Sweden and Finland remained of the greatest significance; but those from the eastern Mediterranean declined whilst out-flows to that area increased, so that by 1980 there was net loss from Sweden in that direction as a result of return migration. In place of Greeks, Turks and Yugoslavs Sweden saw a growth in the numbers from more diversified sources such as Poland, the United Kingdom, Algeria, Morocco, India, Iran and Japan. If we consider the size of net flows experienced by Sweden during the period 1970–80 (Table 4.5) we can see that the greatest net gains were of Finns, Poles, Yugoslavs and Turks, the second of these groups not being 'normal' migrants. Net losses to Italy were of returning migrants who had arrived before 1970, whilst those to Canada and the USA were continuations of traditional overseas emigration. Relatively high gross flows with small balances in relation to the gross figures were experienced with Denmark, France and the United Kingdom. These undoubtedly represent one of the significant phenomena of the 1970s: the evolution of high-level manpower movements between countries at similar stages of economic development and activity, such movement being encouraged by

Table 4.5: Sweden: Net Migration 1970–80

Origin/destination	Total in-migrants	Total out-migrants	Net balance
Finland	166,824	116,638	50,186
Poland	13,950	911	13,039
Yugoslavia	23,476	11,497	11,979
Turkey	11,875	1,957	9,918
Greece	14,986	10,250	4,736
Denmark	42,395	37,821	4,574
United Kingdom	12,489	10,539	1,950
France	5,592	6,137	−545
Italy	5,439	6,611	−1,172
USA	16,079	17,617	−1,538
Canada	2,595	4,425	−1,830
Norway	25,381	27,629	−2,248

Source: *Statistisk Årbog* 1972, 1981

the growing importance of multinational enterprises and the inter-nationalising of much commercial activity (Salt, 1983).

Table 4.6 presents a similar set of data on net movements experienced by West Germany. It is notable here that, despite the attention given in the literature to immigration bans and to return flows, the only three negative balances over the decade as a whole concerned Greece and Spain (both as a result of return migration), and Canada. For all other major migration partners West Germany had a positive net balance of movement between 1970 and 1980 overall. Undoubtedly, however, the patterns of con-nection were changing. Two of the columns in Table 4.9 show the proportion of migration between 1970 and 1980 that was accounted for by the years 1970–4 (in other words, before the oil crisis and the national net outflow of 1975–6). The indications are that immigration from Yugoslavia, Austria, Portugal, Spain and Greece slowed down markedly after 1974. After that year West Germany experienced increased inflows of labour migrants from India and Iran, and also from Poland and the USSR as a result of the movement of ethnic Germans discussed above. As with Sweden, high gross flows in both directions were experienced with certain countries at a similar state of economic development such as the United Kingdom, France, the Netherlands and Switzerland. By the end of the decade significant migrant flows of this kind of about 4,000 per annum were also occurring to and from Japan.

When looked at on a detailed basis, the individual country-to-country migration flows during the 1970s were extremely variable

Table 4.6: West Germany: Net Migration 1970–80

Origin/destination	In-migration Total	In-migration Percent represented by 1970–4	Out-migration Total	Out-migration Percent represented by 1970–4	Net balance
Turkey	1,800,565	53	999,174	38	801,391
Poland	352,994	13	139,339	21	213,655
Yugoslavia	1,011,109	75	863,520	57	147,589
Austria	351,830	71	232,192	54	119,638
Rumania	122,656	42	29,188	53	93,468
USSR	71,745	22	8,394	28	63,351
United Kingdom	198,949	43	139,222	40	59,727
Italy	1,220,053	61	1,163,862	57	56,191
Portugal	159,785	79	111,092	47	48,693
France	198,402	54	152,379	48	46,023
USA	271,734	52	248,916	46	22,818
India	41,058	30	19,573	33	21,485
Czechoslovakia	67,358	41	46,932	43	20,426
Iran	48,019	30	30,563	37	17,456
Netherlands	118,080	56	100,763	50	17,317
Hungary	52,149	45	36,071	44	16,078
Switzerland	100,855	57	90,483	54	10,372
Belgium	52,272	48	46,705	47	5,567
Canada	43,145	60	45,589	51	−2,444
Spain	275,280	82	348,961	57	−73,681
Greece	383,819	74	482,257	45	−98,438

Source: Statistisches Jahrbuch, various years

in their behaviour (see Table 4.7). Some increased in volume, others declined, and many changed their composition even if their size did not alter.

Despite the lack of discernible pattern in Table 4.7 and the complexities of much of the other information available on international movement during the 1970s, it is possible to put forward certain general conclusions concerning flows. Firstly, with few major exceptions (and those in the case of West Germany, see above), no important new sources were drawn into the international migration field of Western Europe during the decade. This was a rather different situation from the 1960s, when a number of countries such as Portugal, Morocco and Turkey were becoming large-scale migrant origins for the first time. The result of this relative stability during the 1970s is that no destination countries have experienced major inflows of new migration streams consisting, as in the 1950s and 1960s, almost entirely of young adult males. The migration streams were generally in

Table 4.7: Selected Migrant Flows 1970 and 1980

From	To	1970	1980	% change 1970–80
Spain	Belgium	2,597	976	−62
Turkey	Belgium	2,600	3,150	+21
Turkey	Denmark	1,675	1,608	− 4
Belgium	France	7,462	7,747	+ 4
Morocco	West Germany	2,760	4,259	+54
Spain	West Germany	62,996	7,681	−88
Turkey	West Germany	177,646	213,126	+20
West Germany	Greece	30,701	23,001	−25
Belgium	Italy	4,792	5,238	+ 9
West Germany	Italy	83,702	80,092	− 4
Italy	Luxembourg	749	494	−34
Indonesia	Netherlands	1,583	2,620	+66
United Kingdom	Norway	1,747	2,309	+32
West Germany	Portugal	5,752	8,666	+51
Belgium	Spain	3,234	1,617	−50
Norway	Sweden	3,247	2,250	−31
Caribbean	United Kingdom	5,100[a]	5,200	+ 2

Note: a. 1971: data from OPCS Monitor
Sources: National statistical yearbooks. Where different figures are obtained from diferent countries for a single flow a mean has been calculated

existence by 1970; the 1970s saw their modification.

A second general conclusion must be that return migration flows first showed up in importance during the decade. These reversed earlier major migration streams such as those from the countries of the northern littoral of the Mediterranean (Spain, Italy and Greece). They also appear to have been important for Eire (although the data sources from that country and the United Kingdom are amongst the poorest in the continent). These return flows were certainly in existence by the start of the decade, but in many cases only became strongly noticeable in the middle of the 1970s.

Thirdly, it became increasingly misleading (but remained unfortunately common) during the 1970s to think of international migration simply in terms of labour flows. Events after the imposition of controls on labour flows in the mid-1970s show the importance of this point. Instead of a consequent reduction of foreigner numbers in most countries such totals increased as immigrant populations became true communities through the continued immigration of families. And this had one vital implication that goes well beyond the simple study of migration: because of family reunification, immigrant populations achieved the likelihood of autonomous growth with no necessity for continued immigration to produce increased numbers. This brings the need to consider the second generation, and to change the nomenclature from discussion of 'immigrants' to discussion of 'ethnic minorities'.

Finally, one type of labour migrant increasingly involved in the deindustrialising economies of the European 'core' — slow-growing though many of these economies may have been — was the highly trained managerial or scientific employee who could be provided only by other countries with similar levels of highly educated and professionally qualified individuals. The image of the international labour migrant as an unskilled industrial worker became outdated and needed replacing with a more complex analysis.

The results of these interacting trends can be summarised by considering the 'foreign' populations of certain countries at the beginning and end of the period. Table 4.8 does this for six countries which are not dealt with in detail elsewhere in this volume; Chapters 5-11 generally provide similar information for other countries. In all the countries listed in Table 4.8 the percentage shift in the proportion of foreigners was less than 2 per cent over the decade. Sweden, Belgium and Switzerland, all of which had significant immigrant populations in 1970, saw these undergo an important degree of stabilisation during the following decade. In part this resulted from the course of migration, but it also reflected levels of naturalisation. It is notable that in the Netherlands and, to some extent, in Belgium the provenance of the dominant groups changed. By the end of the 1970s these were generally fairly stable communities — 'here for good' in the words of Castles (1984) — and that was the case everywhere throughout north-west Europe, even in countries such as Austria which had adhered longest to the guest-worker principle.

On the other side of the continent, by the late 1970s some of the traditional sending countries (Italy, Spain and Greece) had either achieved net migration gains or were on their way towards that position. Only Portugal continued to undergo net outflow. In these southern European countries the returnees are not as distinctive or socially significant as the ethnic minority communities of the north, but they are of considerable importance in the population and economic geography of the areas they have returned to (King, 1986). One final interesting twist in the story of the 'returnee' countries during the 1970s is that they emerged as

Table 4.8: Foreign Residents, Selected Countries, 1970 and 1980

	1970		1980		Percent shift 1970–80
	% foreign	Principal groups	% foreign	Principal groups	
Austria	2.4[a]	—	3.9[b]	—	+1.5
Belgium	7.2	Italy, France, Spain	8.9[b]	Italy, Morocco, France	+1.7
Netherlands	1.6[c]	FRG, Belgium, Spain	3.4	Turkey, Morocco, FRG	+1.8
Spain	0.4	Portugal, France, FRG	0.5[b]	UK, Portugal, FRG	+0.1
Sweden	5.1	Finland, Yugoslavia, Denmark	5.1	Finland, Yugoslavia, Denmark	—
Switzerland	15.9	Italy, FRG, Spain	14.0	Italy, Spain, FRG	−1.9

Notes: a. 1971
  b. 1981
  c. 1968

Sources: National statistical yearbooks

countries of immigration from across the Mediterranean (Vallat, 1980; see also Chapter 9).

Conclusions

It is interesting to look back with the hindsight of the mid-1980s on the international migration history of Western Europe during the 1970s. At the time it was customary (OECD, 1978; Lebon and Falchi, 1980) to identify revolutionary change and to ascribe this to the oil crisis of the years immediately after the Arab–Israeli war of autumn 1973, producing a total halt in movement. This interpretation has been called into question in this chapter for a number of reasons. Firstly, it relies too much on the role of contract guest-workers (who were only ever of real importance in West Germany, Switzerland, Austria and Luxembourg), ignoring other forms of movement. Secondly, it places too much emphasis on economic influences as causal mechanisms. And thirdly, it is an interpretation that ignores some of the detail of dates and events, particularly of the dates of political moves to control migration.

It is notoriously difficult to set up counterfactual positions. However, it is the thesis of this chapter that the economic crisis years of 1974–5 did not bring revolutionary change to the international migration system of Western Europe and that even if such a crisis had not occurred the migration system of 1980 may well have borne certain strong resemblances to the actual system that did in fact develop. The reasoning behind this thesis lies in the structural features and context behind the migration.

By the early 1970s growth in the core economies of Western Europe was already slowing down, and the demand for unskilled industrial labour was no longer growing rapidly as these economies moved more and more towards de-industrialisation. In future the growing sector of the labour market would be that concerning high-level personnel. The development of a new international spatial division of labour, with some industrial decentralisation to relatively peripheral economies, tended to take economic growth to certain of the areas with traditional labour surpluses such as Eire or Portugal. In such conditions it is arguable that unskilled labour immigration into north-west Europe would have been reduced anyway throughout the 1970s, as was indeed already occurring during the early years of the decade.

It is also arguable (King, 1984) that return migration flows to southern Europe and elsewhere were inevitable during the 1970s for reasons that were personal to the migrants concerned, almost irrespective of economic conditions. In practice, much return migration has been to marginal areas of growing economies (southern Italy or southern Spain, for example) rather than to the actual growth centres, but the fact that movement back was occurring before 1974 is of considerable significance. Not all migrant-exporting countries of the Mediterranean were likely to be involved: those (such as Turkey) that had come relatively late into the system would not witness large-scale return moves until a later period — the early 1980s.

The political moves against immigration that many countries took in the period 1973–5 were responses not to economic crisis but to social concern about the effects of immigration. In many countries these bans were unrelated to the oil crisis and recession, although undoubtedly the recession and slower growth rates of the later 1970s helped to turn what in some cases had been designed as temporary bans into permanent restrictions. But the initial bans came in before unemployment rates took off and were thus not a response to labour surplus but to other considerations. New barriers to freedom of movement (or to the relative freedom that had existed previously at least for workers), coupled with the changing aspirations and attitudes of the migrants themselves, then converted temporary flows of labour migrants into longer-term flows of families, creating migrant communities out of groups of migrants. These extensions of migrant time-horizons were, however, already occurring irrespective of political actions by host governments.

Economic rationalist explanations of international migration flows in the 1970s are misleading or partial on several counts. They ignore the increasing diversity of the labour market during the period, and particularly the existence of differential demand for workers of different skill levels. They totally ignore the huge body of migration brought about by external political factors. In viewing international movement solely as labour flow they ignore the extent of familial movement during the decade. And, finally, they tend to see migration solely as a response to external factors; in practice, migration affected its own context by bringing about further change through a variety of feedback processes. For example, both return migration and political actions to reduce movement can be seen as being influenced not by temporary economic conditions but by societal responses (in the one case amongst the migrants and in the other by host populations) to the experience of earlier migration.

International migration therefore developed in the 1970s along lines which were not totally surprising in view of certain developments and changes already occurring by 1970 (the exception being certain of the politically-determined flows of refugees and ex-colonials). The economic, social and political contexts of migration were no longer in the 1970s what they had been in the 1960s, even before the crisis years struck. The results were an evolution of migration trends that can be broadly summed up for individual countries in the two words 'return' or 'consolidation'.

References

Anon (1981) 'L'évolution des migrations européennes selon les analyses du Système d'Observation Permanente sur les Migrations', *Dossier Migrations, 2*
Böhning, W.R. (1972) *The Migration of Workers in the United Kingdom and the European Community*, Oxford University Press, London
Carney, J.G. (1976) 'Capital accumulation and uneven development in Europe: notes on migrant labour', *Antipode, 8*, 38–8
Castles, S. (1984) *Here for Good: Western Europe's New Ethnic Minorities*, Pluto, London
Castles, S. and Kosack, G. (1973) *Immigrant Workers and Class Structures in Western Europe*, Oxford University Press, Oxford
Council of Europe (1983) *Recent Demographic Developments in the Member States of the Council of Europe*, Strasbourg
Courgeau, D. and Pumain, D. (1984) 'Baisse de la mobilité residentielle', *Populations et Sociétés, 179*
Dahya, B. (1973) 'Pakistanis in Britain: transients or settlers?', *Race, 14*, 241–77
Eurostat (1984) *Demographic Statistics*, Statistical Office of the European Communities, Luxembourg
Findlay, A.M. and Godden, J. (1985) 'UK expatriates in the Middle East', *Middle East Economic Digest*, 4 January, p.31
Giner, S. and Salcedo, J. (1978) 'Migrant workers in European social structures' in S. Giner, and M.A. Archer (eds.) *Contemporary Europe: Social Structures and Cultural Patterns*, Routledge & Kegan Paul, London, pp.94–123
Girard, A. (1977) 'Opinion publique, immigration et immigrés', *Ethnologie Française, 7*, 219–28
Johnston, R.J. (1980) 'Xenophobia and referenda. An example of the exploratory use of ecological regression', *Espace Géographique, 9*, 73–80
Johnston, R.J. and White, P.E. (1977) 'Reactions to foreign workers in Switzerland: an essay in electoral geography', *Tijdschrift voor Economische en Sociale Geografie, 68*, 341–54
King, R. (1977) 'Problems of return migration: a case-study of Italians returning from Britain', *Tijdschrift voor Economische en Sociale Geografie, 68*, 241–6
King, R. (1984) 'Population mobility: emigration, return migration and internal

migration', in Williams, A. (ed.) *Southern Europe Transformed*, Harper & Row, London pp. 145–78

King, R. (ed.) (1986) *Return Migration and Regional Economic Problems*, Croom Helm, Beckenham

Kreuzaler, E. (1977) 'The Federal Republic of Germany as host country to foreign guestworkers and their dependants', *International Migration, 15*, 138–42

Kuhn, W.E. (1978) 'Guest workers as an automatic stabilizer of cyclical unemployment in Switzerland and Germany', *International Migration Review, 12*, 210–24

Lebon, A. and Falchi, G. (1980) 'New developments in intra-European migration since 1974', *International Migration Review, 14*, 539–79

Lévi, F. (1977) 'Modèles et pratiques en changement: le cas des Portugaises immigrées en région parisienne', *Ethnologie Française, 7*, 287–98

Lichtenberger, E. (1984) *Gastarbeiter — Leben in Zwei Gesellschaften*, Bohlau, Vienna

OECD (1978) *Migration, Growth and Development*, Paris

Ogden, P.E. (in press) 'Immigration trends in France, 1974–1985' in G. Glebe, and J. O'Loughlin (eds.) *Foreign Minorities in Continental European Cities*, Steiner, Wiesbaden

Paine, S. (1977) 'The changing role of migrant workers in the advanced capitalist economies of Western Europe', in R.T. Griffiths (ed.), *Government, Business and Labour in European Capitalism*, Europotentials Press, London, pp. 199–225

Peach, G.C.K. (1985) 'Immigrants and the 1981 urban riots in Britain' in G.A. Van der Knaap and P.E. White (eds.) *Contemporary Studies of Migration*, Geo Books, Norwich, pp. 143–54

Poulain, M. and Wattelar, C. (1983) 'Les migrations intra-européennes: à la recherche d'un fil d'Ariane au travers des 21 pays du Conseil de l'Europe', *Espace, Populations, Sociétés, 2*, 11–26

Salt, J. (1983) 'Carrières et échanges de cerveaux: un cadre explicatif pour les migrations internationales de travail au sein de l'Europe du Nord-Ouest', *Espace, Populations, Sociétés, 2*, 27–38

Salt, J. (1985a) 'Europe's foreign labour migrants in transition', *Geography, 70*, 151–8

Salt, J. (1985b) 'West German dilemma: little Turks or young Germans?', *Geography, 70*, 162–8

Smith, T.E. (1981) *Commonwealth Migration: Flows and Policies*, Macmillan, London

SOPEMI (1984) *Annual Report 1983*, OECD, Paris

Tribalat, M. (1984) 'L'immigration en Suisse', *Population, 39*, 148–76

Vallat, C. (1980) 'Immigration et sous-prolétariat en Italie', *Méditerranée, 38*, 67–76

Verhaeren, R.E. (1983) 'L'immigration algérienne et la crise économique en France', in Centre de Recherches et d'Etudes sur les Sociétés Méditerranéennes, *Maghrébins en France: Emigrés ou Immigrés?* CNRS, Paris

White, P.E. (1985a) 'Switzerland: from migrant rotation to migrant communities', *Geography, 70*, 168–71

White, P.E. (1985b) 'Levels of intra-urban migration in Western European cities', *Espace, Populations, Sociétés, 1*, 161–9

White, P.E. and Woods, R.I. (1983) 'Migration and the formation of ethnic minorities', in K. Kirkwood *et al.* (eds.) *Biosocial Aspects of Ethnic Minorities*, Journal of Biosocial Science Supplement, *8*, 7–22

5 DENMARK

Yvonne Court

Introduction

The demographic situation in Denmark has changed considerably during the last 15 years. The population has actually declined in numbers and shows accentuated signs of ageing. While the death rate has shown a continuation of earlier trends with a steady rise in the average expectation of life, important changes have occurred in other demographic variables: live births, marriages, divorces and migration (Kulturgeografiske Haefter, 1983).

These changes mirror those which have taken place elsewhere in Europe, but to many Danes they are considered to be dramatic, as shown in extensive media comment in recent years. This chapter outlines the changes which have taken place in the demographic situation of Denmark during the period 1970–83 and considers, briefly, the causes and implications of these changes for other aspects of the economy and society of the country.

Population Size and Growth

From 1970 to 1983 the Danish population increased by 4.3 per cent, from 4,906,900 to 5,116,500 persons. The decline in fertility which started towards the end of the nineteenth century has now effectively reduced the rate of population growth to under 1 per cent per annum (see Figure 5.1).

The question of whether Denmark is becoming 'depopulated' is high on the list of topics currently being publicly debated. According to the lastest (1983) official prognosis, the Danish population will fall by more than 60 per cent in the period up to the year 2082 if the present very low average number of births — 1.38 children per woman (1984) — is maintained. In fact the Danish population began to fall in 1981, and it will take many years to counteract the endemic reduction. Projections for the end of the century indicate that the total population will fall from the current 5.1 million to 4.9 million by the year 2000, a decline of 3.5 per cent.

Figure 5.1: Denmark: Population Growth Per Annum 1930–82

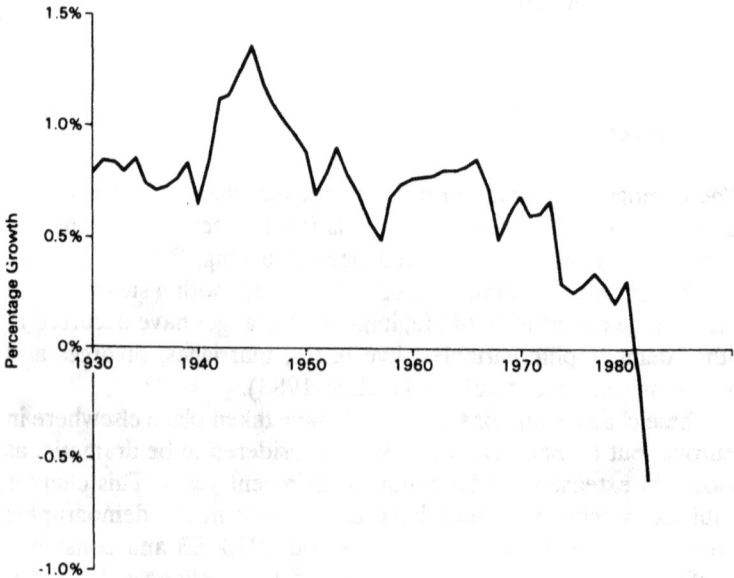

Source: *Befolkningens Bevaegelser*, 1982

Several significant changes occurred in the age structure of the population during the 1970s, changes which are expected to continue in the years ahead. The most characteristic feature of the dynamics of the age structure of Denmark is undoubtedly the accentuation of ageing, but Denmark was not directly involved in World War II and therefore, in comparison with certain other European countries such as France (Figure 7.1) or West Germany, the population pyramid does not show the same signs of war.

On 1 January 1983, 19.4 per cent of the population was under the age of 15, compared with 23.1 per cent on 1 January 1971. The section of the population in the 15–24 age group has now also declined: from 23.7 per cent to 22.7 per cent. In contrast, the proportion of the 30–64 age group has risen from 40.8 per cent to 43.8 per cent, and that of the group over the age of 65 years from 12.4 per cent to 14.7 per cent. Whether measured by the proportion of persons aged 75 or over, or 65 and over, the ageing of the Danish population has become more marked.

The number of elderly is growing faster in the case of women than of men; thus in 1983 more than one woman in five was aged 65 or over and one in eight men 65 or over. Men's higher mortality rate largely explains the less marked ageing of the male population.

If, as expected, the population decreases by the end of the century, the age structure will undergo drastic changes (Danmarks Statistik, 1981). The number of those aged 15–24 will be reduced from 789,908 in 1983 to 591,344 in the year 2000, a fall of more than 25 per cent. Conversely, the group aged 25–64 will increase by well over 10 per cent in the same period, whilst the absolute numbers of those aged over 65 will grow temporarily and then subsequently fall to more or less the same level as in 1983.

Natural Change

Danish birth statistics relate to children born in either Denmark or Greenland to women legally resident in Denmark. Fertility has been declining substantially since the mid-1960s. Figure 5.2 shows

Figure 5.2: Denmark: Total Number of Live Births per Annum 1960–82

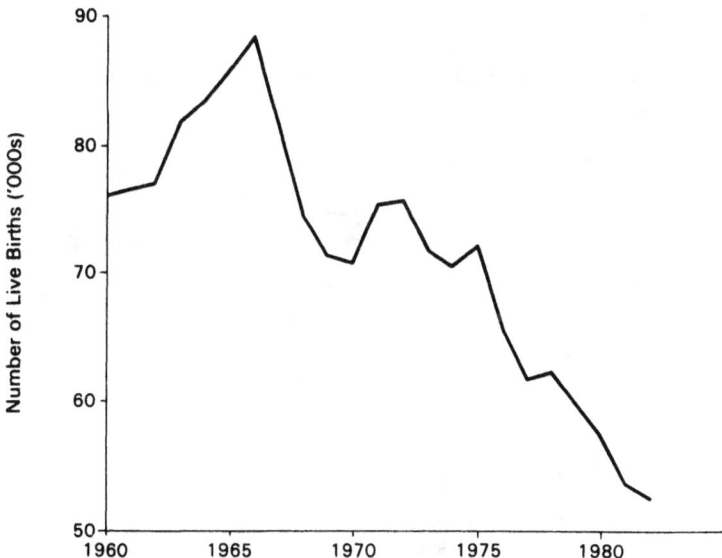

Source: *Befolkningens Bevaegelser* 1982

the annual number of live births from 1961 to 1982. The total has fallen from a peak of over 88,000 in 1966 to 52,700 in 1982, a decrease of 40.1 per cent. As a result the total fertility rate has been reduced to 1.55 children per woman. This marked decrease results from more women remaining childless, fewer women having more than two children, and the age at which they bear children being later. The mean age of women at the time of a first child's birth has risen from 23.7 (1970) to 24.8 (1981); and the mean age at the birth of any child has also risen from 26.2 (1970) to 27.0 (1981). Figure 5.3 shows the changing age-specific fertility rates which have brought this about, the marked reduction in fertility in the group 20–24 being particularly notable.

There are many factors that account for the very low birth figures. Extensive social changes, as well as the development of effective methods of contraception since the mid-1960s and, since 1973, both access to legal abortion and the right to sterilisation to any person over 25 years of age (see Table 5.1) underlie this development in the number of live births (Bertelsen, 1980).

The decisive factors are probably the increase in the number of women in education or in paid employment (evidence for which will be presented later), and the steeply rising costs of child care. This social change has resulted in individual couples finding it

Figure 5.3: Denmark: Age-Specific Fertility Rates 1971–81

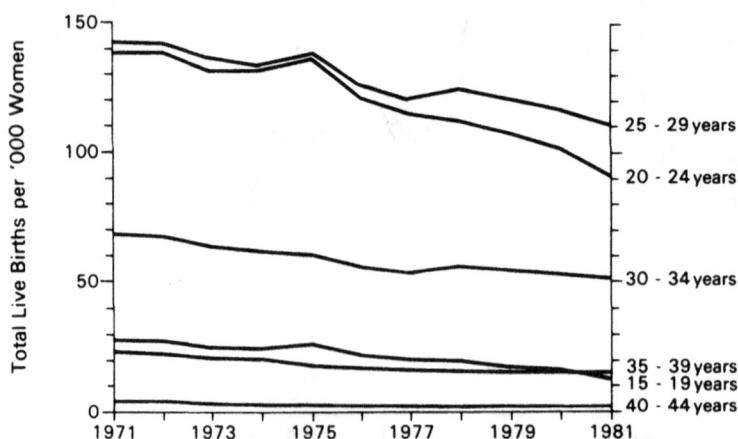

Source: *Statistisk Tiårsoversigt,* 1983

Table 5.1: Denmark: Abortions and Sterilisations 1973–82

A.	Legal abortions				
	1973	1976	1979	1982	% change 1973–82
Total	16,536	26,842	23,193	21,462	+22.9

B.	Human sterilisations			
	1975/6	1979	1982	% change 1975–82
Male	9,657	4,343	4,434	−45.9
Female	4,464	6,888	7,410	+60.2
Total	14,121	11,231	11,844	−16.1

Source: *Statistisk Årbog*, various years

expedient to reduce the size of their families. The number of children must conform with expectations with regard to training and work participation that are now entertained by both partners (Bertelsen, 1981).

The decline in the birth rate will exercise a decisive influence on the future economic, social and political situation in Denmark. It will take years to increase the birth figure decisively, and new legislation would be required to reduce the costs for families. In order to attain the reproduction figure of 2.1 at which the population will remain constant in the longer term, the number of births would have to rise by as much as 50 per cent. Schools and kindergartens are already affected by the problem. It has already been necessary to reduce drastically the number of classes and, hence, lay off teachers. Furthermore, capital investments in the education sector and related sectors, in the form of building, will almost certainly be brought to a halt in the years to come. Political disturbances in Denmark during 1985 were also partly underlain by the growing realisation that the country might no longer be able to afford to maintain its highly regarded social welfare system, partly as a result of demographic changes altering the pressures on it.

In terms of mortality Denmark, like most other European countries, had already attained low rates — by world standards — by the 1930s, and one would have to go back to the 1850s for crude death rate values of over 20 deaths per thousand population. The Danish figure is now just over 10 (10.8 per thousand population in 1982). By world standards, infant mortality in Denmark is also very low (8.2 per thousand live births in 1982). These reflect a combination of very high standards of living and health care.

Denmark recorded higher crude death rates in the 1970s than in the 1950s. This is not a symptom of deteriorating health services or living standards; the cause is a rising average age structure following reduced fertility.

With the present mortality rates in various age groups, a northern European in Denmark can be expected to live to an age of over 74. Average life expectancy at birth has been rising over a number of decades, as shown in Table 5.2.

Even though Denmark is a relatively small country, considerable regional differences in mortality have existed in the past. By and large, there was a higher mortality rate in urban areas than rural areas. However, since the mid nineteenth century regional mortality differences have been greatly reduced. In 1977, the difference between the longest (79.0 in Bornholm) and the shortest (76.3 in all counties except Ribe, South Jutland and Funen) life expectancies for women was 3.6 years. The corresponding difference for men was no less than 6.6 years (Öberg, 1979). Present trends in mortality and life expectancy are of considerable economic and social importance and can hardly be overlooked by the government in its concern with social policies and decisions for the future. These changes already have certain implications in terms of maintenance responsibility for the elderly, and the social welfare costs are likely to increase in the future. At present there is an increasing need for resources in the field of health care: for example, 20 per cent of the 80 years-plus age group are in old people's homes as compared with only 2 per cent of those in the 65–79 age group.

International Migration and the Evolution of Minority Populations

An important feature of the policy content of international migration is that Denmark is a member of both the European Community and of the free labour market constituted since the 1950s by the Nordic countries. In practice, however, the post-war period has generally been characterised by relatively small exchanges of population with other countries. Net migration has fluctuated from positive to negative and back again several times since the 1930s, dependent upon economic conjunctures in the countries concerned. Figure 5.4 shows the trends in international

Table 5.2: Denmark: Life Expectancy at Birth 1931/5–1980/1

	Males	Females
1931–35	62.0	63.8
1951–55	69.8	72.6
1971–75	70.9	76.5
1976–77	71.2	77.1
1978–79	71.3	77.4
1980–81	71.1	77.2

Source: *Befolkningens Bevaegelser*, 1981

Figures 5.4: Denmark: Immigration and Emigration 1970–82

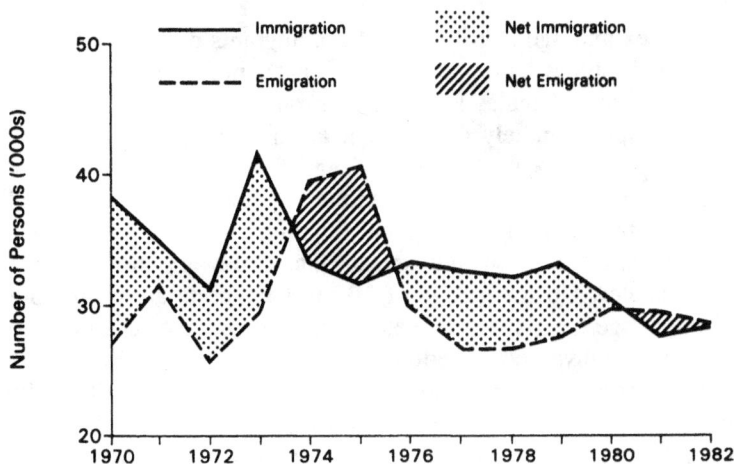

Source: *Statistisk Årbog*, various years

migration during the period 1970–82. Just as there was a net immigration into Denmark during the country's prosperous growth years of the 1960s and early 1970s, there was a net emigration during the most severe years of recession: 1974 and 1975, and again in 1981 and 1982. As elsewhere (see Chapter 4), Denmark imposed a ban on labour immigration from non-EEC and non-Nordic countries in the mid-1970s, but despite the ban immigration has continued, largely as a result of family reunification. Generally, 40–50 per cent of all moves in and out of Denmark involve Danish nationals, and a great number of the moves are to Sweden, Norway and the EEC countries.

During the 1960s migrant workers arrived in appreciable numbers, initially from Spain and Italy and later from Turkey, Yugoslavia, North Africa and Pakistan. In most years since 1960, Denmark has had a net again from other countries. By 1973, migrants from the countries around the Mediterranean accounted for 40 per cent of aliens in Denmark. However, return migration in the years 1974 and 1975 helped to turn the net migration flows into a small loss for those years. The migrant workers were concentrated heavily in Copenhagen, in areas close to the capital (although to a lesser extent), and in the cities of east Jutland, especially Århus. It was these same areas which experienced net migration losses through international migration in 1974 and 1975.

The sex and age distribution of the migrants during the period 1974–81 shows the traditional pattern, with an over-representation of males and a concentration in the youngest age groups. Approximately 40 per cent are in the age group 20–29, and 80 per cent aged between 15 and 59. There seems to be a greater number of mature individuals among the international migrants than among the internal migrants. In the case of international migrants, it would appear that males are more mobile than females. Up to the age of 30 most migrants are single, but after that age the majority are either married or have been married and are now divorced or widowed.

The patterns of international migration inevitably affect the development of minority populations. In fact, as a result of the low rate of net movement Denmark has no large minority populations. Figure 5.5 shows the evolution of foreign nationals resident in Denmark. As would be expected, the numbers of Nordic and EEC nationals are the highest of all groups and have remained fairly constant during the period 1974–84. The number of North Americans increased slightly in the mid-1970s and has since declined. The Yugoslavian trend illustrates the opposite development: decreased numbers in 1975–76 and then a slight but steady rise to a fairly constant level after 1981.

The most dramatic increases have taken place in the numbers of Asians (mainly Pakistanis) and Turks resident in Denmark. The number of Asians has risen steadily from 9,391 in 1974 to almost 16,000 at 1 January 1984. In terms of the represented national

Figure 5.5: Denmark: Foreign Nationals Resident in Denmark
1974–84

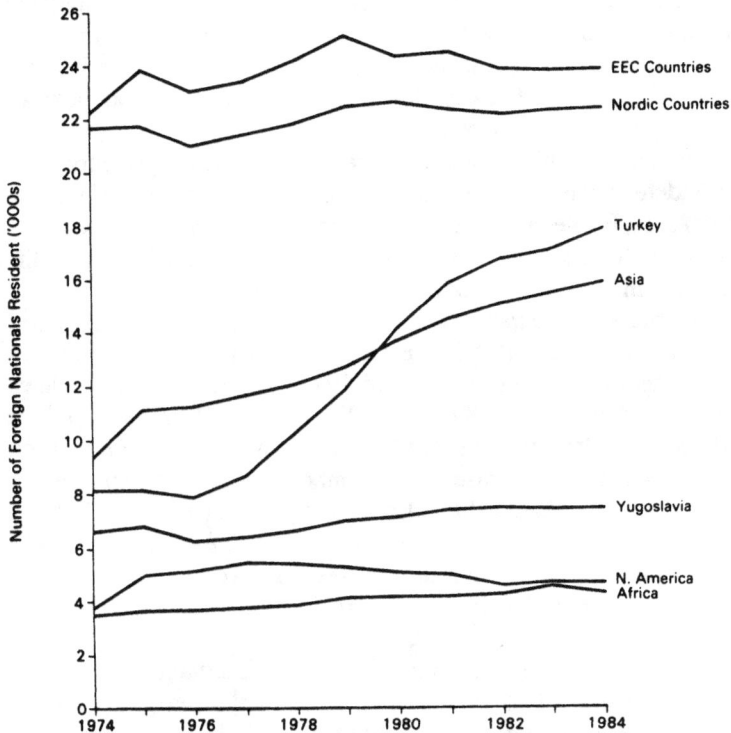

Sources: *Statistisk Tiårsoversigt, 1983*; *Statistisk Årbog,* 1984

groups, it is the Pakistanis and Vietnamese who have accounted
for a large part of this increase. The number of Pakistanis has
almost doubled in this period (6,653 in 1984 against 3,733 in
1974). Since 1978 the number of Vietnamese has risen almost
ninefold, from 384 in 1978 to 3,390 in 1984. This reflects
Denmark's absorption of 'boat people' in the years after the end of
the Vietnam war (see also Chapter 4).

The number of Turks resident in Denmark was fairly constant
until 1976, when there was a dramatic increase which has continued into the 1980s, although there are now signs that this
increase is slowing down.

Internal Migration and Counterurbanisation

The statistics of internal migration comprise all persons changing residence from one Danish local government district (*kommune*) to another. With effect from 1979, the statistics also comprise persons changing residence within their *kommune*, so that now all internal migration is covered.

Migration within Denmark is becoming increasingly important as a determinant of regional population development, since the difference between the number of in-migrants and out-migrants can vary to a greater extent and with greater rapidity than differences in the numbers of births and deaths.

Denmark has experienced a marked change in its migration patterns during the last 15 years. The total number of moves in 1982 was 27 per cent less than in 1971. Inter-county moves have also decreased from 248,652 in 1970 to 173,516 in 1982 (minus 30 per cent). It is possible that this decline in the level of migration is the result of an increase in the numbers of those commuting.

A dramatic change has also taken place in the regional net migration pattern. The 1960s saw a continuation of a well-established pattern of migration losses from west Jutland, and net migration gains in the Copenhagen region and in the urban areas of east Jutland, especially Århus.

The early 1970s saw a major change in this situation (see Figure 5.6). At the level of the county, those in the periphery (North Jutland, Ringkøbing, Ribe and South Jutland) showed net migration gains, and it is the capital region and the urban areas of east Jutland that have lost population through migration. However, the early 1980s show a different pattern again. The Copenhagen region's losses begin to decrease until, in 1982, there was a small net gain. The peripheral counties display net losses of varying degrees.

A far clearer picture of population change can be derived if population changes at the local or municipality level are considered. Figure 5.7 shows the overall patterns of population change in Denmark at this scale. A high level of positive change can be seen in the rural and small town areas of Jutland, and the other areas of the metropolitan region, whereas a high negative change has taken place in the core area of Copenhagen, its surrounding municipalities and parts of the islands (Møn, Falster and Lolland) south of Zealand.

Figure 5.6: Denmark: Net Migration by County 1970–82

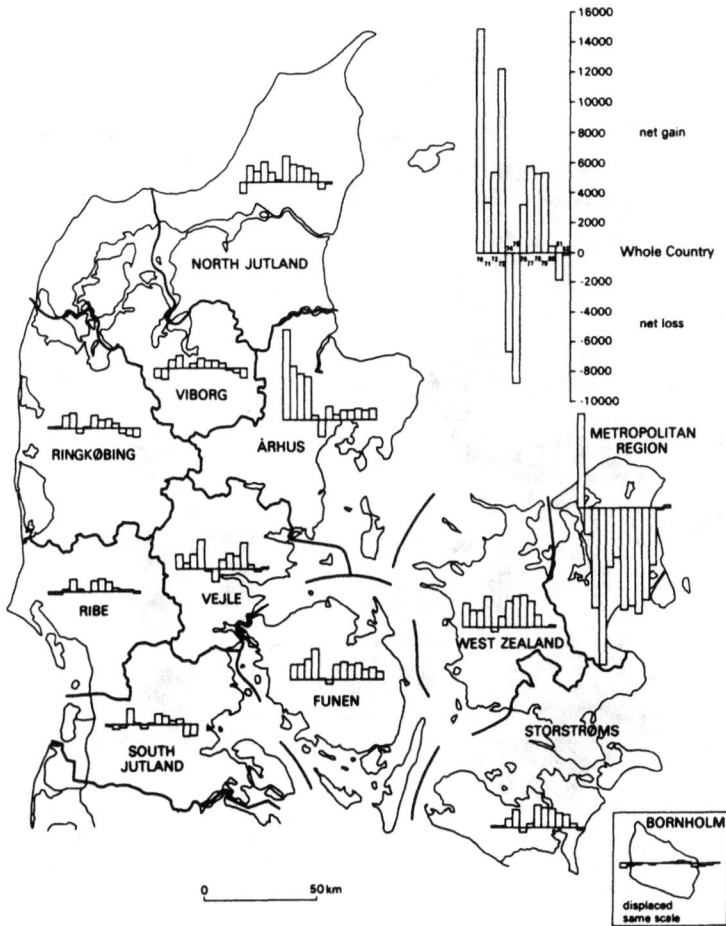

Figure 5.8 shows the relative importance of the components of population change, and demonstrates that migration has become the most important component of population change. In most rural areas in-migration is greater than natural increase, whilst the capital region and some urban areas of east Jutland show population losses through out-migration. There has been a general westward movement away from the core area and suburbs of the metropolitan region, and from urban areas of east Jutland, such as Århus and Horsens.

Figure 5.7: Denmark: Percentage Population Change by
Municipality 1970–83

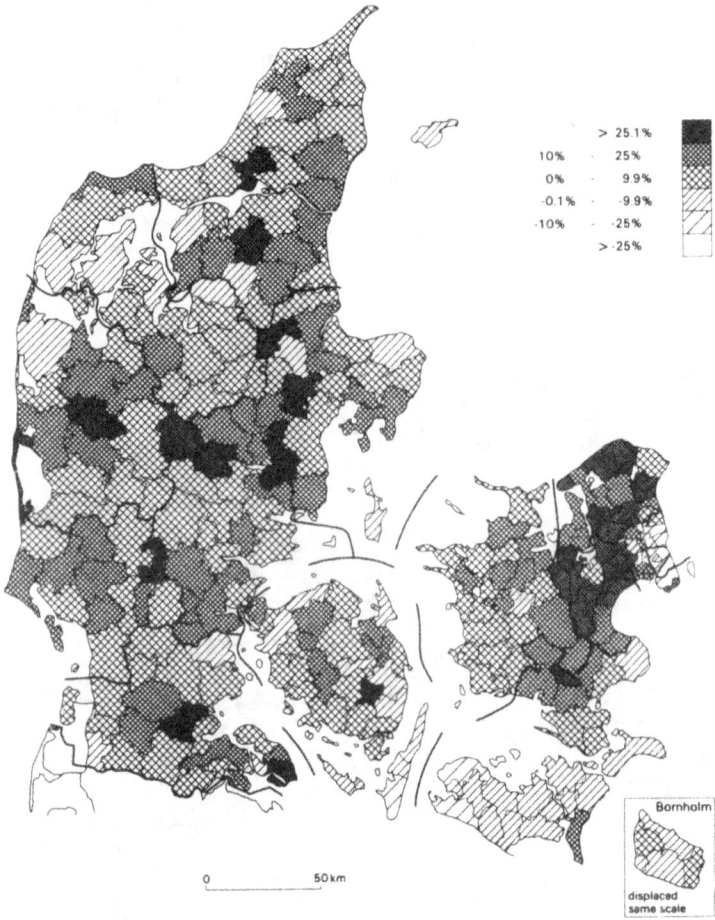

The trend in Denmark throughout this century has been
towards a highly urbanised population. By 1979, 83 per cent of the
population lived in urban areas (officially defined as continuous
built-up areas of over 200 persons). The size distribution of different settlements illustrates the dynamics of these changes in
different sizes of settlements (see Table 5.3)

The Copenhagen metropolitan region's share of population has
decreased, and the large towns are also losing their share.
Medium-sized towns are increasing their share, although the settle-

Figure 5.8: Denmark: Population Change by Component 1970–81

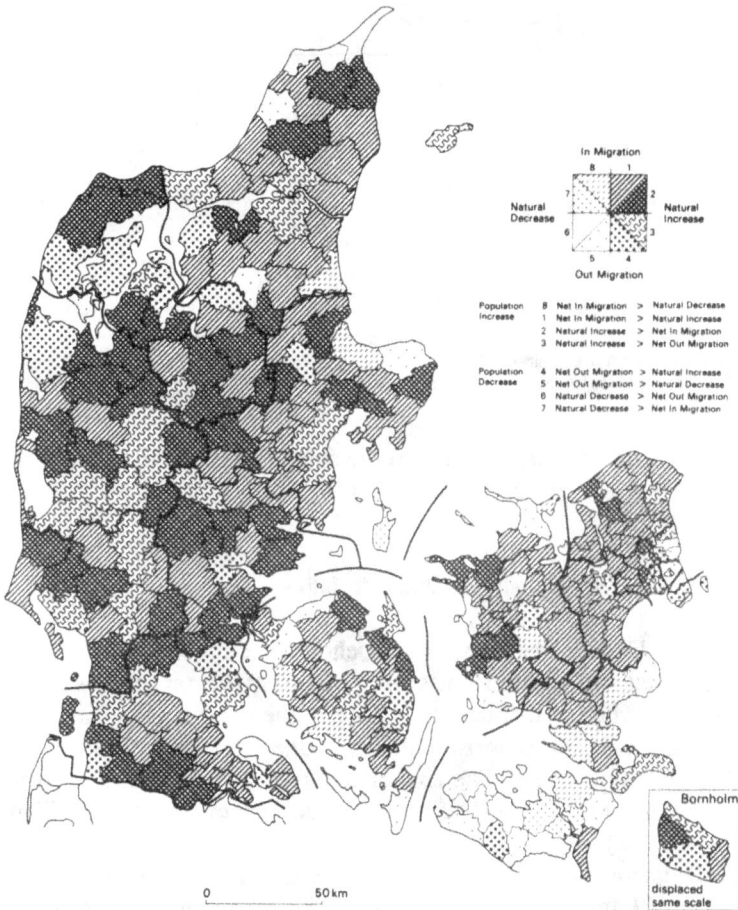

ments of between 10,000 and 19,999 were losing after 1976.

Therefore one can detect evidence at a municipality level for a turnaround in population evolution, although there are now signs that, as mobility decreases, the turnaround is not as strong as it was. Whereas before the early 1970s migration had been (a) from rural to urban, and (b) from rural periphery to metropolitan regions, migration from the early 1970s was

(i) from urban to rural and more peripheral areas of the country, and

Table 5.3: Denmark: Percentage of Population Living in Urban
Areas of Different Population Sizes

	1960	1970	1976	1980
Capital region	27.5	27.9	25.5	24.9
Other urban				
20,000+	21.0	23.6	23.2	22.7
10,000-19,999	6.2	6.2	6.9	5.8
5,000-9,999	4.0	4.0	4.6	4.6
1,000-4,999	7.2	10.6	13.7	14.4
500-999	8.1[a]	8.5[a]	4.5	4.5
Outside urban areas	26.0	19.2	21.6	23.1

Note: a. Urban areas sized 200-999
Source: *Statistisk Årbog*, various years

(ii) from the larger towns to the small and medium-sized towns
(Court, 1982; 1984).

Household Composition Characteristics

In the Danish statistics, a household is defined as all people
registered with the Central Population Register at the same
address, whether or not they belong to the same family. Therefore
a household can comprise more than one family yet still be classified as a household. The size of the average household fell from
2.75 persons in 1970 (Danish National Agency for Physical Planning, 1982) to 2.42 in 1983.

Data concerning household size are unobtainable for the period
1970–79, but developments during 1980–84 indicate some likely
trends (see Table 5.4). The most notable feature of the table is the
proportion of single-person households. The only other size categories to show any absolute increase are those of two- and three-
person households; all larger categories have decreased.

Recent trends in marriage and divorce reinforce the developments within different types of household (see Table 5.5). The
number of contracted marriages has declined from 32,801 in 1971
to just over 24,000 in 1982. The number of divorces rose from
rather more than 6,000 per annum at the start of the 1960s to
13,400 in 1971 and 14,600 in 1982. In connection with this there
has been a significant increase in common law marriages, where

Table 5.4: Denmark: Household Size 1980 and 1984

Number in household	1980 Number	%	1984 Number	%	% Change 1980–84
1 person	601,074	29.1	663,761	31.1	+10.4
2 persons	642,793	31.2	677,503	31.7	+5.3
3 persons	325,658	15.8	331,498	15.5	+1.8
4 persons	331,663	16.1	326,434	15.3	−1.6
5 persons	117,739	5.7	101,468	4.8	−13.8
6 and over	43,221	2.1	34,908	1.6	−19.2
Total number of households	2,062,148	100.0	2,135,572	100.0	+3.5

Sources: Statistisk Tiårsoversigt, 1983; Statistisk Årbog, 1984

two persons of opposite sex keep house together and cohabit without undergoing a legal form of marriage ceremony. The number of people cohabiting in 1977 was 343,000; this rose to 449,000 in 1981, an increase of 30 per cent. Approximately 75 per cent of these people were single, 19 per cent divorced and the remainder widowed. In 1981, consensual unions accounted for 17 per cent of all existing unions (Council of Europe, 1983). The ability to earn her own living has made contracted marriage less necessary for a woman as a security for her own (and her children's) maintenance (Andersen, 1976).

Labour-Force Characteristics

Labour-force statistics are compiled on the basis of extracts from administrative registers held by Danmarks Statistik and a 10 per cent random sample of the population. The potential labour force is that share of the population which is of working age: those between 15 and 74 years old. Several aspects of Denmark's demographic situation relate directly to the character of the labour market.

The size of the labour force has increased to a greater extent than has the share of the population which is of working age (see Table 5.6). This, first and foremost, is the result of the heavy influx of women into the labour force; the female labour force increased by over 240,000 from 1971–81, and now accounts for 44 per cent of the labour force in comparison to 39 per cent in 1971. The male labour force grew by only 20,000 over the same period.

Table 5.5: Denmark: Relative Distribution of Family Type by
Households 1980 and 1983 (%)

	1980		1983	
1. *Households with one family:*	84.9		84.5	
Single persons without children	29.2		30.5	
of which women		17.6		18.3
men		11.6		12.2
Married without children	20.6		20.0	
Single with children	4.6		5.0	
of which women		3.9		4.3
men		0.7		0.7
Married with children	29.8		27.3	
Cohabiting with children	0.7		1.7	
2. *Households with two or more families*	10.1		10.4	
2 single persons of opposite sex	8.4		8.6	
without children		6.3		6.8
with children		2.1		1.8
2 single persons of same sex	1.7		1.8	
without children		1.5		1.6
with children		0.2		0.2
3. *Other households*	5.0		5.1	
Total households	100.0		100.0	

Source: Statistisk Tiårsoversigt, 1983

Table 5.6: Denmark: Number of Persons of Working Age and in the
Labour Force 1971–81

		Thousands			% Change 1971–81
		1971	1976	1981	
Number of persons of working age:	M	1,784	1,825	1,883	+5.5
	F	1,806	1,848	1,902	+5.3
	T	3,590	3,673	3,784	+5.4
Number in labour force:	M	1,466	1,481	1,486	+1.4
	F	943	1,014	1,188	+25.9
	T	2,409	2,495	2,674	+11.1

Source: Statistisk Tiårsoversigt, 1983

This increasing female labour-force participation can also be illustrated by activity rates. While the male activity rate fell from 83.2 to 78.9 per cent between 1970 and 1981, female activity rates increased from 50.8 to 62.5 per cent during the same period. Some interesting features of these rates become apparent if they are examined by age characteristics.

During the 1970s male activity rates overall were much lower than during the 1950s and 1960s. These decreased levels of participation are undoubtedly the result of changes in the occupational activities of both the youngest and oldest men. In part, these are to be accounted for by developments towards an increasing length of education in the post-war years, and by an increased tendency among the young to undertake an advanced academic or practical education. Also influential has been the fact that social welfare for the elderly has undergone a marked development in recent years: for example, the number of persons receiving disability pensions has increased substantially.

More significant changes have occurred with respect to women (see Table 5.7). One of the most conspicuous developments is that the gap between the activity rates of married and single women has narrowed. The trend is primarily due to the fact that the activity rate of married women has increased. At one time a woman's marriage or the birth of a first child almost automatically meant her withdrawal from the labour market, but that is no longer the case. In 1981 the number of married women of working age in the labour force was 728,590 in comparison with 589,000 in 1970.

Table 5.7: Denmark: Female Activity Rates by Age 1970–81 (%)

	1970	1978	1981
Married women: age			
14–24	55	83	90
25–29	39	74	77
60+	7	21	15
Total	34	65	66
Unmarried women: age			
14–24	52	54	63
25–29	75	81	79
60+	12	16	13
Total	44	54	58

Source: ILO Yearbook of Statistics, various years

The total number of married women aged between 15 and 74 years was 1,153,479 in 1981 and 1,202,000 in 1970. The increase in activity rates in this group is, clearly, the result of recent developments in industry and the expansion of public administration as both have provided women with greater possibilities for obtaining employment.

One of the most important characteristics of married women's economic activity is to be found in the extent to which they take part-time employment. At the time of the labour-force sample survey in 1981, approximately 50 per cent of the married women who were economically active were employed in part-time positions. Among all economically active women in 1981, 46.5 per cent were employed part time. Among the total economically active population only 23.7 per cent had part-time employment.

The division of female activity rates by age shows that the largest increase is caused both by an increased labour force entry on the part of the younger age groups, and a fall in the number of persons withdrawing from the labour market up to the age of 50. A comparison between the two sexes shows that, as for the young age groups, the gap between the activity rates of men and women has narrowed in recent years. The activity rate of men reaches its highest point at a higher age (97.3 per cent at 30–44 years) than that of women (88.6 per cent at 25–29 years).

Figure 5.9 shows the distribution of the labour force since 1955. The declining importance of agricultural employment is evident, as is the development of the public sector which has resulted in a pronounced expansion in the employment in 'services'. The various sectors of the labour market can also be differentiated by gender. Agriculture, the manufacturing industries, building and construction tend to be dominated by males; the public sector and services by females. Changes in the pattern during the 1970s and early 1980s have been very small, and the lack of mobility is one of the reasons why it has been difficult to reduce the present high level of unemployment. Table 5.8 illustrates these developments; it is especially characteristic that an increasing number of women hold jobs in the public sector and a decreasing number in the manufacturing industry, whereas the share of men working in the latter remains relatively constant.

In absolute terms, there has been a decline in the number employed in the manufacturing industries throughout the period as a result of economic stagnation, whereas demand for labour in the

Figure 5.9: Denmark: Economically Active Population by Sector 1955–81

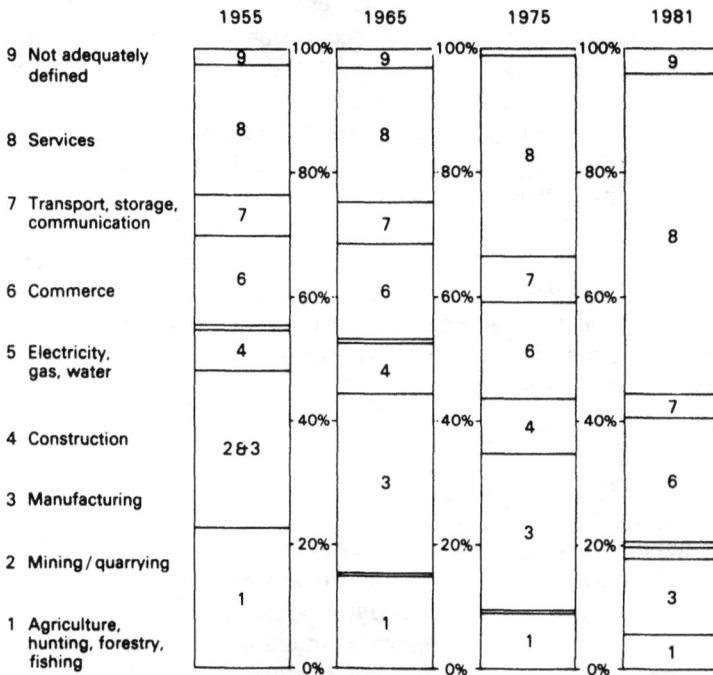

Source: *ILO Yearbook of Labour Statistics*, various years

Table 5.8: Denmark: Employed Women as a Percentage of the Total Number Employed in Each Sector

Sector	1974	1976	1981
Agriculture, fishing	27	27	26
Manufacturing	27	26	31
Building and constructing	8	8	11
Administrative, managerial and professional services	65	65	64
Miscellaneous services	45	44	46
Industry or occupation not stated	24	37	65
Total	41	41	45

Source: Statistisk Årbog, various years

public sector has increased. This increase in demand has absorbed the growth of the female labour force.

There has been a relative decline in the number of self-employed among the economically active in the period 1970–81. This decline has taken place in all occupational branches, but it has been most pronounced in the agricultural sector, which includes the greatest number of these people.

The group including salaried employees has expanded greatly in size, whilst the group of unskilled manual workers has decreased in size. In addition, there have been noticeable declines in the relative number of skilled manual workers since 1970. The majority of women are employed as salaried employees or unskilled workers, and very few women (one in nine) are self-employed in comparison with men, of whom one in six belong to this category. Men are more equally distributed in occupational groups with a bias in favour of salaried employees.

Conclusions

A number of changes have taken place in Denmark during the last 15 years, many of which are similar to developments in the rest of Europe but have nevertheless caused great concern amongst the Danes. The changing demographic situation has given rise to a great deal of media comment, but political reaction has, as yet, been relatively insignificant. This is probably because the general opinion in Denmark is that population figures are manipulated by social-political interests.

The reduced birth rate is, undoubtedly, one of the key changes and the one which is causing greatest concern. There are obvious implications, in terms of child care and for the education sector as well as for the labour and housing markets. The slowly changing age structure of the population and the increased death rate will entail changes in terms of maintenance responsibility for the elderly.

Relatively few changes have taken place in the pattern of international migration, certainly in comparison with other European countries. As a consequence of the small numbers involved it is of limited significance in the overall patterns of population change.

Migration within Denmark is an important determinant of regional and local population change, despite the overall decline in mobility. There is definite evidence that counterurbanisation was in progress during the 1970s, although there are now signs that the trend is slowing down during the 1980s.

References

Andersen, D. (1976) *Papirløst Samliv Blandt de 20–29 Årige*, Socialforskningsinstituttet, Copenhagen
Andersen, O. (1977) *The Population of Denmark*, CICRED, Paris
Bertelsen, O. (1980) *Den Unge Familie i 70 'Erne*, Socialforskningsinstituttet, Copenhagen
Bertelsen, O. (1981) *Det Faldende Fødselstal*, Socialforskningsinstituttet, Copenhagen
Council of Europe (1983) *Recent Demographic Developments in the Member States of the Council of Europe*, Steering Committee on Population, Strasbourg
Court, Y.K. (1982) *Migration in Denmark, 1950–80*, unpublished MA dissertation, University of Sussex
Court, Y.K. (1984) 'Recent demographic change in Denmark, 1970–82', *South Hampshire Geographer, 16*, 1–11
Danish National Agency for Physical Planning and the Danish Ministry of Housing (1982) *The Human Settlements Situation and Related Trends and Policies*, Copenhagen
Danmarks Statistik (1981) *Landsprognoser 1980–2010 og Regionale Fremskrivninger 1980–2000*. Statistiske Undersøgelser 38, Copenhagen
Kulturgeografiske Haefter (1983) *Befolkning og Samfund*, vol. 8, no. 24, Copenhagen
Öberg, S. (1979) *Internal Migration: Facts and Theories within Denmark, Norway and Sweden*. Paper presented at seminar 'Impact of Current Population Trends of Europe's Cities and Regions', Council of Europe, Strasbourg

6 EIRE

John Coward

Introduction

The 1970s witnessed many major changes in the demographic and socio-economic characteristics of the population of the Irish Republic. Some of these changes, such as net migration gain, rapid population growth and the shift towards counterurbanisation represent newly-established trends in the recent history of the Irish population; while other changes, such as reductions in family size, increasing nuptiality and declining household size represent a continuation of trends that have been in progress for some time. This chapter focuses on some of these features by briefly summarising the characteristics of the available data and then highlighting and explaining the major national and regional demographic characteristics which evolved during the 1970s.

The recent census of population in the Republic of Ireland was taken on the night of 5 April 1981, at the same time as those in Great Britain and Northern Ireland. Prior to this the most recent, fully detailed census had been in 1971, although a complete enumeration of the population using only a small number of questions had been carried out in April 1979. There was no mid-term census in 1976 (although there will be in 1986), and thus the censuses of 1971 and 1981 provide the most important means of documenting some of the recent major socio-demographic changes.

There was a quite considerable range of questions asked in the 1981 census, and in addition to the more standard questions of a typical census information was sought on such matters as religious denomination, the fertility of married women and ability to speak Irish. Certain questions were also included for the first time in an Irish census, including those on present economic status and address of place of work.

While the census data are available for a number of spatial scale levels (Figure 6.1), the finest level for which published information on most topics is available is that of the county and county borough. There are 27 county units and five urban boroughs, and

Figure 6.1: Scales of Data Collection and the Irish Counties and County Boroughs

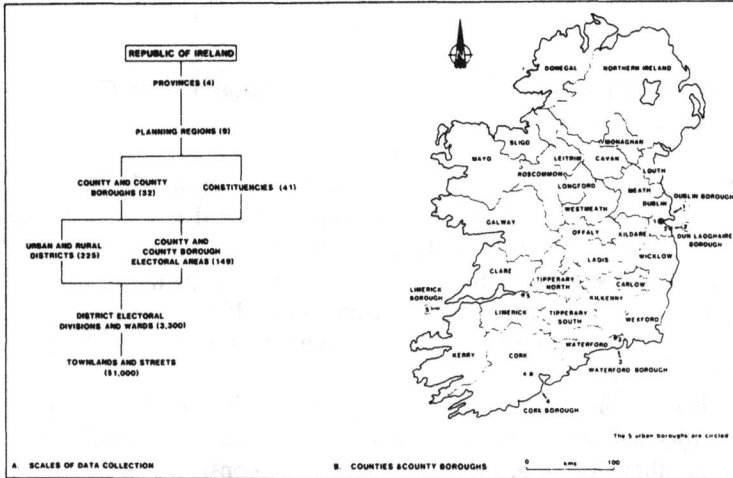

A. SCALES OF DATA COLLECTION   B. COUNTIES & COUNTY BOROUGHS

this spatial grid provides a reasonably detailed mesh for which most census data are readily available. Furthermore, there have been few boundary changes over time. In 1981 the mean population size of these 32 units was 110,000, while the median size was 75,000. There is considerable variation in the population size of these areas, ranging from 28,000 in County Leitrim to over half a million in Dublin Borough. Due to recent urban growth in some areas there are now several urban areas which merit the status of urban borough (and separate information in the census reports) but which are still included with their containing countries. For example, Galway Metropolitan Borough (population 40,000) has a larger population than Waterford County Borough and yet is still subsumed within Galway County at the county/county borough level of aggregation (Figure 6.1).

Ideally, for the purposes of detailed geographical research, more published information is needed at scales finer than that of the county and county borough. The next finer levels of aggregation, for example, are those of the urban and rural districts (of which there are 225) or the county and county borough electoral areas (149). Little information is published at these levels, however, and thus the range of published data at quite fine scales is limited. On the other hand, researchers have fairly good access to unpublished data at some of these finer scales, although there have been problems concerning delays in the tabulation of results at these levels.

National Population Change: Trends in Natural Increase and International Migration

While the major demographic characteristic for which the population of the Irish Republic has been renowned is that of population decline due to high levels of out-migration, recent periods have witnessed a turnaround in this feature. Thus the population declined in each inter-censal period from 1841 to 1961 (with the exception of 1946–51) but has increased over the last 25 years (Table 6.1).

Natural increase has remained quite high over the last half-century and has generally increased from one inter-censal period to another (Table 6.1). This is due to the considerable decline in the death rate together with the fact that the birth rate remains at quite a high level (over 20 per 1,000 population). The maintenance of high birth rates during the twentieth century has been one of the characteristics which has set Ireland apart from many of her West European neighbours and can be attributed to a variety of demographic, socio-economic and cultural factors, including the relatively low level of modernisation and the particular strength of Roman Catholicism (Kennedy, 1973; Coward, 1978, 1982).

Table 6.1: Eire: Population Change 1926–84

Period	Population at end of period (000s)	Average annual change per 1,000 population		
		Population	Natural Increase	Net Migration
1926–36	2,968	−0.1	5.5	−5.6
1936–46	2,955	−0.4	5.9	−6.3
1946–51	2,960	+0.4	8.6	−8.2
1951–61	2,818	−4.9	9.2	−14.1
1961–71	2,978	+5.5	10.2	−4.7
1971–79	3,368	+15.4	11.1	+4.3
1979–81	3,443	+11.1	11.8	−0.7
1981–84[a]	3,535	+5.4	10.6	−5.2

Note: a. Estimated figure
Source: Censuses of population and reports on vital statistics

However, the most outstanding feature of population change over the period 1971–79 was the overall net gain of population through migration (Table 6.1). This was the first time that such a feature had occurred since the advent of census-taking in 1821. A variety of factors explain this phenomenon, the most important being the period of relative economic prosperity in the Irish Republic during part of the 1970s associated with EEC membership and strenuous attempts by the government to attract foreign-owned manufacturing industry. Moreover, the increasingly difficult economic situation in Britain — the major destination for Irish emigrants — meant that the well-used safety valve of migration to that country offered less secure prospects than before. These factors certainly helped to reduce the outflow of migrants as well as encouraging return migration to Ireland. These overall patterns obscure considerable variations by age, and Garvey (1985) shows that for a period 1971–81 there was still a net out-movement amongst those aged 15–24 and, to a lesser extent, 25–34. During the 1970s there was also a net cross-border gain from Northern Ireland reflecting the latter's particularly severe economic problems as well as the effects of the troubles. Overall during the 1970s the Republic experienced a net gain of population through migration of approximately 100,000 people, (Garvey, 1985) and the importance of the migration of family groups should be noted, given that by 1981 37 per cent of the net flow consisted of those aged under 14 while 31 per cent were aged between 35 and 44. The movement of the elderly represented an important but not major element, accounting for 14 per cent of the net movement during the 1970s. More recently, however, the overall balance has swung back to net loss of population through migration (Table 6.1), reflecting the rapidly rising cost of living in the Republic coupled with increasing unemployment, particularly amongst those seeking their first job. The 1970s may well prove to have been an exceptional period in Ireland's demographic history.

The rising natural increase and unprecedented migration gain during the decade did of course result in rapid population growth. By 1981 the population had increased to 3.44 million, increasing by 15.6 per cent over the period 1971–81. It is ironic that while in this decade many West European countries were attaining low, zero or negative growth rates the population of the Irish Republic was increasing at a particularly rapid rate. Furthermore, these changes had a profound effect on the age structure such that, when

compared with an earlier period, such as 1961, the relative growth
of the population aged 15–34 is particularly marked (Figure 6.2).
These changes reflect past fluctuations in natural increase and, in
particular, recent trends in migration. As a result of the high birth
rate and the in-migration of many children, the present age
structure of the population is remarkably youthful (Figure 6.2): for
example, in 1981 30 per cent of the population were aged under
15 and almost 50 per cent under 25. In England and Wales, by
comparison, just over one-third of the population were aged under
15 in 1981. The increases in the young adult age groups ensured
that overall age dependency declined from 1961 to 1981, although
age dependency is still high by European standards (Garvey,
1983). The increases in population and changes in age structure
have immense consequences for the demand for education, social
services and employment (Horner and Daultrey, 1980; Courtney
and McCashin, 1983; Courtney, 1985).

As far as future population prospects are concerned it is likely
that growth rates will decline somewhat in the near future. For

Figure 6.2: Age Structure of the Population 1961 and 1981

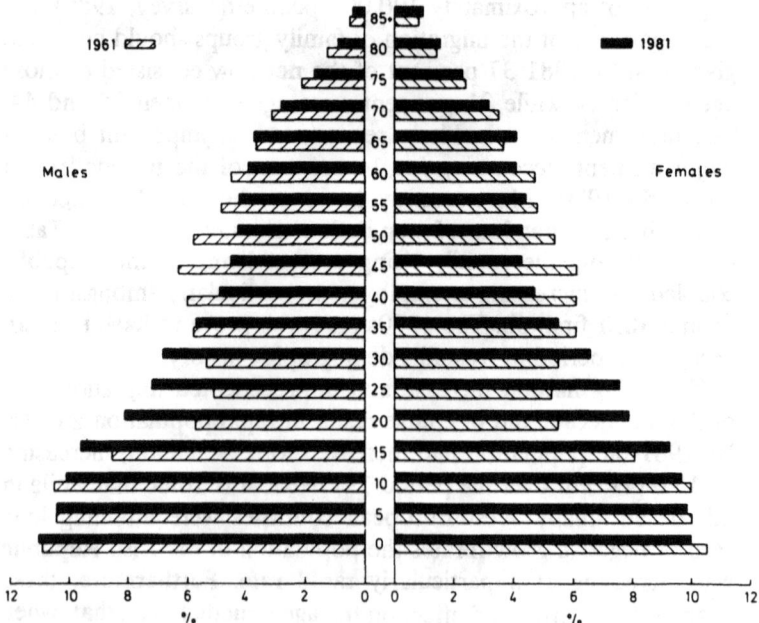

example, the birth rate has fallen considerably since 1981 (in 1983 it fell below 20 for the first time in 50 years), while net migration loss is likely to remain the dominant migration trend. The youthful age structure of the population ensures, however, that the potential for further increase is still very considerable.

Regional Variations in Population Change

There are major variations in population change within Ireland which can be observed at a variety of scale levels. Traditionally, during the era of population decline prior to the 1960s the most striking division was that between eastern and western halves of the country (Cousens, 1968), but the newly-emerged demographic trends are also partly associated with a differing set of regional patterns of population change. This section pays particular attention to variation at the county and county borough level of analysis, focusing on the separate spatial patterns of natural increase and migration before considering their combined effects expressed in overall population change.

Variations in Natural Change

As mentioned previously, the Irish Republic is still associated with relatively high rates of natural increase by West European standards as a result of the high birth rate. During the 1970s the average annual natural increase was eleven per thousand population, comprising an average birth rate of 22 and an average death rate of eleven. There are considerable spatial variations around this level, with the populations of some counties registering an average of less than 3 per cent over the decade and, at the other extreme, some recording a natural increase in excess of 20 per cent (Figure 6.3). At this scale of study, variations in age structure (reflecting past trends in natural increase and, more importantly, variations in migration) play a key role in influencing the patterns of natural increase. This is seen particularly clearly for many of the eastern counties around Dublin affected by in-migration from both Dublin City and other parts of the country. In Dublin County, for example, dominated by the extensive suburbs around the capital and where over 60 per cent of the population were aged below 30 in 1981, the average birth rate during the 1970s was 27 while the death rate was five, producing a rate of natural increase in excess

Figure 6.3: Variations in Natural Change, Net Migration and
Population Change 1971–81

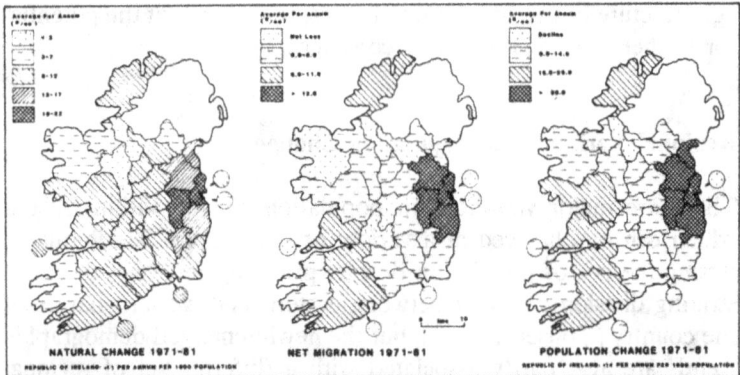

of 2 per cent per annum. At the other extreme, some of the
counties in the north-west of the country with particularly elderly
age structures — those characterised by poor economic conditions
and sustained migration loss — have much lower rates of natural
increase. In County Leitrim,for example, the average birth rate of
16.5 was considerably below the normal average of 21.6, while the
death rate of 16.2 was well above the national level. Apart from
age structure, a variety of socio-economic factors contribute to
these variations in natural increase. There are, for example,
distinctive variations in mortality, reflecting — rather surprisingly
— the generally lower rates in the poorer, more rural north-
western counties (Pringle, 1982). Similarly, there are very marked
differences in nuptiality; and it is the more prosperous and
urbanised areas that display the highest levels, as seen in the
eastern counties around Dublin (Coward, 1978; 1982). Finally,
variations in marital fertility are quite pronounced, reflecting the
lower rates in those eastern areas around Dublin which have relatively high proportions of the population in urban areas and
engaged in white-collar occupations (Coward, 1982). All in all
there are considerable variations in natural increase at the county
level, and these have important consequences for overall population growth rates and the demand for service provision.

Regional Variations in Net Migration

Detailed information on migration from the 1981 census was not yet published by 1985; therefore it was not possible to examine trends in migration in terms of either gross flows or the origins and destinations of internal migrants. Net migration can, however, be calculated from the balancing equation — the difference between overall population change and natural increase — and this section summarises the major features of the 1970s at the county and county borough level of aggregation.

Nine of the 32 areas experienced a net outflow of migrants during the 1970s. Such areas tended to be either the urban boroughs or some of the more rural isolated counties in the midlands and north-west (Figure 6.3). The highest rates of net migration loss occurred within the urban boroughs (four of the five boroughs had a net outflow), with particularly large losses from the capital and primate city of Dublin. Here, inner city redevelopment, decentralisation and the expansion of suburban housing outside the city boundaries resulted in considerable net migration loss, averaging almost 2 per cent per annum over the decade. Of those areas gaining migrants, by far the largest relative gains were evident for those counties close to Dublin: particularly County Dublin, and also Meath, Kildare and Wicklow (Figure 6.3). It is these areas that have attracted many of the migrants from Dublin City (and from other parts of the country too) and which generally fall within the commuting zone of the capital. The greatest gains in net terms occurred within Dublin County, with net migration gain averaging 3.6 per cent per annum over the decade. The other areas experiencing net migration gain displayed rates of increase considerably lower than those of the four eastern counties around Dublin (Figure 6.3). One important feature is that for the first time in well over a century some counties in the western half of the country experienced net migration gains over an inter-censal period. A variety of factors have influenced this turnaround, but the dominant process here has been the improved economic conditions in many of these areas, partly reflecting the effects of EEC membership (since 1973) and the fairly successful attempts by central government to disperse foreign investment in manufacturing industry throughout most parts of the country (Gillmor, 1982). Indeed, a sizeable proportion of new manufacturing jobs have been located in the rural areas, and the greatest relative increases in manufacturing jobs during the 1970s occurred within some of the more rural regions of the west (Gillmor, 1982). Return migration to Ireland has also helped to establish the trend of net migration gain in many areas, and some areas (such as the border county of Donegal) have attracted migrants from Northern Ireland. Thus the spatial pattern of net migration flows depicted in Figure 6.3 reflects a continuation of some well-established trends whilst at the same time displaying certain newly-established features concerning net migration within the Irish Republic.

Regional Population Change

While the 1970s represented an important era in national population change, this period also witnessed distinctive changes in the pattern of change at the regional level. The major feature here is that the demographic vigour at the national scale reflected population growth for most parts of the country at the county/county borough level of analysis. There were also, of course, variations in the intensity of change which gave rise to considerable spatial differentials.

At this level of analysis, the major characteristic is that most parts of the country experienced population growth as a result of quite substantial natural increase and net migration gain (Figure 6.3); indeed, only two of the 32 areas experienced population decline, a notable departure from earlier trends. The broad patterning of variation reflects a long-established feature in that the highest rates of growth were in the eastern counties around Dublin, where both natural increase and net migration gain were particularly high. Growth rates were highest in County Dublin, averaging almost 6 per cent over the decade in question. However, population growth was also quite high in many other parts of the country, particularly in certain counties of the west such as Galway, Clare, Limerick, Cork and Donegal. In some respects these regional patterns reflect a turnaround in spatial population change, because certain areas experienced population increase during an inter-censal period for the first time in over a hundred years; moreover, many other counties registered unprecedented rates of growth compared with earlier periods this century. In the case of seven counties, the years 1971–81 saw an inter-censal population increase for the first time since 1900. These counties — among them Kerry, Mayo and Donegal — all benefited from the improvements in economic conditions that took place during the 1970s, as reflected in the small net migration gains in these areas (Figure 6.3). The more 'normal' pattern, consisting of net migration loss more than compensating for a natural increase, disappeared during this period. In one county, the trend of population decline continued into the 1970s: County Leitrim, in the north-west of the country, generally acknowledged as the poorest county in Ireland. Here, population decline reflected net migration loss coupled with very low natural increase. The latter was a product of the more elderly age structure of this county and also of its relatively low proportion of married people — a function of the rurality and poor economic conditions — which contributed to a depression in the birth rate. The only other area to experience population decline was Dublin Borough, where the modest natural increase failed to compensate for the particularly high rates of migration loss during the 1970s. The other four urban boroughs experienced modest population growth as a result of moderate natural increase exceeding net migration loss or, in one case, moderate natural increase and migration gain.

Many of these basic patterns are also seen at finer scales of analysis, with the growth of suburban areas fringing Dublin and some of the other large urban areas (Cork, Limerick, Waterford and Galway) being particularly noticeable. Even at finer scales, the widespread nature of population growth in Ireland during the 1970s is readily apparent. Thus Horner and Daultrey (1980) show that the population of 81 per cent of the 157 rural districts (incorporating any urban populations) increased from 1971–79, compared with 8 per cent and 38 per cent during the 1950s and 1960s respectively. Horner and Daultrey (1980) also show that the changeover from decline to increase took place earlier in districts with large towns and in those districts in the eastern half of the country, suggesting that the shift in population growth diffused down the urban hierarchy and from east to west.

Thus the basic trends in population change are seen to be broadly similar throughout the country as a whole, with national trends being reflected at regional level. There is considerable evidence of a turnaround in population trends for many parts of Eire during the 1970s, and this can be attributed to changing economic conditions, EEC membership and government policy aimed at attempting to develop all parts of the country. These changing patterns of population growth are of immense importance in the planning of service provision, infrastructure, education and employment.

Counterurbanisation and Population Redistribution

Compared with those of many of her West European neighbours, Ireland's population is not markedly urbanised. In 1981, the urban population (concentrations of population greater than 1,500 persons) represented 56 per cent of the total. Although it might be expected that urbanisation still represents the major form of settlement change, there is now evidence to indicate that a shift towards counterurbanisation has occurred. This section briefly reviews the recent trends and summarises some of the salient features of changing population distribution.

The processes of urbanisation and counterurbanisation can be judged quite well from the existing census material. Thus information on total population is available for a variety of scale divisions and for the main urban areas including their suburban populations. Moreover, the 1981 tabulations include information for 1971 on the basis of the same areas as those defined in 1981. In overall terms, the population of the Irish Republic has become more urbanised this century. For example, the proportion of the population living in urban areas in 1926 and 1971 amounted to 32 and 52 per cent respectively, compared with 56 per cent in 1981. The aggregate urban areas grew by 32 per cent between 1971 and 1981, compared with 10 per cent for the aggregate rural areas.

During the 1950s and early 1960s the dominant process of settlement change was that of urbanisation, with the greatest gains occurring in the largest urban areas and with overall losses in the rural areas. These trends altered during the 1970s, and there are now some signs of the occurrence of counterurbanisation (Table 6.2). For example, population growth during the 1970s for three of the four main urban areas was less than the overall average, while the rates of growth for smaller urban areas were greater than average. This growth was particularly marked for the middle range of urban areas (populations numbering between 3,000 and 10,000), where it amounted to almost 40 per cent over the decade. Some of these towns are close to major urban areas and thus reflect the wider spread of suburbanisation among the population in general (and particularly around Dublin), but many others are located well away from such urban centres. Finally, the rural areas, in overall terms, grew at a rate approximately half that of the national rate. By Irish standards, however, this is a feature of major importance because the general trend prior to the 1970s was one

Table 6.2: Eire: Population Change by Type of District 1971–81

Type of District[a]		Population in 1981 (thousands)	% change 1971–81
Greater Dublin		915	+14.2
Cork Borough + suburbs		150	+10.6
Limerick Borough + suburbs		75	+19.0
Waterford Borough + suburbs		40	+13.8
Other towns (and number)			
>10,000	(13)	254	+26.9
5,000–10,000	(32)	250	+40.4
3,000–5,000	(27)	119	+38.1
1,500–3,500	(38)	97	+26.3
1,000–1,500	(61)	83	+24.4
<1,000	(383)	180	+25.9
Country districts		1,282	+7.4
All areas		3,443	+15.6

Note: a. Includes suburbs and environs, where applicable.
1971 data refer to the same areas as measured in 1981
Source: Census of Population 1981, vol. 1

of population decline in these areas.

The findings presented here are similar to those of Fielding (1982), whose study concentrated on population change through net migration for the nine planning regions during the period 1971–79. Thus while the population of the Irish Republic continues to become more urbanised there are some signs that counterurbanisation has been occurring, as reflected in the considerable growth of middle-order towns and the increasing demographic buoyancy of the rural areas. There has been a shift towards counterurbanisation as a result of decentralisation, suburbanisation and attempts to encourage economic growth outside the largest urban centres.

As far as broad trends in population redistribution are concerned, the most noteworthy feature is the increasing proportion of the population in the eastern half of the country and, in particular, in the Dublin area. Between 1926 and 1981, for example, the proportion of the population living in the eastern half of the country (the province of Leinster and the counties of Cavan and Monaghan) increased from 44 to 55 per cent, while those living in Dublin (County and County Borough) increased from 17 to 29 per cent. These trends were a product of the relatively low natural increase and net migration loss in much of the western half of the country, and it is only more recently that such patterns have broken down. However, the fastest rates of population growth are still in the eastern part of the country, around Dublin (apart from Dublin Borough itself), and this is placing considerable pressure on the services and infrastructure of this area. Government policy has attempted to limit the drift to the east, and although this had some success during the 1970s it is still the case that the eastern half of the country is growing at a faster rate than the west.

Labour-Force Characteristics

The census remains the most detailed data source on the labour force although additional, more frequent, Labour Force Surveys are now conducted in order to supplement census sources. The Labour Force Surveys, introduced in 1975, were conducted bi-annually up to 1983 and have been annual since then. They are based on a 5 per cent sample and do not provide spatially disaggregated information at detailed scales of analysis, although separate tabulations are available for the nine planning regions. This section briefly summarises some of the broad patterns of labour force participation and highlights the changing trends during the 1970s.

In terms of the sectoral composition of the labour force, the major features are the continued decline in agriculture and expansion of the industrial and service sectors. Between 1961 and 1981, for example, the size of the agricultural labour force was halved while the two remaining sectors each increased by approximately 40 per cent. In relative terms, this has resulted in considerable changes: in 1961 the proportions of the labour force engaged in agriculture, industry and services were 35, 25 and 40 per cent respectively, whereas the corresponding proportions in 1981 were 16, 32 and 52 per cent. Thus over half the labour force are now engaged in the service sector.

Unemployment has increased markedly in recent years. The level of unemployment was relatively low (less than 7 per cent) during the 1960s and early 1970s, but had risen to 9 per cent by 1981 and to 14 per cent by 1983. The rapid growth rates and young age structure of the population have created particular problems in terms of providing employment opportunities in recent years, added to which the recession in Britain has made emigration to that country a riskier venture than in the past.

The other major feature is that women, particularly married women, now represent an increasing proportion of the paid work-force. The most marked change has been the increasing participation of married women in the labour force as the result of a variety of social and economic factors, including the removal of the marriage bar, earlier ages at marriage, the delay of childbearing in early married life and the growth of the service and industrial sectors. Between 1971 and 1981 the number of married women in the labour force more than doubled, increasing from 14 to 32 per cent of the total female labour force. This increase in participation has been most marked amongst younger married women: for example, the participation rate of married women aged 25–34 increased from 9 to 22 per cent between 1971 and 1981 (Garvey, 1983).

There are considerable regional variations in each of these labour-force characteristics. Thus variations between the nine planning regions in 1981 indicate that only in the eastern region (consisting of Dublin County and County Borough) are less than 5 per cent of the labour force engaged in agriculture, while in other regions the figure varies from 19 to 32 per cent. Even the highest proportion engaged in agriculture, 32 per cent in the western region (consisting of counties Galway and Mayo), indicates that agriculture no longer dominates the labour-force structure. This 'most rural' region has one quarter of its labour force in industry and over 40 per cent in the service sector. All regions have undergone increases in unemployment, although in 1981 the regional rates were somewhat lower than the average of 9 per cent in the midlands, south-west and eastern regions. The north-west region (Counties Leitrim and Sligo) had a particularly high rate of unemployment — 15 per cent — in 1981.

Household Composition

Published census data on household composition are not yet available for 1981, but it is planned to replicate the classification used in 1971 based on number of persons per household, presence of children, type of family unit and number of family units per household. During the 1960s the greatest relative increases in household types were amongst one-person, husband-and-wife and conjugal family households. Data concerning the number of households and average household size are available for the more recent period and indicate that the number of households increased by 23 per cent during the 1970s, reflecting, in particular, the return migration of family units and the trend towards earlier ages at marriage and household formation. These increases were particularly marked in the counties around Dublin. reflecting the importance of this area as a destination for migrants as well as the higher nuptiality and younger ages at marriage in this area.

There has been a reduction in the average size of private households over the 1970s: from 3.9 in 1971 to 3.6 in 1981. It is difficult to explain this change without access to household structure data, but it is likely that the previously mentioned trends of higher nuptiality, younger ages at marriage and reductions in marital fertility have all played contributory roles. In 1981 the smallest average household sizes occurred in some of the poorest western parts of the country most affected by out-migration, as well as in the main urban areas. The reduction in average household size during the 1970s was evident in all counties and county boroughs, with the greatest declines occurring within Dublin Borough. The particularly marked declines in Dublin Borough reflect a variety of factors, including the reduction in average family size, the continued in-migration of young single persons (many of whom live in single-person households) and the out-migration of family units to suburban areas beyond the city.

Minority Populations

Two 'minority' groups deserve attention here, one being based on religion and the other on an ability to speak the Irish language. Within the Irish Republic the predominant religion is Roman Catholicism, with the other groups for which a religion is stated (mainly Church of Ireland and Presbyterian) constituting approximately 4 or 5 per cent. The relative size of this minority group is currently declining as a result of its lower natural increase, older age structure and the effects of the Catholic Church's decree on mixed marriages. Interestingly, while the Irish population is noted for its high level of religious adherence, figures for 1981 indicate relatively large increases in the number of people either stating no religion or not supplying information on their beliefs. These still represent, however, a relatively small proportion of the population overall: 3 per cent in 1981.

It is difficult to make a clear estimate of the number able to speak Irish, because the census question was phrased in very general terms. It distinguished 'speak Irish only', 'speak Irish and English', 'read but cannot speak Irish' and was based on individual self-assessment, which presumably reflects differing yardsticks and ideologies. The proportion of the population (aged three and over) who speak Irish has generally increased since the 1920s: rising from 19 per cent in 1926 to 28 per cent in 1971. On a county basis, the proportion of Irish speakers in 1971 was highest in those counties containing the Gaeltacht areas — notably, the west coast counties of Galway (45 per cent), Mayo (36 per cent), Kerry (35 per cent) and Donegal (35 per cent). All counties had at least 20 per cent of their populations who were Irish speakers, and the lowest proportions occurred in the south-eastern counties of Wicklow (20 per cent), Wexford (21 per cent) and Carlow (23 per cent).

Conclusion

The inter-censal decade 1971–81 was one of tremendous social, economic and demographic change in the Republic of Ireland. The most outstanding demographic characteristic was the rapid increase in population as a result of high natural increase and, until 1979, net migration gain. Most parts of the country experienced population growth, but spatial variations in the components of population growth led to considerable differentials in population change throughout the country, partly reflecting a continuation of previous patterns but also heralding certain newly-established features in recent regional population patterns. Various other important socio-demographic features are seen to have evolved over this period, including the changing age structure of the population, the shift towards counterurbanisation, the changing nature and structure of the labour force and also the decline in average household size. The rapid population growth which characterised the 1970s is unlikely to continue at the same pace throughout the 1980s; reductions in natural increase and a return to net migration loss represent the more typical features of this decade. The changes that took place in the 1970s, at both national and regional levels, in terms of population characteristics, associated as they are with numerous social and cultural factors, indicate that this period will represent an exceptional era in Ireland's demographic history.

Acknowledgements

The author thanks the following for their help in connection with the preparation of this chapter: Damien Courtney, Tony Fielding, Donal Garvey, Arnold Horner and John Stephens.

References

Courtney, D. (1985) 'Demographic patterns in the Irish Republic' in L. O'Dowd and P. Clancy (eds.) *A Sociology of Modern Ireland,* Institute of Public Administration, Dublin

Courtney, D. and McCashin, A. (1983) *Social Welfare: the Implications of Demographic Change*, National Economic and Social Council, Dublin

Cousens, S. (1968) 'Population trends in Ireland at the beginning of the twentieth century', *Irish Geography, 1*, 387–401.

Coward, J. (1978) 'Changes in the pattern of fertility in the Republic of Ireland', *Tijdschrift voor Economische en Sociale Geografie, 69(6)*, 353–61

Coward, J. (1982) 'Fertility changes in the Republic of Ireland during the 1970s', *Area, 14*, 109–17

Fielding, A. (1982) 'Counterurbanisation in Western Europe', *Progress in Planning, 17*, 1–52

Garvey, D. (1983) A profile of the demographic and labour-force characteristics of the population-sample analysis of the 1981 census of population. Read to the Statistical and Social Inquiry Society of Ireland, Dublin, April 1983

Garvey, D. (1985) 'The history of migration flows in the Republic of Ireland', *Population Trends, 39*, 22–30.

Gillmor, D. (1982) *Manufacturing Industry in the Republic of Ireland,* Bank of Ireland, Dublin

Horner, A. and Daultrey, S. (1980), 'Recent population changes in the Republic of Ireland', *Area, 12*, 129–36

Kennedy, R. E. (1973) *The Irish: Emigration, Marriage and Fertility*, University of California Press, Berkeley

Pringle, D. (1982), 'Regional disparities in the quality of life: the Republic of Ireland 1971–77', *Irish Geography, 15*, 22–34

7 FRANCE

Philip Ogden and Hilary Winchester

Introduction

The French have long had a fascination with demographic issues. The years since the Second World War have given them much to think about, with profound changes in population growth, internal and international migration and socio-economic structure. A rapidly expanding economy, matched by unexpectedly high population growth in the two decades after 1945, transformed a characteristically rural and agricultural society into an urban and industrial one. The agenda of social research was thus heavily slanted towards discovering the mechanisms behind urbanisation, the originality of Paris as its focus, and the consequences for the countryside of declining peasant agriculture and rural depopulation. In addition, heavy reliance on external immigration to supplement the labour force added a new dimension to the social geography of the city, and provoked research on the process of labour migration and the formation of ethnic minorities. Whilst the social history and demography of France between 1945 and 1975 are by no means fully understood, the last decade has seen a change in emphasis. Urban growth has slowed, or gone into reverse; the fate of the declining countryside seems not so clearly sealed; the centralised influence of Paris is questioned; and immigration has slowed to a trickle. These, and other trends in the labour force and household, have taken place against a background of slowing economic and population growth. Equally, and whilst there are still significant differences, France has shared many experiences common to the other major states of Western Europe (Hall and Ogden, 1985).

This chapter looks at five sets of broadly demographic issues for the period 1975–1982. It relies in the main on the results of the 1982 population census which had just become available as the chapter was being written, the tabulations being broadly comparable to previous post-war censuses held in 1975, 1968, 1962, 1954 and 1946. The census forms an unrivalled source of detailed information and the chapter has, in part, the aim of illustrating its uses.

Natural Population Change

The legal population of metropolitan France rose from 52,593,000 in 1975 to 54,334,871 by 1982 (Table 7.1a). The rate of population growth was just over 3 per cent during the inter-censal period, which showed a marked decrease from the two preceding inter-censal periods (Ogden, 1981; Noin, 1984a). The annual rate of total population increase, which had been over 1 per cent in the 1960s, fell to 0.8 per cent in 1968–75, and to only 0.5 per cent in 1975–82. The greater part of the increase in the French population was accounted for by natural growth rather than migration (Table 7.1). Nonetheless, the rate of excess of births over deaths (accumulating to 1.5 million during the inter-censal period) was substantially lower than at any time in the preceding 20 years.

The decline in rates of natural growth has been caused by a pronounced fall in fertility rates. Crude birth rates averaged 14 per thousand in 1975–82, and the total fertility rate fell from a peak of 2.8 children per family in 1964 to stabilise at about 1.9 in 1980 (Noin, 1984a). Natural growth rates are little affected by changes in mortality rates, although these have continued to show slow and regular improvement. Life expectancy for men is about 70.8 years and for women 78.9, the difference being attributable, at least in part, to an excess of alcohol-related deaths for men. The pro-

Table 7.1: France: Components of Population Increase

A. Total change 1975–82

Legal population 20 February 1975	52,593,000
Legal population 4 March 1982	54,334,871
Growth 1975–82	1,741,871
Natural growth (from civil registration)	1,485,703
Migration balance (by residual method)	256,168

B. Annual rates of change 1962–82

	Per cent variation per annum		
	1962–8	1968–75	1975–82
Total increase	1.2	0.8	0.5
Natural increase	0.7	0.6	0.4
Net migration	0.5[a]	0.2	0.1

Note: a. Inflated by the return of repatriates from North Africa
Sources: Recensement 1982, Principaux Résultats, Sondage au 1/20ème: France Métropolitaine, p.86; Ogden, 1985a, p.25

nounced fall in fertility rates has occurred despite the continuing pronatalist stance of the French government, although France had one of the highest birth rates in Western Europe in the early 1980s (Huss, 1980). The decline in fertility is inextricably bound up with changes in household structure, family pattern, and the occupation and status of women.

Historical population development and the changes in birth and death rates are reflected in the age and sex structure of the population (Figure 7.1). The recent reduction in the birth rate has brought about a relative diminution in the younger age groups, especially those aged under ten. The population 'bulge' has now moved into the 30–39 age group, reflecting the elevated birth rates of the 1950s. The population numbers in the 40–45 and 60–65 age group are severely depleted because of the reduced birth rates during the war years of 1939–45 and 1914–18. The proportion of the very old — those aged over 75 — has continued to rise as a result of increasing life expectancy: they now form 6.6 per cent of the total population compared to 5.6 per cent in 1975.

The imbalance in the age structure is complicated by an imbalance in the sex structure of the population, with overall only 954 men to 1,000 women. The majority of old people are women as a result of their greater longevity, and this imbalance is exacerbated by the effects of the First World War, which caused the premature deaths of many men who would now be in their seventies and eighties. By the age of 50, women are in the majority, and the imbalance is accentuated with increasing age: by the age of 75, 60 per cent of the population are women; by the age of 80, 70 per cent are women. In the under–50 age group men are in the majority, partly because of the greater number of male births, and partly because the majority of foreign immigrants are male. There are marked regional differences in age and sex structures related to variations in both natural growth and migration. For example, while 13.8 per cent of the total population is aged 65 or over, this figure rises to 16.6 per cent for rural communes (20 per cent for those outside the ZPIU — urbanised zones, *zones de peuplement industriel et urbain*) and falls to 12.8 per cent for urban areas (11.7 per cent for the Paris agglomeration). There is still a strong geographical contrast between a relatively young population in the north and an aged population in the south.

Figure 7.1: France: Total Population by Age and Sex, 4 March
1982

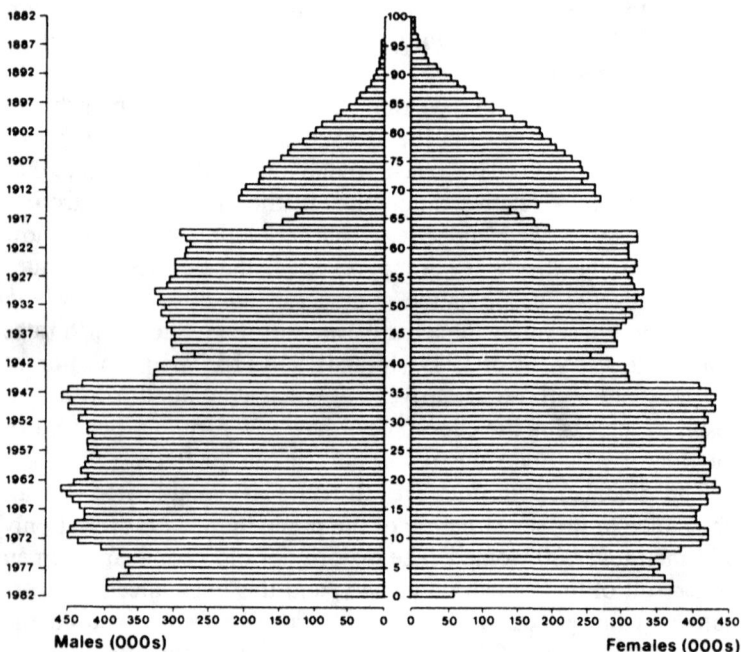

Males (000s)   Females (000s)

Characteristics of the Labour Force

The labour force or 'active population' is defined as the employed
or unemployed population, whereas the 'inactive population' consists of children, pupils and students, those on military service, the
retired, and those declared inactive. The active population is classified in three ways: according to employment status, according to
socio-professional grouping, and according to the type of
economic activity undertaken. Firstly, employment status is categorised into eight groups, one of which is the unemployed. The
other groups distinguish employers, independent non-salaried
workers, apprentices, family helpers and employees in the private
sector, public sector, and for the state. Secondly, socio-
professional status is categorised into six major groups and takes

account, at least in part, of the distinction between independent non-salaried people and those who are employees. Three socio-professional categories recorded in previous censuses have been reallocated in the 1982 census because of their diminishing importance, namely agricultural labourers, workers in domestic service and the motley group previously recorded under the heading of 'clergy, army, police and artists'. Finally, economic activity is classified into 14 major categories including agriculture, various types of industry, construction, transport and groups of services.

Between 1975 and 1982 the active population increased from 21,774,860 to 23,525,120, an increase of 8 per cent. This rapid increase in the labour force is related to the large numbers of young people reaching working age, born in a period of higher birth rates. At the other end of the age spectrum, relatively few were retiring in the late 1970s as these were the small generations born in the years of the First World War (1914–1918). The numbers in the work-force were, however, offset to some extent by the lengthening of the period of education and the tendency towards earlier retirement (Huet and Schmitz, 1984).

Part of the increase in the labour force is attributable to the increasing participation of women in the paid labour force outside the home. From 1975 to 1982 the number of women in the labour force increased from 8,132,185 to 9,584,720, rising as a proportion of the total labour force from 37 to 41 per cent. The move into paid labour is particularly noticeable for younger women: in 1975, 58 per cent of women aged 30 were in the labour force; while by 1982, 69 per cent of women aged 30 were either in employment or actively seeking employment (see Figure 7.2). Moreover, when tracing cohorts through the previous censuses it is clear that participation rates have increased for all age groups. For example, of the women born in 1940, 48 per cent were active in 1968 when they were 28 years old and 52 per cent were active in 1975 when they were 35 years old, but the proportion had increased to 62 per cent in 1982 when these women were 42 years old. This participation in the paid labour-force results from changing attitudes and expectations of women which are seen also in changing household and family structures. However, many women now undertake the dual burden of unpaid domestic and childrearing work together with paid work in the labour force. Women's participation in the labour force exhibits marked regional variations, with the lowest levels in the Mediterranean

Figure 7.2: France: Activity Rates for Women by Age Group 1962–82 (women in or actively seeking work)

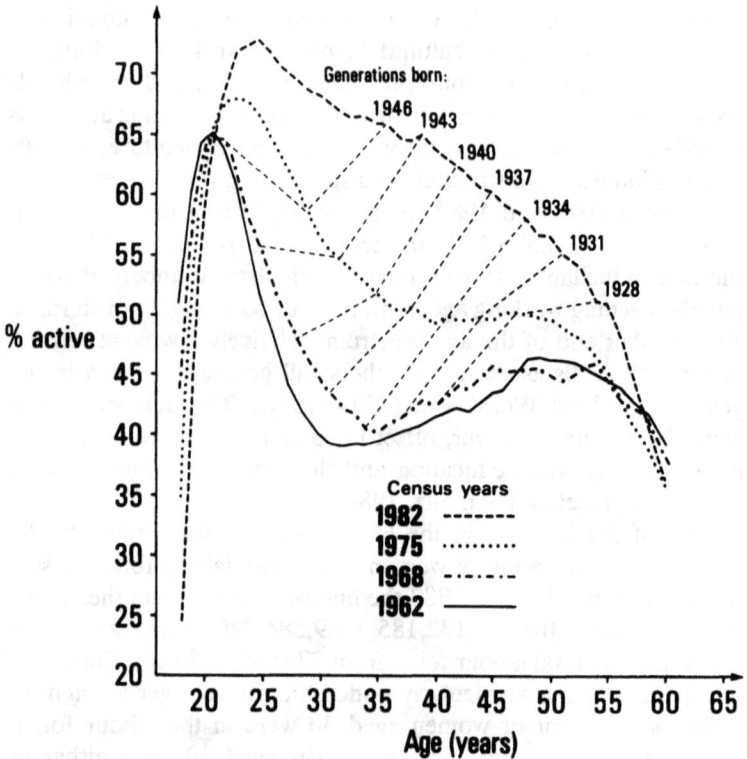

Source: Recensement 1982, Principaux Résultats, Sondage au 1/20ème: France Métropolitaine, p.86

zone and the highest in the Ile-de-France, around Paris.

A breakdown of female employment by economic activity shows that women are numerically dominant in retail services (where they make up 53.8 per cent of the labour force), in insurance (55.4 per cent) and in non-retailing services (54.8 per cent). They are therefore severely under-represented in the other branches of economic activity, particularly in agriculture (34 per cent); production and distribution of energy (15.8 per cent); construction (7 per cent); and most types of industry (29.6 per cent). Women's employment has therefore become concentrated in the

growing service sector; the classifications by employment status
show that this concentration was particularly marked in state
enterprises, including HLM (housing) offices and public hospitals
but not including those industries nationalised by the Socialist
government in 1982.

The oil crisis of 1973 and the restructuring of French industry
has led to job losses in almost all sectors of manufacturing employment, with jobs in industry and construction declining by 9.8 per
cent between 1975 and 1982. Jobs in agriculture continued to
decline, showing a loss of 16.6 per cent in the inter-censal period.
Increases in service employment of 14.9 per cent over the same
period failed to compensate for jobs lost in other sectors. As a
result, the level of unemployment increased sharply from 3.8 per
cent in 1975 to 8.8 per cent by 1982. Unemployment rates are
particularly high for young people: in the 15–19 age group, 25.4
per cent of men were unemployed and 45 per cent of the women
(Table 7.2b); in the 20–24 age group, the rates were 15.7 per cent

Table 7.2: France: Unemployment

A. Total unemployment, by sex 1962–82

	Males	Females
1962	108,943	86,731
1968	239,040	197,072
1975	374,530	456,430
1982	934,120	1,125,040

B. Unemployment rates (per cent), by sex and age 1982

Age	Males	Females
Total	6.7	11.7
15–19	25.4	45.0
20–24	15.7	23.3
25–29	6.6	12.0
30–34	4.6	8.8
35–39	3.8	7.1
40–44	4.0	6.3
45–49	3.9	6.1
50–54	4.3	6.6
55–59	6.4	8.5
60–64	7.0	7.4
65–69	2.0	2.3
70+	1.4	1.5

Source: Recensement 1982, Principaux Résultats, Sondage au 1/20 ème:
France Métropolitaine, pp.55, 62

and 23.3 per cent respectively. Unemployment levels decline steadily with age, to reach their lowest levels at age 45–49. Unemployment rates for women are consistently higher than for men, reflecting their position as a marginal labour force.

The high birth rates of the 1950s and early 1960s have brought about a profound rejuvenation of the work-force. In total, 58 per cent of the work-force is now aged under 40, whereas this proportion was only 50 per cent 20 years previously. At the same time, the labour force is becoming more highly educated and there are increasing proportions in the higher socio-professional groups. The youthfulness and increasing upward social mobility of the work-force is further accentuated by a growing trend towards early retirement, facilitated by the availability of special benefits available in particular sectors of employment, such as agriculture, or iron and steel. This trend will accelerate from 1983, when the normal age of retirement became 60 years.

Characteristics of Household Composition

Ordinary households are defined as occupants of private dwelling units which are used as 'principal residences'. The members of a household defined in this way are not necessarily related. Each household is required to have a 'reference person' (one and one only): therefore the number of principal residences, ordinary households and reference persons is one and the same. Within a household there can be one family, or more. A family can consist of at least two people, who may be a couple (whether married or not) with or without unmarried children under 25; alternatively, it may consist of a single parent (who is unmarried, separated, widowed or divorced) with unmarried children under 25, constituting a single-parent family. Members of a household who do not belong to a family are termed 'isolated' persons; this category may include unmarried children over 25, even when living in the same household as their parents or siblings, and also includes single elderly relations.

The reference person of the household is defined according to a list of criteria used in descending order, related to the family structure, gender, whether in active employment, and age. If there is a family within the household the reference person is the male of the couple, or the adult without spouse in the case of a single-parent family. If there is no family within the household the reference person is the oldest of the active members of the household, or if there is no active person then the oldest inactive person. In households with multiple families these criteria, in descending order, are used to define the reference person. Inevitably, the majority of reference persons are middle-aged married men.

The majority of French people live in ordinary households, 52,981,320 of 54,273,000, or 97.6 per cent. Those not in ordinary households are in institutions of various sorts, are lodgers or are living in mobile homes (Table 7.3). The number of ordinary households has increased markedly between 1975 and 1982, from 17,744,985 to 19,590,400 — an increase of 10.45 per cent in the total number of households, compared to an increase in the total population of only 3.2 per cent. Correspondingly, there has been a decrease in the average size of households from 2.9 persons per household to 2.7. The change in household structure is particularly noticeable in the increase in one-person households (which now represent a quarter of all households) and in the reduction both in the number of households comprising five persons or more and of complex households, comprising more than one family (Table 7.4). Similarly, the number of families has increased by 8.1 per cent from 13,177,400 to 14,118,940. Over half of these families have no children aged under 16, and there are relatively fewer families with three or more children aged under 16, a fact that is related to the recent reduction in the birth rate (Table. 7.5).

The increase in the number of single-person households particularly concerns women, who make up 65.4 per cent of these households. This is primarily a result of the imbalances between

Table 7.3: France: Population by Household Type 1982

Population in ordinary households	52,981,360
Population not in ordinary households	1,291,840
of which:	
In institutions (e.g. prisons, psychiatric hospitals, barracks)	418,840
Elderly in rest homes	329,880
Workers accommodated in hostels	203,920
Students in hostels	128,360
Members of religious communities	86,440
Population in mobile homes, including houseboats	124,400

Source: Recensement 1982; Principaux Résultats, Sondage au 1/20ème:
   France Métropolitaine, p.100

Table 7.4: France: Persons per Household

	Per cent of total households	
	1975	1982
1 person	22.2	24.6
2 persons	27.8	28.5
3	19.2	18.8
4	15.4	16.1
5	8.2	7.4
6 or more	7.2	4.6
(Mean number of persons per household	2.88	2.70)

Source: Recensement 1982, Principaux Résultats, Sondage au 1/20ème:
   France Métropolitaine, p.70

Table 7.5: France: Number of Children (Aged 0–16) Per Family

	Per cent of total households	
	1975	1982
0	48.3	50.5
1	23.0	22.7
2	16.7	17.7
3	7.3	6.5
4	2.7	1.7
5 or more	2.0	0.9

Source: Recensement 1982, Principaux Résultats, Sondage au 1/20ème:
   France Métropolitaine, p.99

the sexes at older ages, and of the greater longevity of women. There are almost three million single-person households comprising individuals aged over 55 and of these 77.3 per cent are women. There are over one and a quarter million single-person households aged over 75, and of these 81.5 per cent are women. Men form the majority of single-person households in the age group 25–54. This is related to an increasing rate of celibacy and a later age of marriage, particularly prevalent in the higher socio-professional groups (Fouquet and Morin, 1984); it is not necessarily synonymous with a solitary life-style.

Since 1975 there has been an increase in the number of single-parent families: from 723,000 in 1975 to 846,820 in 1982. Of these, 85.4 per cent consist of a single woman with children, predominantly in the 35–44 age group. The causes of this increase are related to a rising divorce rate, which has doubled since 1968, facilitated by changes in the law in 1975 (Boigeol *et al.*, 1984): divorce rulings still tend to give custody of the children to the mother. There is also an increasing trend for couples to live together without marriage. A total of 17 per cent of the female single-parent family heads were unmarried mothers, but it is suggested that the character of illegitimate births is gradually changing from one of clandestine unwanted births in low-status sectors of the population to one of positive choice for higher-status groups (Deville and Naulleau, 1982).

There are obvious relationships between the changing structure of fertility, changes in households and families, and developments in the characteristics of the labour force. For the majority of couples under 55, both partners are economically active. Lower fertility levels are producing smaller families and households, releasing more women for work outside the home. Changing patterns of fertility and labour-force participation, and rising trends in celibacy, divorce and illegitimacy are changing the traditional family and household structures, and bringing the patriarchal norms of society into question.

Regional Differentials in Population Change

The 1982 census results indicate some marked shifts in regional population structure, intensifying trends already noted at the time of the previous census in 1975 (see, for example, Courgeau, 1978; Courgeau and Lefèbvre, 1982). Most notable is the steady reversal of urban growth and the beginnings of rural rejuvenation, under the process loosely defined as 'counterurbanisation' (Ogden, 1985a). Certainly the 1982 results confirm that the dominant image of post-war France as increasingly divided between burgeoning, and particularly Parisian, urban growth and a declining countryside is now out of date.

The national decline in rates of population increase noted above has had a generally depressing effect on growth at the *département* scale, although sharp contrasts persist in total growth and in rates of natural increase and migration. Of the 96 *départements* 20 had fewer inhabitants in 1982 than in 1975. This compares with 18 which lost population between 1968 and 1975. But there has been a change in the composition of these *départements*, with an increase in the number of declining urban areas and a return of some rural districts to relative demographic health. Thus Figure 7.3a shows population loss in a few residual rural areas in the Massif Central and the Pyrénées, in the industrial regions of the north-east and in the inner Paris basin. Population growth, on the other hand, is a feature of, first, the outer parts of the Paris basin; second, a broad swathe of *départements* in the south-east, along the Rhône valley and along the Mediterranean coast; and, lastly, in many parts of Brittany, Normandy and the Western littoral.

Figures 7.3b and c reveal the complex interplay of natural increase and migration. Figure 7.3b shows that 28 *départements* experienced an excess of deaths over births between 1975 and 1982 (compared to only three for 1962–68 and twelve for 1968–75). This reflects both the national trend and also the long-term decline of total population — and consequent ageing — in many rural areas. In all 96 *départements* the annual excess of births over deaths was smaller between 1975 and 1982 than between 1968 and 1975; but there was a pronounced, and long-established contrast between high rates of natural increase in the north and low rates in the south. Figure 3c shows how important therefore was the influence of migration in shaping overall population change: out-migration from the north-east, from the inner Paris basin and cities like Lyons and Saint-Etienne outweighed their natural increase rates. In-migration, on the other hand, was particularly notable in the south-east, in the outer Paris basin and, most significantly, in many rural *départements* of 'traditional' out-migration. A process begun during the 1968–75 period in Brittany, for example, has been firmly consolidated since. The rather crude picture in Figure 7.3 does suggest, then, the operation of two processes: decentralisation of growth to the outer fringes of the urban areas, particularly Paris; and deconcentration, where many areas with a very long, continuous outflow of population have seen that trend reversed.

The details of these processes may be seen by looking at the urban and rural districts in turn. Figure 7.4 shows how dramatic the turnaround has been in both cases during the last inter-censal period. All size categories of rural *commune* showed an improvement during the period 1975–82 compared to other post-war inter-censal periods. For urban areas, the heady days of growth in the 1950s and 1960s have been replaced by a slump in growth rates for nearly all size categories by the 1970s: for the period 1975–82 all but the smallest towns were growing either very

Figure 7.3: France: Regional Patterns of Population Change
1975–82
(a) Population change by *département*, per cent per annum
(b) Natural change (excess of births over deaths), per cent per
annum
(c) Migratory balance, per cent per annum

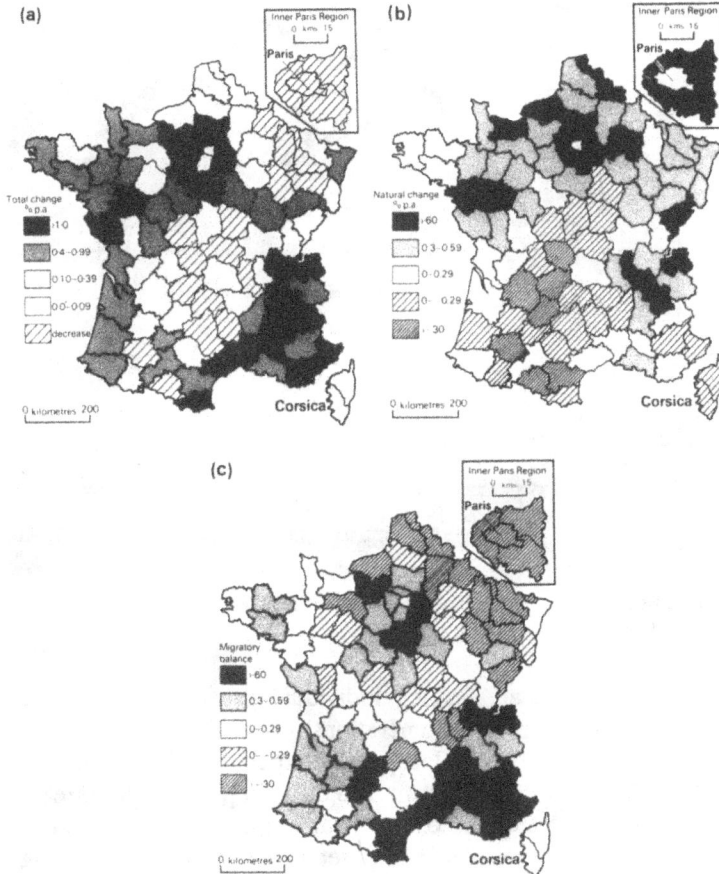

Source: Ogden, 1985a, p. 27

Figure 7.4: France: Evolution of Population Growth Rates of Rural and Urban *Communes* 1962–82

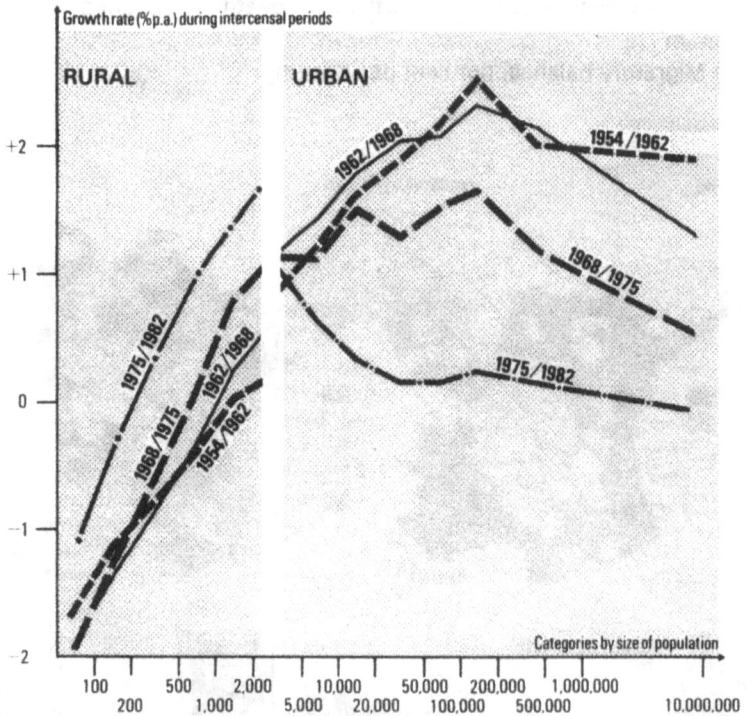

Source: Recensement 1982, Principaux Résultats, Sondage au 1/20ème: France Métropolitaine, p.84

slowly or not at all. Taking individual urban *communes* (the central areas of urban agglomerations) of the 109 with more than 50,000 people in 1975 86 lost population between 1975 and 1982, and of the 39 with more than 100,000 people only 5 increased. Table 7.6a illustrates the exodus from central city areas and the slowing of growth also in the wider urban districts of the eight principal French agglomerations. Table 7.6b shows for Paris that population loss is most intense in the central districts and is the product of strong out-migration rather than natural decrease. Detailed analysis shows that it is only in the outer parts of the Paris basin that population grew, largely as a result of in-migration (see,

Table 7.6: France: Dimensions and Components of Urban Decline

A. Growth Rates in Urban Areas (*Unités Urbaines*) and Urban *Communes*

	Overall urban area		Urban *commune*	
	% change 1968–75	% change 1975–82	% change 1968–75	% change 1975–82
Paris	3.6	−0.5	−11.1	−5.8
Lyons	7.5	−0.1	−13.5	−9.6
Marseilles	5.9	0.9	2.3	−3.9
Lille	5.1	−0.1	−8.8	−10.7
Bordeaux	7.5	2.6	17.5	−6.7
Toulouse	14.1	2.5	0.7	−8.1
Nantes	11.8	2.5	−0.9	−6.2
Nice	11.4	2.7	6.5	−2.3

B. Components of Population Change, Ville de Paris 1975–82

		Annual rate of change %		
Arrondissements	Total change (thousands)	Total	Natural change	Migration
1– 4 Centre	−21.6	−2.5	0.0	−2.5
5–11 Near-Centre	−54.3	−1.4	0.2	−1.6
12–20 Outer	−55.0	−0.5	0.3	−0.9
Paris	−130.9	−0.8	0.3	−1.1

Sources: Boudoul and Faur, 1982; Fleury, 1982, p.9

for example, Fleury, 1982; Bonvalet and Lefèbvre, 1983; Bonvalet and Tugault, 1984; Noin *et al.* 1984b).

Urban decline is certainly reflected in renewed population growth in the countryside, although there is a need to be cautious in interpretation: this is not the dawn of a new age of the peasantry but rather represents a more expansive form of urbanisation. Table 7.7 thus shows that there is still a broad swathe of the countryside in the grips of depopulation: 44.5 per cent of all rural *communes* lost population between 1975 and 1982 (although many through natural decrease rather than out-migration). Yet if we divide rural *communes* into three categories according to their status within, near to or entirely outside the ZPIU or urbanised zones, a more subtle view emerges. It is the *communes* in the first category which are growing most quickly. In the second category, more than half experienced population increase, and it is only in the third category that population decline is still endemic.

In general, then, as Boudoul and Faur (1982) have shown, old divisions between rural and urban are becoming obsolete as

Table 7.7: France: Rural Population Change by Type of *Commune* 1975–82

| | Per cent of total *communes* | | | |
| | Increasing | | Decreasing | |
	Total	by more than 15%	Total	by more than 15%
All rural *communes*	55.48	23.35	44.52	8.97
Those within ZPIU[a]	74.08	37.81	25.92	3.07
Those not within ZPIU				
(a) near to ZPIU[b]	55.13	22.85	44.87	8.81
(b) entirely outside ZPIU	39.10	11.04	60.90	14.66

Notes: a. *Zone de peuplement industriel ou urbain*
     b. Where at least one *commune* in a *canton* belongs to a ZPIU
Source: Calculated from Boudoul and Faur, 1982, Table 7

urbanisation becomes more expansive. There is still a rural 'heart-land' in decline, but the rural depopulation which has for so long been a dramatic influence upon the geography of France's popu-lation seems to be almost at an end. The census has also allowed us to question the idea of an ever more mobile population: Courgeau and Pumain (1984), for example, have tentatively indicated a decline at least in residential mobility during the later 1970s.

Immigrants and Minority Population

The counting of immigrants and ethnic minorities reveals perhaps one of the greatest weaknesses in the French census, since the information is limited in both scope and reliability. The questions in the census on place of birth and nationality provide the main source, with some supplementary information from cross-tabulations by previous place of residence on 1 January 1975. There are no specific questions on race or ethnicity. The major published tables relate to nationality, with extensive cross-tabulations by demographic, social and economic variables. Infor-mation is also tabulated for households with a foreign head, giving a rather broader picture of the 'foreign' population. The main difficulty relates to underestimation, as many foreign nationals are difficult to count, not least because many are illegal residents who wish to evade the census or any other form of enumeration. It is possible that there were, in 1982, as many as 300,000 illegal immigrants in France. Therefore any study of ethnic minorities must also rely on supplementary information, for example figures from the Ministry of the Interior based on the issue of work permits.

The official census count in 1982 was of 3.68 million foreign nationals with an additional 1.42 million French by naturalisation. This compared with an estimate of 4.46 million foreign from the Ministry of the Interior for the end of 1982 (Ogden, 1985b). Despite governmental control there was an increase of some 7 per cent between 1975 and 1982; but this compares with an increase of some 40 per cent during the preceding eight years and with a decline in the number of foreigners in employment by some 11.5 per cent over the period 1975–1982. The number of unemployed foreigners has tripled, from 73,100 in 1975 to 218,140 by 1982. Of great significance for the general political debate has been the changing balance of nationalities revealed by the census (Table 7.8). Whilst only a little over one-third of the foreign population is North African, thus contradicting the popular equation of immigrants and the 'Arab' problem, their proportion in the total has been rising. A sharp decline by some 17.4 per cent in foreigners from traditional 'Latin' sources (Italy, Spain and Portugal) has been matched by an increase of 32.6 per cent in those from the

Table 7.8: France: Population Composition by Nationality 1982

	Total	Per cent change 1975–82	Average household size[a]	Average no. of children 0–16[b]
Total population	54,273,200		2.70	0.90
French (1) by birth	49,167,180		2.66	0.86
(2) by naturalisation	1,425,920		2.77	0.75
Foreign: Total	3,680,100	+6.9	3.34	1.54
Italian	333,740	−27.9	3.06	0.91
Spanish	321,440	−35.4	2.99	0.93
Portuguese	764,860	+0.8	3.63	1.51
Algerian	795,920	+12.0	3.99	2.46
Moroccan	431,120	+65.8	3.91	2.52
Tunisian	184,400	+35.5	3.60	2.03

Notes: a. In 'ordinary households' where 'person of reference' (head of household) is of that nationality
b. Per family defined as ordinary households as in 'a'

Sources: Recensement 1982, Principaux Résultats, Sondage au 1/20ème: France Métropolitaine, pp.70, 71; Structure de la Population, pp.88–9

Maghreb and Turkey. Whilst the under-recording in the census naturally influences the conclusions that can be drawn, the results do confirm further changes in the social and demographic structure of the foreign population.

For example, while males of working age still predominate and there are still marked imbalances in sex ratios at most ages (Figure 7.5), recent trends towards family reunification (Jones, 1984; Blanchet, 1985) have lessened these contrasts. Of the 3.68 million total foreign population, 2.10 million are males but 1.23 million of the total are aged 19 or under (and of these 750,000 were born in France). On all measures, there are great contrasts by nationality; for example, average household size (Table 7.8) varies from 2.66 for households where the 'reference person' was French by birth to 3.99 when he or she was Algerian. This was principally because of higher numbers of children.

If, indeed, we look not simply at the strictly-defined population of foreign nationality but at the population living in households headed by a foreigner, the total number rises to 4.06 million; and 1.39 million under-16s live in such households. This is as near as the census gets to 'ethnic minorities' as opposed to 'immigrants'. Cross-tabulations by social indicators (see Table 7.9) show that well-established patterns endure: acute overcrowding and low amenity levels.

Occupational data confirm the established pattern of foreigners

Table 7.9: Selected Social Indicators for Households with a Head of Foreign Nationality 1982

	All households per cent	Average	Foreign per cent	Average
Owner-occupiers	50.68		20.87	
Renting: unfurnished non-social housing	26.04		39.28	
Renting: unfurnished social housing	13.48		23.58	
In buildings of 20+ dwellings	13.83		22.81	
With telephone	74.42		50.33	
Inside lavatory	84.95		76.13	
Severe overcrowding	2.50		11.90	
Number of persons per room	0.74		1.09	
Number of rooms per dwelling	3.65		3.06	

Source: Recensement 1982, Principaux Résultats, Sondage au 1/20ème: France Métropolitaine, p.73

Figure 7.5: France: Sex Ratios Amongst Foreign Population in 1982 Compared with Total Population (males per hundred females by age)

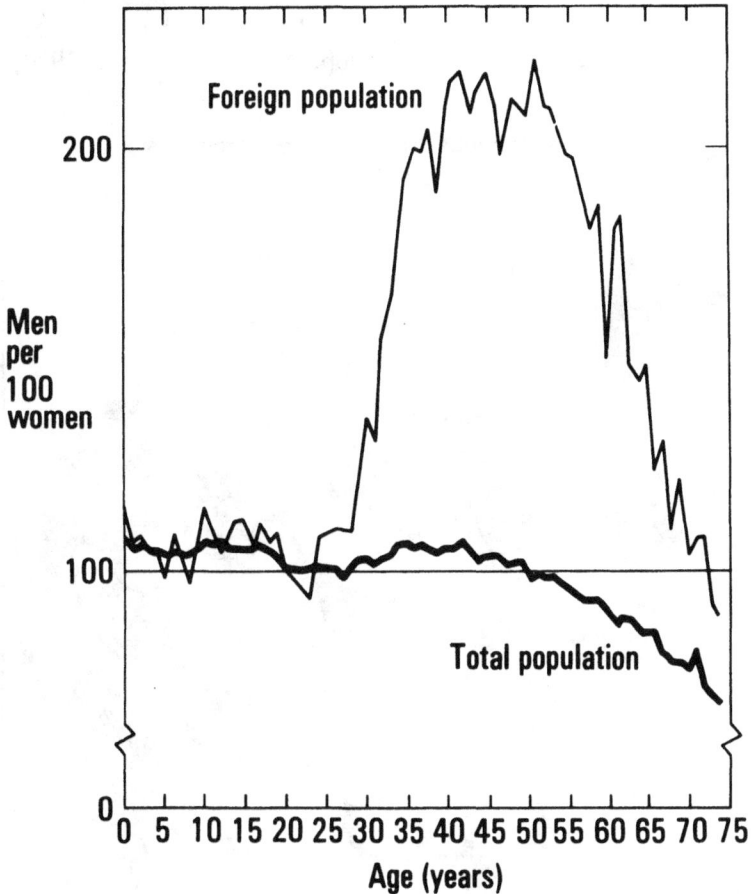

Source: Tribalat, 1985, p.134

taking a great part in the industrial sectors of the economy and, above all, in building and public works. Thus foreigners accounted for 6.2 per cent of the total labour force, 3.4 per cent of those in agriculture, 8.1 per cent in industry, 17 per cent in building and public works and 4.3 per cent in services. The recession has hit hard at immigrants in the labour force: by 1982, some 22 per cent of all Algerians living in France were unemployed (Tribalat, 1985, p. 148).

Finally, marked geographical concentration of the foreign population was also very apparent (Figure 7.6). Some 57 per cent were in the three regions of Ile-de-France, Rhône-Alpes and Provence-Côte d'Azur in 1982 (compared to 41 per cent in 1954).

Figure 7.6: France: Regional Importance of Foreigners as a Percentage of Total Population 1982

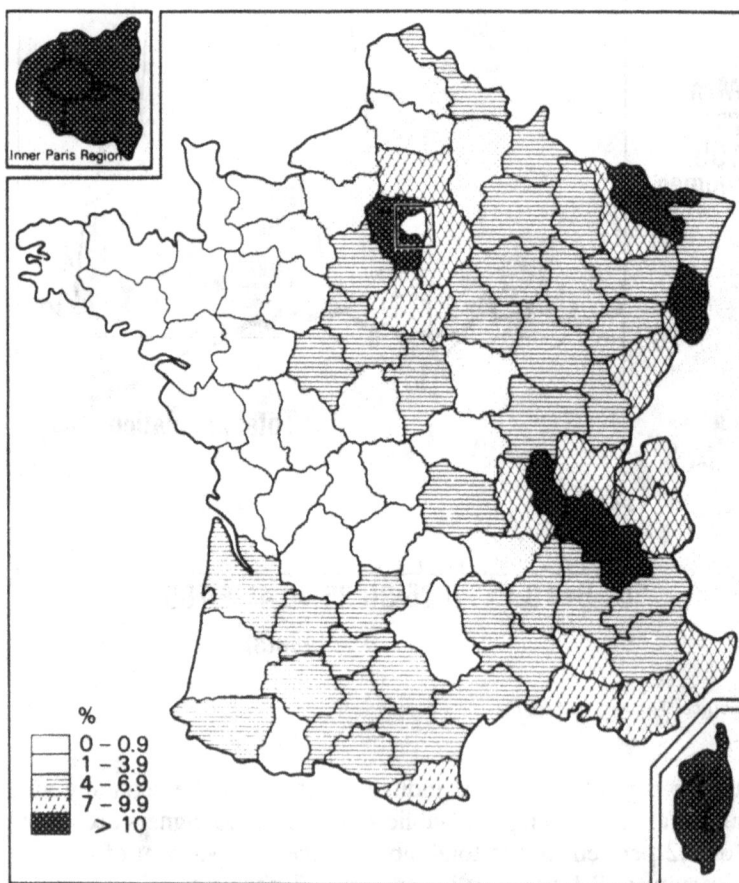

Source: Recensement 1982, Principaux Résultats, Sondage au 1/20ème: France Métropolitaine, p.91

There has been an increasing tendency for urban concentration, particularly amongst recent immigrants and therefore the 'newer' nationalities. Some 17 per cent of Paris's population was foreign in 1982, the highest figure for any *département* in France. Unpublished data from the census show that of the 36 cities of more than 100,000 population in 1982, 13 had more than 10 per cent foreigners in their population and a further 10 more than 7 per cent. Again, differences within the foreign population were very marked when detailed patterns of segregation and concentration are examined: for example, three out of four Tunisians and two out of three Algerians live in the top three regions mentioned above.

Further information, whose increasingly complex interpretation is not attempted here, may be obtained from the published cross-tabulations of nationality and birthplace data and migrations both into France since 1975 and within the country. For example, of the 1982 resident population more than six million were born outside France (reflecting the large-scale immigration of French ex-colonials as well as of foreigners); 1.32 million people had come into the country since 1 January 1975; and of the 3.6 million foreign nationals 832,000 had been born in metropolitan France, only 718,000 had been living outside France in 1975 and 1.56 million were living in the same dwelling in 1982 as in 1975.

Conclusion

In several respects, therefore, the population of France has been undergoing intriguing changes which set the period 1975–82 apart from the generality of change in the post-war years. There is certainly much work to be done in determining how fundamental these changes have been and to what extent they conform to the wider European view sketched elsewhere in this volume. For example, the slow-down in population growth largely produced by a decline in the birth rate is both evident and a cause for concern to commentators and government. Yet compared to other West European countries, natural increase is still at a relatively high level and further investigation, along the lines recently indicated by McIntosh (1983) and Chesnais (1985), into the relationship between demographic trends and government policy-making would clearly be rewarding. This is of relevance not only to the formulation of specific pro-natalist policies but also to the sensitivity of policy on education, housing or pensions to cope with short-term and long-term demographic trends.

In addition, the processes underlying what may well prove to be the most fundamental shift in the geography of the French population during the 1970s — counterurbanisation — merit very detailed research which will become possible as the small-area data from the 1982 census become available. Growth in some rural populations (noted in 1975 and confirmed in 1982) and the decline of the central city will lead to major revisions of textbook stereotypes. Finally, the 1970s and 1980s certainly mark a turning-point in the nature of international migration. There are many elements here which place France within the common experience of neighbouring countries of traditional labour immigration: a decline in new entries, a shift towards family reunification and a general tendency for the supposedly impermanent immigrant to become the permanent ethnic minority. Yet France is likely to remain distinctive here also, partly because of the national origins of the immigrants which give a particular flavour to the debate, and partly because of the detail of governmental policy and political reaction. The rise in the early 1980s of the National Front has indicated the strength of the immigration issue and forced a reassessment of policy amongst all the leading political parties. This issue, and many of the other questions raised in this chapter, illustrate very forcefully the need for considered and detailed study of population characteristics and evaluation both in the short and the long term.

References

Blanchet, D. (1985) 'Intensité et calendrier du regroupement familial des migrants: un essai de mesure à partir de données agrégées,' *Population*, *40*, 249–66

Boigeol, A., Commaille, J. and Munoz-Perez, B. (1984) 'Le divorce', *Données Sociales*, 428–46

Bonvalet, C. and Lefèbvre, M. (1983) 'Le dépeuplement de Paris 1968–75. Quelques éléments d'explication', *Population*, *38*, 941–58

Bonvalet, C. and Tugault, Y. (1984) 'Les racines du dépeuplement de Paris', *Population*, *39*, 463–82

Boudoul, J. and Faur, J.P. (1982) 'Renaissance des communes rurales ou nouvelle forme d'urbanisation?' *Economie et Statistique*, *149*, I–XVI

Chesnais, J-C. (1985) 'Les conditions d'efficacité d'une politique nataliste: examen théorique et exemples historiques', *International Population Conference IUSSP, Florence, Proceedings*, vol. *3*, 413–25 (Liège)

Courgeau, D. (1978) 'Les migrations internes en France de 1954 à 1975. I: Vue d'ensemble', *Population, 33*, 525–45

Courgeau, D. and Lefèbvre, M. (1982) 'Les migrations internes en France de 1954 à 1975, II: Migrations et urbanisation', *Population, 37*, 341–69

Courgeau, D. and Pumain, D. (1984) 'Baisse de la mobilité residentielle', *Population et Sociétés, 179*

Deville, J.C. and Naulleau, E. (1982) 'Les nouveaux enfants naturels et leurs parents', *Economie et Statistique, 145*

Fleury, M. (1982) Fort ralentissement de la croissance démographique de l'Ile-de-France: résultats provisoires du recensement. *Aspects Economiques de l'Ile-de-France, 5*, 3–9

Fouquet, A. and Morin, A-C. (1984) 'Marages, naissance, familles', *Données Sociales*, 408–27

Hall, R. and Ogden, P.E. (1985) *Europe's Population in the 1970s and 1980s*, Cambridge University Press, Cambridge

Huet, M. and Schmitz, N. (1984) 'La population active', *Données Sociales*, 26–34

Huss, M-M. (1980) *Demography, Public Opinion and Politics in France, 1974–80* (occasional paper 16) Department of Geography, Queen Mary College, London

Jones, P. (1983) 'International migration and demographic change: some evidence from the Rhône *département*', in P.E. Ogden (ed.) *Migrants in Modern France, Four Studies* (occasional paper 23) Department of Geography, Queen Mary College, London, 9–28

McIntosh, C.A. (1983) *Population Policy in Western Europe: Responses to Low Fertility in France, Sweden and West Germany*, Sharpe, New York/London

Noin, D. (1984a) 'La population de la France au début des années 1980', *Annales de Géographie, 517*, 291–302

Noin, D. *et al.* (1984b) *Atlas des Parisiens*, Masson, Paris

Ogden, P.E. (1981) 'French population trends in the 1970s', *Geography, 66*, 312–15

Ogden, P.E. (1985a) 'Counter-urbanisation in France. The results of the 1982 population census', *Geography, 70*, 24–35

Ogden, P.E. (1985b) 'France: recession, politics and migration policy', *Geography, 70*, 158–62

Tribalat, M. (1985) 'Chronique de l'immigration', *Population, 40*, 131–54

8 THE FEDERAL REPUBLIC OF GERMANY

Jürgen Bähr and Paul Gans

Introduction

The beginning of the 1970s marked a turning-point for the population development, in both quantitative and qualitative respects, of the Federal Republic of Germany. In quantitative terms, the marked decline in the birth rate from the late 1960s led to a negative balance of natural change after 1972. Admittedly this could be more than balanced, up to the halting of recruitment of foreign workers at the end of 1973, by the high annual net immigration flow; however, further legal measures to control the arrival of foreigners produced, in the succeeding period, a somewhat irregular pattern in the development of the population total (see Figure 8.1). Thus the population of the Federal Republic on 1 January 1985 (61.0 million) was scarcely more than at the time of the last census on 27 May 1970 (60.7 million); the maximum population total so far recorded, however, was of over 62 million at the start of 1974. From then began a gradual reversal which was not broken until the beginning of the 1980s, when there was a temporary slight increase. Despite temporary migration losses, the total foreign population rose strongly during the period. At the beginning of 1985, 4.36 million foreigners were registered in the Federal Republic in comparison with only 2.98 million in September 1970 (Figure 8.1) — an increase of 46 per cent.

In qualitative terms, the following have been the most important developments. Firstly, as a result of the influx of more and more foreign workers and their families spatial segregation in certain districts of the big cities has become much more clearly marked, necessitating the stronger development of integration policies, especially with respect to the second and third generations of 'guest-workers'. Secondly, changes in the characteristics of household composition and the general trend towards smaller families are increasing housing problems in the big cities. Thirdly, the already strained employment situation was made worse by the growing number of young people entering the labour force: despite economic improvement from 1983 onwards, jobs were still being

142

Figure 8.1: Federal Republic of Germany: Population Development
1971–84

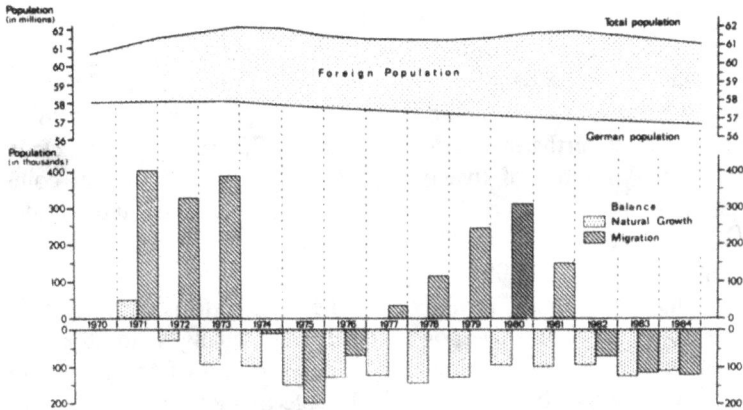

lost through rationalisation measures.

The evolutionary tendencies and problem areas that have been briefly outlined here will be considered in greater detail in the following sections of this chapter through the use of basic statistical data. Although the principal task is to consider the Federal Republic as a whole, it is important not to overlook the considerable regional differences that exist. Examples include the growth of population in administrative districts around the big cities as a result of suburbanisation, and the movement of population from north Germany to individual areas of the south as a consequence of the increasing level of economic contrast within the country. However, these developments, in part on a small scale, are very difficult to demonstrate conclusively. Firstly, the 1970 reform of local government led to a new and very different composition of administrative areas. Secondly, the microcensus (at 1 per cent cover with spot checks at 0.1 per cent) does not permit continuous regional updating of results and cannot therefore replace the missing population census as a proper tool for geographical research.

Natural Population Change Since 1970

In international comparisons West Germany has the lowest birth rate in the world. Whilst in the mid 1960s crude birth rates of 18 per thousand were reached, today the rate is less than 10 per thousand (in 1984, 9.5 per thousand). The only other country with a similar low birth rate is Denmark, at 9.9 per thousand (see also Chapter 5). Coupled with a stagnating, or even temporarily slightly increasing, crude death rate of between 11 and 12 per thousand (11.3 per thousand in 1984), the result has been an excess of deaths over births in every year since 1972 (see Figure 8.2). In 1984 the number of live births was less than 600,000 in comparison with more than 1 million in 1967. In contrast, the number of deaths stood at 700,000 so that the annual birth deficit reached approximately 100,000.

This considerable reduction in the birth rate is only in small measure explained demographically by changes in the age structure of the population. Indeed, at the end of the 1970s the arrival of larger birth cohorts at the age of marriage and fertility had very little effect on the numbers of births.

Change in the fertility behaviour of different generations is confirmed by consideration of standardised indices of natural population evolution. As early as 1970 the net reproduction rate fell

Figure 8.2: Federal Republic of Germany: Natural Population Change 1815–1983

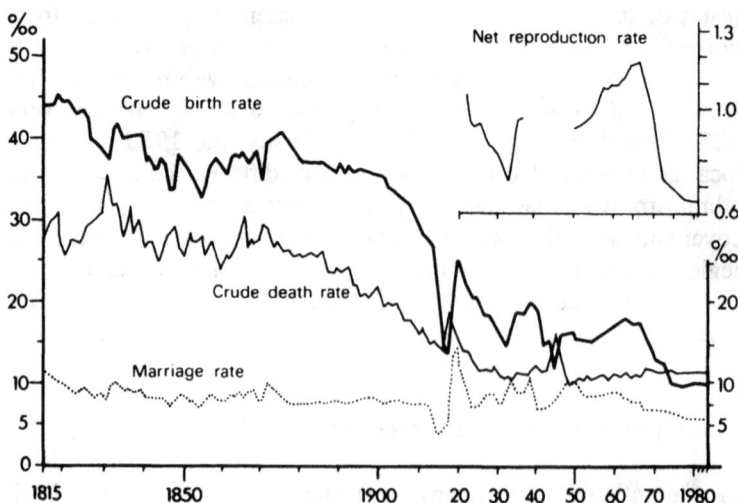

below the replacement level of 1.0, and it was continually reduced throughout the 1970s to stand at 0.65 at the end of the decade. This corresponded to a total fertility rate (TFR) of approximately 1.4, so that on average a woman behaving according to the fertility characteristics of that period throughout her reproductive years would bring only 1.4 children into the world (inter-generational continuity of cohort sizes is not reached until TFR equals 2.2).

Changing attitudes to child production are especially clearly shown when one considers the fact that 29 per cent of marriages contracted in 1960 were to result in three or more children but that this proportion has diminished to 17 per cent for the marriages of 1975. A variety of overlapping factors can be put forward as a basis for these changes in behaviour. These include economic motivations, the employment of married women, the absence of an environment favourable to child rearing, the evolution of secular-isation processes and also improved access to contraceptive methods. Changes in marriage patterns must be considered in greater depth, as these are directly related to changes in the development of household sizes.

Despite a steady increase since the mid-1960s in the proportion of couples living together without being married (from 4.7 per cent in 1965 to 9.1 per cent in 1984), more than 90 per cent of children born today are born within marriage. However, in the most recent period the proportion of married individuals has clearly been diminishing and the age at first marriage has increased. At the same time both the divorce rate and the number of those living together but unmarried are increasing. The latter trend can be described as being particularly spectacular. The 1972 micro-census recorded only 136,500 unmarried couples, whilst ten years later there were more than half a million (515,000 in 1982) — an increase of 277 per cent. In addition, there has been considerable change in the age composition and family status of those involved. In 1972 those over 55 were the dominant group, whilst in 1982 it was those under 35; and in 1972 the proportion of actual single people amongst unmarried couples was only 30 per cent, whereas in 1982 they had been 63 per cent of the total.

The balance between birth and death totals would have become even more extreme were it not for the effect of the high rate of natural increase amongst the foreign population. Their crude death rate is strongly influenced by the characteristics of their age com-position and thus is extremely low (1.8 per thousand in 1982); this together with a high (although rapidly and continuously falling since 1974) crude birth rate (15.5 per thousand in 1982) causes a relatively high rate of natural increase, which was over 20 per thousand per year prior to 1976 and still reached almost 14 per thousand in 1982. Even if the influences of age structure are eliminated there still exist considerable differences with respect to the evolution of fertility amongst Germans and foreigners. Thus the total fertility rate for the foreign population still just exceeded replacement level in 1981 (at 2.278 agains 1.359 amongst Germans). Certainly over the course of time a marked convergence towards German fertility practices can be recognised which finds expression in the swift decline of the TFR, parallel to the decline in the crude birth rate. Already for almost all nationalities TFR has sunk below the threshold level of 2.2; only the rate for the Turkish population (3.485) lies considerably above that.

All population projections for West Germany start from the assumption that in the foreseeable future there will be no new basic changes in reproductive patterns; instead, further decline in fertility is to be expected. It follows from this that the population decline in the Federal Republic will continue into the future (Table 8.1). According to the best estimates of likely fertility and migration, however, this population loss will be only of slight importance quantitatively by the year 2000 as a result of the influence of the foreign population. The assumption at present is of a decline of the German population by 9 per cent and of the total population by 4 per cent. According to these projections it would be only in the period after the turn of the century that dramatic changes would be noticeable. If present reproductive behaviour were to continue in the long term the population of West Germany would fall by 26 per cent (in comparison with its level in 1982) by the year 2030, to a figure of 45.7 millions. The number of Germans would be reduced by a third, to only 38.2 millions, and the proportion of foreigners in the population would rise from 7.6 per cent in 1982 to 16.3 per cent in 2030.

Population decline has already started to produce significant consequences in terms of changes in age-structure composition. Most marked in the future will be a rapid decline in the proportion under 20 which still today represents more than a quarter of the population, declining to less than 20 per cent by the end of the century; there will be an approximately balancing increase in the proportion of those over 59 (see Table 8.1). Admittedly as a result

Table 8.1: Federal Republic of Germany: Population Projection
Estimates by Age Groups 1982–2030

	1982	1990	2000	2010	2020	2030
German population[a]						
Total (thousands)	56,992	54,893	52,140	47,929	43,339	38,275
Index	100	96	91	84	76	67
Per cent under 20	25	20	20	18	16	16
20–59	54	58	56	56	55	49
60+	21	22	24	26	28	35
Foreign population[b]						
Total (thousands)	4,721	5,747	7,003			
Index	100	122	148			
Per cent under 20	36	32	28			
20–59	61	63	64			
60+	4	5	9			
Total population[c]						
Total (thousands)	61,713	60,640	59,143	55,481	50,993	45,741
Index	100	98	96	90	83	74
Per cent under 20	26	21	21	19	17	17
20–59	55	50	57	57	56	50
60+	20	20	22	24	27	33
Private households[d]						
Total (thousands)	25,100[e]	26,000	25,330			
Index	100	104	101			

Notes: a. Assuming constant net reproduction rate of 0.627 (1978 level)
　　　b. Assuming decline of net reproduction rate to 0.84 in 2000; no mortality
differences between Germans and foreigners from 1990 onward; annual migration
gain of 55,000 persons, with 85,000 per annum between 1988 and 1992 because of
expansion of the European Community
　　　c. The projections for 2000–2030 do not consider international migration
　　　d. Included in the assumptions here are changes in household formation behaviour
　　　e. 1981
Source: Bundesinstitut für Bevölkerungsforschung, 1984

the dependency ratio (the number of children and old people compared to those in the employed age groups) will only change slightly and will temporarily decline only up to 1990. However, the changing age structure will result in an obvious change of emphasis from the provision of education and training to pensions and other services. Present-day discussions about the maintenance of nurseries and schools on the one hand and the protection of pensions on the other show that a corresponding reorientation of financial expenditure will be very difficult to achieve in practice.

The Evolution of Characteristics of the Labour Force

During the 1970s the size of the labour force rose faster than the size of the total population. During the 1960s the activity rate first began to fall, to reach a minimum level of 43.8 per cent of the total population in 1971; since then it has risen continuously, to reach 47.1 per cent in 1984 (see Table 8.2). The basis for these changes lies equally in demographic, social and economic influences. The reduction in the activity rate since 1961 is a result of three factors: firstly, a reduction in the number of persons in the employed age groups; secondly, the continuing trend lengthening the period of an individual's education, whether at school or university; and thirdly, the improved possibilities for early retirement as a result of the establishment of laws on pension provision. The more recent increase in activity rate is explained above all by the arrival on the labour market of larger cohorts born in the 1950s, and also by the growth of employment amongst women. The proportion of females in the labour force rose sharply during the 1970s and now lies at 39 per cent.

The fact that the number in employment now is approximately equal to that in 1970 but that the activity rate has clearly grown indicates that there is also a growing number of unemployed. As in other western countries, rising unemployment has become the most important economic and social problem of the early 1980s. Whilst the unemployment rate in 1970 was insignificant at 0.4 per cent, by 1984 it stood at 7.7 per cent. Alongside this it must also be remembered that in certain population groups, above all those

Table 8.2: Federal Republic of Germany: Population, Labour Force and Employment 1961–83

	1961		1970		1980		1984	
	Thousands	%	Thousands	%	Thousands	%	Thousands	%
Population	56,175		60,651		61,516		61,196	
Labour force	26,821		26,610		27,640		28,815	
Activity rate		47.7		43.9		44.9		47.1
Females		37.0		35.8		37.9		39.1
Employed	26,713		26,494		26,874		26,608	
Unemployed	108		117		766		2,207	

Sources: 1961 and 1970: censuses; 1980: micro-census; 1984: results of a European Community labour force sample survey

with low levels of educational or professional training, this rate is considerably exceeded (for example, unemployment amongst females is 9.7 per cent and amongst foreigners of both sexes 12.8 per cent). On a regional basis there is a clear contrast between the coastal areas together with the coal, iron and steel districts, with their crisis-affected branches of industry such as steel production and shipbuilding, and parts of south Germany in which the modern, dynamic industries of the future are located. Here the unemployment rate lies at only half the level of that in the first-named set of areas.

Unrelated to fluctuations in the activity and unemployment rates, the structure of employment has continued to change from an industrial to a service basis. To date these changes are only in small measure recognisable through labour-shedding in agriculture and forestry; much more important are shifts from the secondary to the tertiary sector. The reduction in the importance of productive industry has been such that its share of total employment has fallen from 48.8 per cent in 1970 to only 41.6 per cent in 1984. The year 1980 was the first one to see more than half of all employed persons occupied in the service sector. The significance of services was founded above all on the expansion of financial institutions and insurance activities, of holding companies and of social security offices as well as of other organisations of a non-profit-making nature, including the various activities of government. Already this subcategory within the tertiary sector (which could, indeed, be identified as a 'quaternary' sector) absorbs more than one-third of all employment (Table 8.3). Analysis of year-by-year figures shows that this growth is independent of all general economic influences. Short-term variations in the total employed in this sector are very largely absent, unlike those that can be seen in the levels of employment in productive industry (such as in the 1967 recession, in the mid-1970s and at the beginning of the 1980s).

The steady absolute and relative expansion of tertiary activity is not only a result of growing prosperity and increased free time leading to strongly growing demands for services of all kinds; it is also the case that to date rationalisation processes in this sector have been much smaller than in both the other sectors.

Information on the employment status of occupied persons provides a good indicator of the development of a service-based economy (Table 8.4). In the last two decades the proportion of the

Table 8.3: Federal Republic of Germany: Gainfully Employed
Persons by Economic Sectors

| | Percentages | | | |
	1961	1970	1980	1984
Agriculture and forestry	13.6	8.5	5.5	5.4
Manufacturing industries including mining and construction	47.6	48.8	44.2	41.6
Commerce and transport	17.5	17.5	18.4	18.3
Other services	21.3	25.2	31.9	34.7

Sources: Hassmanns *et al.*, 1983; Statistisches Jahrbuch 1985

self-employed and their families has fallen not only in agriculture
but also in other economic sectors, whilst the proportion of civil
servants and other white-collar employees has grown steadily. The
proportion of manual workers, which had remained relatively constant for a long time, has shown a clear decline in the most recent
period. In 1983 the proportion of manual workers fell below 40
per cent for the first time; this is compared with a combined total
for civil servants and white-collar workers which, amongst the total
employed population, stood at only just under 50 per cent (47.3
per cent in fact) and which was already clearly above that level as
far as female employment is concerned.

The Evolution of Characteristics of Household Composition

Despite the fact that the total population of West Germany
changed little during the 1970s and early 1980s, the number of
private households grew significantly. During the decade from
1972 to 1982 there was a growth of more than 10 per cent, to a
total of 25.3 million households. As a result the average household
size now is less than 2.5 persons (in 1982 it was 2.43 in comparison to 2.74 in 1970). However, it is more useful to consider
the distribution of household sizes rather than just this average
value. Table 8.5 shows that at the present time almost one-third of
all households are one-person households (31.3 per cent in 1982)
and that this group also has the fastest rate of increase. Amongst
two-person households their relative proportion overall has grown

Table 8.4: Federal Republic of Germany: Gainfully Employed
Persons by Employment Status

	Percentages			
	1961	1970	1980	1984
Employers	12.1	9.7	9.0	9.4
Unsalaried family workers	10.0	6.3	3.6	3.4
Civil servants	5.8	7.3	8.9	9.5
Employees	24.1	31.1	36.5	38.0
Manual workers	48.0	45.6	42.0	39.7

Sources: Bundesinstitut für Bevölkerungsforschung, 1984; Statistisches Jahrbuch 1985

Table 8.5: Federal Republic of Germany: Private Household
Structures 1961–82

Years	Percentages of households					Average
	1 person	2 persons	3 persons	4 persons	5 persons	household size
1961	20.6	26.5	22.6	16.0	14.3	2.88
1970	25.1	27.1	19.6	15.2	12.9	2.74
1980	30.2	28.7	17.7	14.6	8.8	2.48
1982	31.3	28.7	17.6	14.4	8.0	2.43
Sizes of settlements 1982						
Up to 5,000	20.2	26.1	19.8	19.0	14.9	2.92
5,000–20,000	24.1	27.9	19.8	17.5	10.7	2.68
20,000–100,000	29.2	28.9	18.7	15.5	7.7	2.47
Over 100,000	40.3	30.0	15.1	10.3	4.3	2.10

Sources: 1961 and 1970: censuses; 1980 and 1982: micro-censuses

only slowly since 1970, and it has remained stable in more recent
years. All other households size categories display a continuous
decline, which is especially marked for households of five or more
persons. These trends correspond not only to the falling birth rate
but also to the fact that young adults are now leaving their parental
homes at an earlier age and that households consisting of three or
more generations have become very rare (accounting for only 2
per cent of all households).

Changes in the characteristics of household composition can be
more clearly seen if the category of one-person households is sub-

jected to closer scrutiny, Although it is true that the dominant group are the widowed, at 47 per cent of such households (against 52 per cent in 1972), it is also true that the trend of living alone has experienced above-average growth amongst never-married people. These now make up 37 per cent of one-person households, in comparison with only 32 per cent in 1972. The bases for these trends can be found in a low marriage rate and in the growing weakening of traditional family ties.

The next decade is expected to produce a continuation of these trends (see Table 8.1). That would mean that even at the turn of the century the number of households would still be greater than at the present day, despite the falling population. Average household size would by then have fallen to 2.2 or 2.3 persons, and the proportion of one-person households would have risen to 35 per cent.

General decline in household sizes has not affected the persistence of a notable urban-rural contrast. This reflects a number of factors, such as different life-styles and demands, particularities of industrial structure and employment opportunities and associated migration streams (with emigration linked to bigger households in outer areas, immigration to smaller households in the big cities), as well as variations in attitudes to the family and to marriage. The proportion of one-person households is highest in the big cities: here, such households already made up somewhat over 40 per cent of the total by 1982, whilst in the smaller and medium-sized cities they formed 25 per cent, and very much less than that in settlements with a population of less than 5,000 (see Table 8.5). The recent, and much discussed, emergency housing need in the big cities is at least in part explained by these trends.

Regional Variations in Population Evolution and Internal Migration Trends

The most noteworthy regional divergences from general trends of population evolution are to be seen in the high rate of population decline in the inner cities of the larger agglomerations as well as in the developing differences between northern and southern parts of West Germany.

In terms of the former tendency, the big cities (those with populations of over 100,000) are especially affected by declines in their German populations alongside a substantial growth in the numbers of foreigners. The total German population of these cities declined between 1970 and 1982 by 5.1 per cent (despite considerable administrative area expansion brought about by the incorporation of outlying settlements), whilst the number of foreigners grew by 62.4 per cent. This differential evolution also resulted in a clear difference in terms of the proportion of foreigners in the total population: between 1970 and 1982, this rose in the big cities from 6.3 per cent to 11.3 per cent, substantially faster than their overall growth in the Federal Republic from 4.9 to 7.6 per cent of the total population.

The above-average rate of population decline in the big cities is explained by the fact that here, amongst the German population, the reducing birth rate and out-migration into the nearby surrounding areas are superimposed. The coincident considerable influx of foreigners into the cities could not generally balance this loss of the German population. The exceptions were composed of those large cities with an above-average power of migration attraction — not just for foreigners but above all for Germans. These were almost exclusively cities in which the economic basis was determined by the tertiary sector. These were predominantly administrative or university cities: for example, Münster, Göttingen, Heidelberg, Bonn, Aachen and Wiesbaden. The significance of the especially wide-ranging educational opportunities for the outstanding importance of these cities as migration destinations must not be overlooked.

By contrast, the urban cores of all the great agglomerations fell into the category showing an especially marked decline in numbers both of the German and of the total population. Within this group there were cases where the birth deficit had the greatest influence (such as West Berlin or Hamburg), as well as those where the negative migration balance was critical (for example, Duisburg and other cities of the Ruhr, Düsseldorf, Frankfurt, Stuttgart or Mannheim). In the economically fragile coal and steel cities of the Ruhr, the migration loss of the German population was twice as high as the birth deficit. The simultaneously low rate of immigration showed the low level of attractiveness of these cities as places of residence, both for families and also for young people in training. On a wider scale, these trends also show the influence of a broader economic gradient from the south to the north of the country (see below).

At a higher level of spatial aggregation — the *Länder* and the administrative districts — differences in natural population growth have scarcely any effect, and small-scale migration patterns are largely covered up. Despite this, certain substantial deviations from the average can be observed at this level (see Figure 8.3). Eleven of the 31 *Länder* and administrative districts (*Regierungsbezirken*) of the Federal Republic had a negative population balance between 1970 and 1983. In a further four the increase was less than the average for West Germany, and in each case the rate of change has become negative in the most recent period.

The spatial pattern of Figure 8.3 shows two important regularities. The first is that all the city-states (Hamburg, Bremen and West Berlin) displayed high population loss. The second is that population development in north and south Germany is beginning to move in different directions. If one ignores the special case of West Berlin, the drawing of the boundaries of the federal *Länder* plays a decisive influence in the case of the first; for the suburbanising areas of the cities of Bremen and Hamburg belong administratively, in large part, to the bordering *Länder* of Lower Saxony and Schleswig–Holstein. Thus observed population increases in the administrative districts of Weser–Ems and Lüneburg and in *Land* Schleswig–Holstein are very largely explicable in terms of receipt from urban-rural migration. The four north German coastal districts taken together recorded a below average population increase during the period, at 0.6 per cent in comparison with 1.3 per cent for the Federal Republic as a whole.

By contrast, the existence of positive population change throughout southern Germany (with the single exception of Oberfranken) is explained above all by long-distance migration movements. Alongside the already mentioned city-states, the old industrial *Länder* of North Rhine–Westphalia and the Saar also show considerable migration loss at the present day. In opposition to these patterns, high-net receipts of migrants are most significant in Bavaria, but they also occur in Baden–Württemberg, Rhineland–Pfalz and in Hesse. Consideration of the most important net-migration flows (Figure 8.4) leads to the observation that the *Länder* of Hesse and Rhineland–Pfalz represent a sort of threshold within this spatial partitioning of population change from north to south. Whilst these *Länder*, in their connections with North Rhine–Westphalia or the Saarland, experience net in-migration, they also send out people to the bordering *Länder* of Baden–Württemberg and Bavaria.

Figure 8.3: Federal Republic of Germany: Population Change by
Länder and *Regierungsbezirke* 1970–83

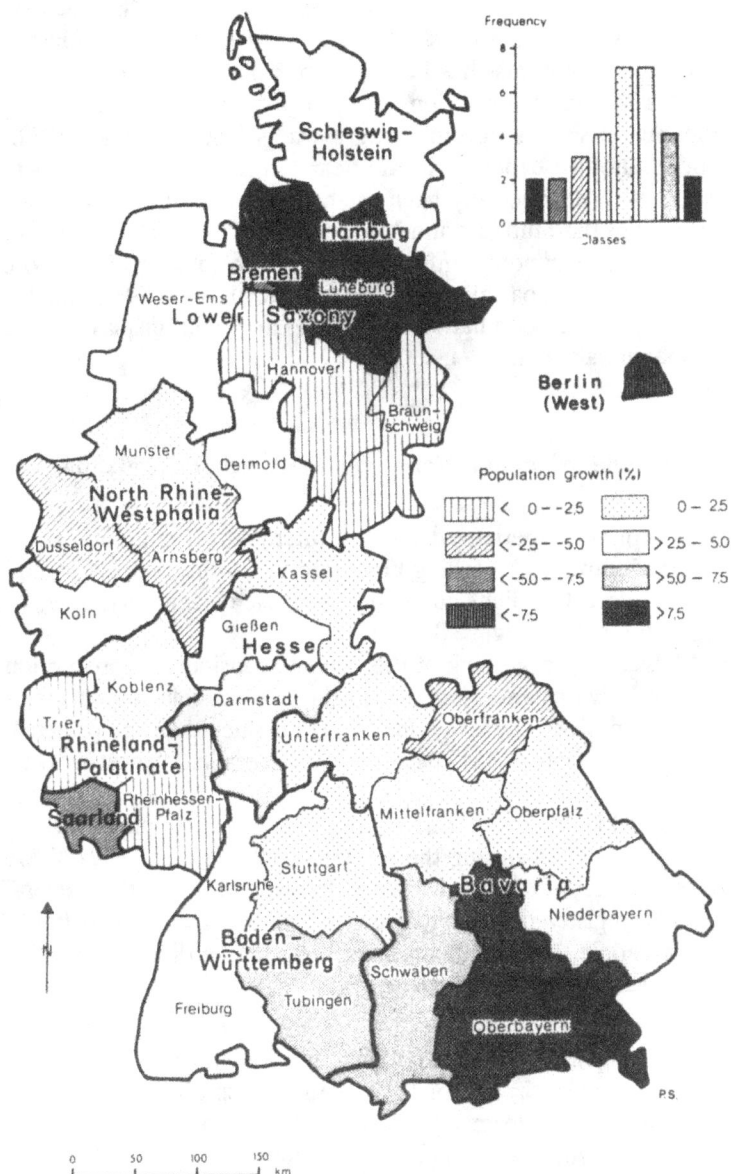

The migration balances between the Federal *Länder* indicate, just as do the closely-related unemployment rates already mentioned, that the economic problem areas of West Germany lie predominantly in the northern and western parts of the country: the areas associated with shipbuilding or with the steel industry. This regional contrast has become increasingly marked in recent years as the relative position of the regions most affected by the economic crisis has become progressively worse. Change in this trend cannot be expected in the near future, for modern growth industries have especially been established in southern Germany, above all in the Stuttgart and Munich areas. The existence here of the necessary economic infrastructure will in future pull in more people from the coastal areas and from North Rhine–Westphalia, thus leading to population evolution that will display strong regional imbalances.

International Migration Trends and the Foreign Population

High surpluses experienced through international migration more than made up for the falling birth rate up to the mid-1970s and also produced the slight population increase evident at the beginning of the 1980s (Figure 8.1).

Whilst at the beginning of the 1960s a considerable proportion of the positive balance was due to the still-possible settlement of people from East Germany, in the period since then the principal determining factor has become the so-called 'guest-worker' migration (Figure 8.5).

This influx from the European periphery (including Turkey) was first disrupted during the recession of 1966/7, but it quickly recovered very strongly. In the years around 1970 the Federal Republic registered an annual net in-migration of around half a million people. Developments since then can be divided into four clearly marked phases (Figure 8.5):

(i) The period up to the halting of recruitment of guest-workers at the end of 1973, with considerable fluctuation in manpower (from equally high levels of in and out movement) and maximum rates of migration gain.

(ii) The economic crisis of the mid-1970s, during which new

Figure 8.4: Federal Republic of Germany: Principal Net Migration
Streams Between *Länder* 1980–82

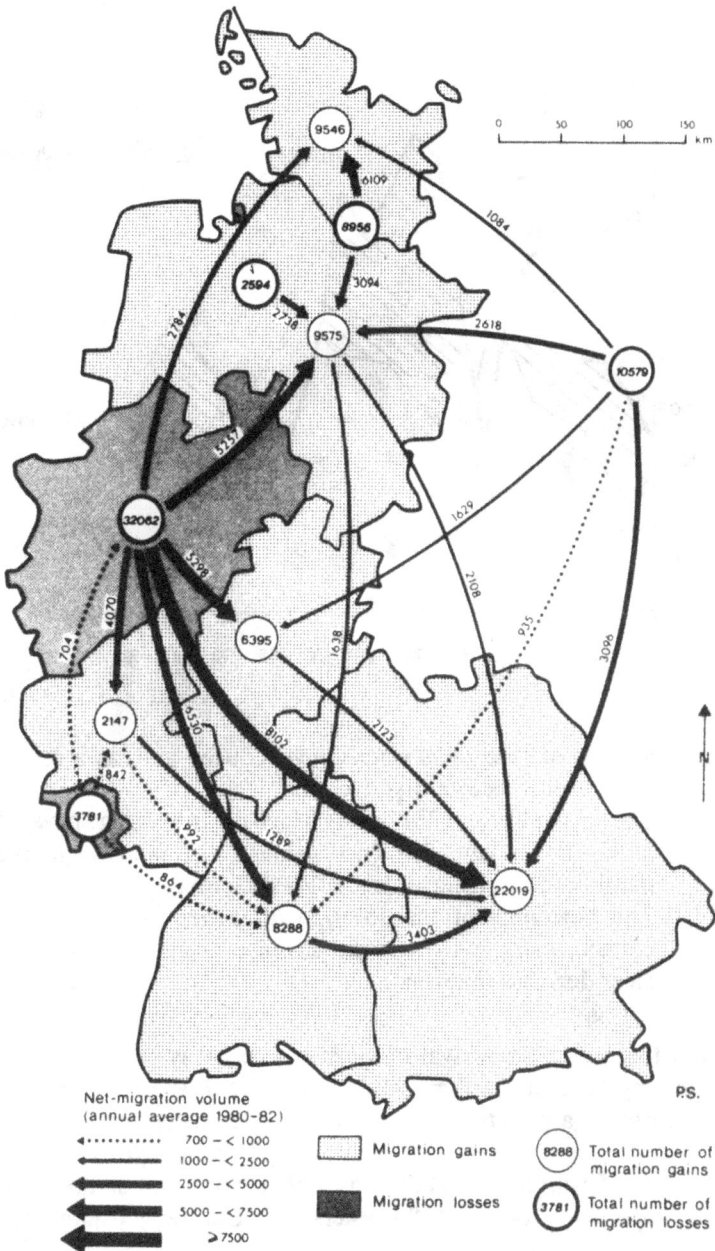

Net-migration volume
(annual average 1980–82)

700 – < 1000
1000 – < 2500
2500 – < 5000
5000 – < 7500
≥ 7500

Migration gains
Migration losses

8288 Total number of migration gains
3781 Total number of migration losses

P.S.

Figure 8.5: Federal Republic of Germany: Migration to and from Other European States (including Turkey) 1960–83

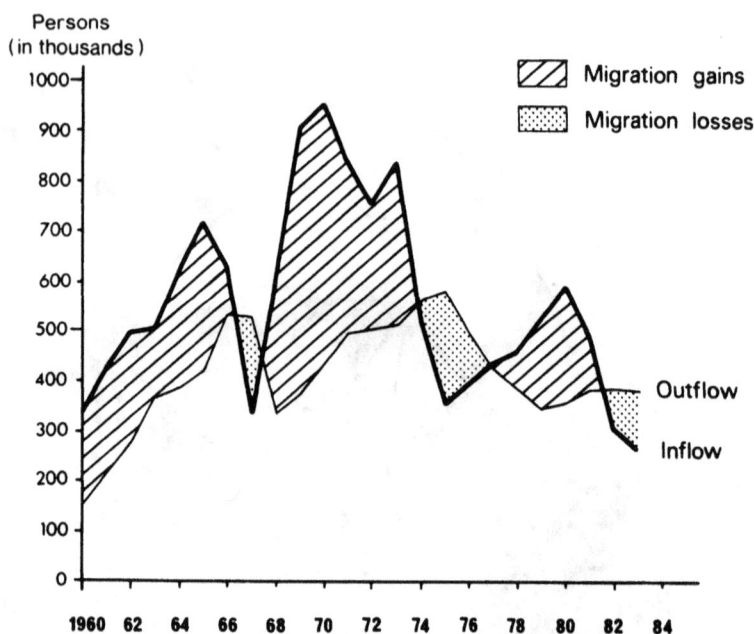

arrivals of foreigners were much reduced and, as a result, the balance became negative.

(iii) The years 1977 to 1981 during which the increasing arrival of family dependants led once again to an increase in the number of foreigners living in West Germany.

(iv) The beginning of the 1980s, with a new change in the pattern, marked by a slight increase in departures and a clear decrease in arrivals.

From the outset the arrival of guest-workers was controlled and steered by governmental measures. The Federal Republic had not seen itself as a country of immigration, and hence the influx of foreigners was controlled by bilateral agreements (for example, that of 1955 with Italy, that of 1961 with Turkey, and that of 1968 with Yugoslavia). Since 1968 workers from European Community countries have enjoyed freedom of movement between the individual member-states and legal equality with their respective citizens.

After the halting of recruitment in 1973 the migration of guest-workers was again influenced by legal regulations. Without doubt the raising of child allowances in 1975 for guest-worker children living in the Federal Republic, and the easing of regulations in 1979 on the employment of family members, favoured the arrival of dependants. Working against such measures were immigration controls, such as those of 1981, whereby entry was restricted to dependants below the age of 16, and the offering of repatriation grants from 1982, which have encouraged increasing return movement since that year.

As a result of the various waves of migration, the areas of origin and the demographic structure of the foreign population have altered considerably. Until the end of the 1960s the Italians were the biggest group; later, there was strong growth in immigration from Greece and Yugoslavia; and today it is Turks who are the most numerous, at over a third of all foreigners ahead of the Yugoslavs and Italians (see Table 8.6). As the employment and thus the immigration of foreigners occurred in the form of a progressive spatial diffusion process from south to north, federal *Länder* in south Germany record particularly high proportions of foreigners (for example, 9.5 per cent in Baden–Württemberg, 9.2 per cent in Hesse in contrast to 3.5 per cent in Schleswig–Holstein and 4.0 per cent in Lower Saxony); whereas the growth rate in the north is consistently above the average for the country as a whole: for example, growth between 1978 and 1983 of 39.7 per cent in Lower Saxony, 29.4 per cent in West Berlin, in comparison with 5.8 per cent in Baden–Württemberg and 9.9 per cent in Bavaria. The temporal shift in the proportions of different nationalities has been superimposed on these trends so that in areas affected relatively late by this diffusion process — in other words, northern Germany and the Ruhr — Turks are of particular importance: in 1983 they represented 55 per cent of all foreigners in Bremen, 44 per cent in West Berlin, 41 per cent in Schleswig–Holstein and 39 per cent in North Rhine–Westphalia, in comparison with Hesse, Baden–Württemberg and the Saarland, where they formed less than 30 per cent.

The composition of the foreign population according to sex, age, family status and length of residence (Table 8.7) displays how,

Table 8.6: Federal Republic of Germany: Foreign Population by Nationality

	Total Foreigners in thousands	Nationality (%)				
		Turkish	Yugoslav	Italian	Greek	Spanish
1961	686	1.0	2.4	28.7	6.1	6.4
1968	2,381	13.5	13.9	21.6	11.4	8.7
1971	3,431	19.0	17.3	17.2	11.5	8.2
1974	4,127	24.9	17.2	15.3	9.9	6.6
1981	4,630	33.4	13.8	13.5	6.5	3.8
1984	4,364	32.7	13.8	12.5	6.6	3.6

Source: Bähr, 1983; Statistisches Jahrbuch 1985

Table 8.7: Federal Republic of Germany: Demographic Structure and Length of Residence of the Foreign Population 1973 and 1983

	1973	1983
Age groups:		
Per cent under 18	18.8	28.2
18–34	49.6	32.5
35 and over	31.6	39.3
Sex:		
Per cent male	62.6	57.5
Marital status:		
Per cent single	43.3	51.5
Length of residence:		
Less than 1 year	12.2	3.3
1–4 years	40.2	16.2
4–8 years	24.9	17.3
8 years or more	22.7	63.2

Sources: Bähr, 1983; Statistisches Jahrbuch 1984

after the halting of recruitment in 1973, true immigration — or at least a pattern of long-term movement — developed out of the predominantly temporary and generally single person migration of workers. In 1983 almost two-thirds of foreigners had already been living in the Federal Republic for more than eight years, and the demographic structure, which for a long time showed a marked imbalance in favour of single men in the employed age groups, has been considerably altered during the past decade by the arrival of females and those aged under 18. It therefore follows that the foreigners are no longer simply temporary guests but must be considered immigrants. This applies especially to the second and third generations, who are already strongly oriented to the social system of West Germany. Because the legal implications of this situation have not yet been drawn out into the open a series of temporary provisions are still in existence that have now lasted for over 30 years, and any future discussion of integration or repatriation seems likely to be controversial.

Bibliography

Bähr, J. (1983) *Bevölkerungsgeographie: Verteilung und Dynamik der Bevölkerung in Globaler, Nationaler und Regionaler Sicht*, Ulmer, Stuttgart

Bähr, J. and Gans, P. (1985) 'Bevölkerungsveränderungen und Migrationsmuster in den Grosssdädten der Bundsrepublik Deutschland seit 1970' in J. Freidrichs (ed.) *Die Städte in der 80er Jahren: Demographische, Okonomische und Technologische Entwicklungen*, Westdeutscher Verlag, Opladen, pp. 70–116

Birg, H. (1983) *Verflechtungsanalyse der Bevölkerungsmobilität zwischen den Bundesländern von 1950 bis 1980*, IBS-Materialien 8, Bielefeld

Bolte, K.M., Kappe, D. and Schmid, J. (1980) *Bevölkerung: Statistik, Theorie, Geschichte und Politik des Bevölkerungsprozesses* (4th edn) Leske, Opladen

Bundesforschungsanstalt für Landeskunde und Raumordnung (1983) 'Regionalstatistische Informationen aus der laufenden Raumbeobachtung', *Information zur Raumentwicklung*, 5, 1147–1254

Bundesinstitut für Bevölkerungsforschung (1984) 'Demographische Fakten und Trends in der Bundesrepublik Deutschland' *Zeitschrift für Bevölkerungswissenschaft*, 10, 295–397

Buttler, G. (1979) *Bevölkerungsrückgang in der Bundesrepublik: Ausmass und Konsequenzen*, Materialien des Instituts der Deutschen Wirtschaft 2, Cologne

Fleischer, H. (1983) 'Die demographische Entwicklung in der Bundesrepublik Deutschland und in der DDR seit 1979', *Schriftenreihe des Bundesinstituts für Bevölkerungsforschung, 11*, 241–55

Gatzweiler, H.P. and Schliebe, K. (1982) 'Suburbanisierung von Bevölkerung und Arbeitsplätzen-Stillstand?', *Informationen zur Raumentwicklung*, 4, 883–913

Giese, E. (1978) 'Räumliche Diffusion ausländischer Arbeitnehmer in der Bundesrepublik Deutschland 1960–1976', *Die Erde, 109*, 92–110

Hussmans, R., Mammey, U. and Schulz, R. (1983) 'Die demographische Lage in der Bundesrepublik Deutschland', *Zeitschrift für Bevölkerungswissenschaften, 9*, 291–362

Koch, F. (1983) *Innerregionale Wanderungen und Wohnungsmarkt*, Forschungsberichte des Instituts für Bevölkerungsforschung und Sozialpolitik, 5, Frankfurt

Köllmann, W. (1983) 'Bevölkerungsentwicklung in der Bundesrepublik' in M.R. Lepsius and W. Conze (eds.) *Sozialgeschichte der Bundesrepublik Deutschland*, Stuttgart, pp. 66–114

Mammey, U. (1984) 'Bevölkerungsentwicklung in den beiden deutschen Staaten', *Geographische Rundschau, 36*, 553–9

Marschalck, P. (1984) *Bevölkerungsgeschichte Deutschlands im 19. and 20. Jahrhundert*, Suhrkamp, Frankfurt

Mertins, G. (1983) 'Zwischen Integration und Remigration: die Gastarbeiterpolitik der Bundesrepublik Deutschland nach 1973 und deren Rahmenbedingungen', *Geographische Rundschau, 35,* 46–53

Nipper, J. (1983) *Raumliche Autoregressivstrukturen in Raum-Zeitvarianten Sozio-Ökonomische Prozessen,* Giessener Geographische Schriften, *53*

Norte, H. (1981) 'Entwicklung und Bedeutung von Arbeitsmigranten und Ausländerbeschäftigung in der Bundesrepublik Deutschland zwischen 1950 und 1979', *Bochumer Historische Studien, 24,* 537–60

Rupp, S. (1981) 'In der Bundesrepublik Deutschland lebende ausländische Arbeiter, ihre Haushalte und Familien', *Schriftenreihe des Bundesinstituts für Bevölkerungsforschung, 10,* 183–204

Schmid, J. (1984) *Bevölkerungsveränderungen in der Bundesrepublik Deutschland,* Kohlhammer, Stuttgart

9 ITALY

Russell King

Introduction

As befits its transitional position between the more developed
countries of Western Europe on the one hand and the less
developed realm of Mediterranean Europe on the other, Italy's
recent demographic evolution reflects features from both parts of
the subcontinent as well as its own unique traits. Declining fertility
portends a static or declining population by the end of the century
in spite of a drastic fall-off in emigration, the country's traditional
demographic safety-valve. Counterurbanisation trends have
appeared in certain areas, especially in the north, following the
model already established in most other European countries north
of the Alps. On the other hand, in the south of Italy family size,
though shrinking, remains significantly above the West European
norm and rural–urban migration continues at rates reminiscent of
France in the 1950s. An entirely new trend, present in both north
and south, is the appearance over the last 15 years of large
numbers of labour migrants from North Africa and the Third
World.

Some of these trends could hardly have been predicted 20 years
ago. In the two standard English language texts on the geography
of Italy, Walker (1964) wrote that a large annual population
increase seemed certain 'for a long time to come', and Cole (1968)
could not see an end to the rapid process of rural-urban migration
which had boosted urban growth so spectacularly during the inter-
censal decade 1951–61. Clearly, the 1970s saw the need to
reappraise judgements such as these, although the current picture
remains highly complex with marked regional variations in the
incidence and rate of demographic changes.

Although this chapter will make reference to all the themes
which are the subject of this book, the degree of emphasis will vary
substantially among these topics. The reason for this selectivity is
the intrinsic interest of certain aspects of Italian demography, such
as migration and regional differentials in population change. The
regional context is particularly important in the case of Italy:

national data and trends are often misleading compromises between the very different demographic realities of north and south. Compared to earlier censuses the 1981 census shows that north-south contrasts have ameliorated or are to be seen now in different terms; nevertheless they remain fundamental to any discussion of Italy's population geography.

Population Change 1971–1981

The twelfth Italian Census of Population, 25 October 1981, enumerated 56,243,935 persons *de jure* (*popolazione residente*) and 56,336,185 *de facto* (*popolazione presente*). This is the first time in the history of Italian censuses — which date back to 1861 — that the *de facto* population has exceeded the *de jure* one, indicating in 1981 a substantial temporary presence of foreigners in the country, in contrast to the past when Italy always had a larger number of its own nationals temporarily resident abroad (for example, as seasonal workers in Switzerland). Following the Italian convention the rest of this chapter will deal only with the *de jure* population.

The increase in population between the 1971 and 1981 censuses was 2,107,388, or 3.9 per cent. This increase is decidedly smaller than previous inter-censal increases of 6.9 per cent during 1961–71 and 6.6 per cent during 1951–61, and is all the more remarkable considering the dramatic fall-off in Italian emigration in the 1970s compared to the high levels of exodus during 1951–71. In fact in most years since 1971 Italy has experienced net immigration, due largely to the influx of returning migrants but partly to a growing number of foreigners entering the country. The 1971–81 inter-censal population increase was the lowest ever save for 1911–21 (when a rate of 2.5 per cent was heavily affected by the First World War).

The main reason for Italy's declining rate of demographic increase is the falling birth rate which, continuing the long-term post-war trend, fell from around 17 per thousand in 1970–72 to 11 per thousand in 1981. The birth rate is probably now down to below 10 per thousand, thus approaching the death rate which has fluctuated in recent years around 9.4 to 9.7 per thousand. In Italy now birth control is considered to be a right which has been finally won and cannot be questioned (Dagradi, 1980). The falling birth rate in turn produces an increasing proportion of old people in the age pyramid and, because of the greater life expectancy of females, an increasing feminisation of the population. Thus, whilst the male inter-censal (1971–81) population increase was 3.5 per cent the female was 4.3 per cent, leading to an excess of females over males of 1.45 million. The number of males per hundred females has progressively diminished over the long term from 103.6 in 1861 to 95.0 in 1981.

As a prelude to a more detailed discussion of regional variations later in this chapter, we can state that the 1971–81 increase in population was considerably higher in the south (5.3 per cent) than in the north (2.6 per cent) and centre (4.4 per cent) macro-regions of the country. In fact very nearly half the inter-censal increase (1 million out of 2.1 million) was accounted for by the south, which contains only 35 per cent of the Italian population. This broad pattern of regional population change represents a complete reversal of the previous (1961–71) inter-censal pattern, which saw stagnation in the south (1.6 per cent increase) and rapid growth in the north (10.2 per cent) and centre (9.7 per cent), fed largely by the massive south-north transfers of population which characterised this earlier decade.

As a result of these developments the macro-regional distribution of population has changed somewhat. Over the decade 1971–81 the north's share of the total population has fallen from 46.1 per cent to 45.5 per cent, whilst that of the south has risen from 34.9 per cent to 35.4 per cent. The centre's share has remained more or less constant (19.0 per cent in 1971, 19.1 per cent in 1981). These changes are due to the continuing, though declining, higher southern birth rate and the drying-up of inter-regional migration streams.

Household Structures

ISTAT (The Italian census authority) fails to make a clear distinction between 'household' and 'family', presenting all such data under the label *famiglie*. In practice in the Italian situation, 'family' is generally coterminous with 'household', although there are some exceptions. The 1981 census recorded 18,536,570 'families' containing 55,768,593 people. This latter figure is 475,342 less than the total *de jure* population, the difference being accounted for by individuals who are long-term residents in hospitals, rest homes, colleges, barracks, religious institutions, prisons, hostels and hotels. In 1981 the mean 'family' (really 'household') size was 3.0, a marked decrease from the 3.3 of 1971 and 4.0 of 1951. In addition to the declining birth rate alluded to above this is also a reflection of the trend towards nuclear rather than extended family households. Again, however, macro-regional variations are evident, the mean family/household size being, in 1981, 2.8 in the north, 3.0 in the centre and 3.3 in the south (with a high of 3.57 in Naples province).

Between the 1971 and 1981 censuses the index of overcrowding — measured by dividing the number of family/household members into the number of occupied rooms (excluding those used for study, workshop or other 'non-living' purposes) — improved from 1.0 to 0.8. The macro-regional variation in this index (0.9 in the south, 0.7 in the north and centre) is now rather less marked than it was two decades ago (1961: 1.5 in the south, 1.1 in the centre, 1.0 in the north), indicating substantial improvements in housing conditions in the south.

Population Characteristics

Table 9.1 shows data on a selection of variables concerned with characteristics such as population age, employment and education. The first two columns concern age structure. Southern regions have a significantly younger population, as measured by the percentage under 14 years, than most central and northern regions. Higher percentages of the older age groups (those over 65) are found in the north and centre. The most dramatic contrast is between Liguria and Campania. Linguria is the only region with more people aged over 65 than under 14, a function largely of its role as a retirement region, for here is to be found the Italian Riviera. Campania, on the other hand, has three times more young people (under 14) than old (over 65), the Naples urban region experiencing the highest birth rate of any part of the country (Achenbach, 1983).

The changing age structure of the population has fundamental social and economic implications. In 1981, 13.0 per cent were over 65 (compared to 11 per cent in 1971); the forecast is 14.5 per cent in 1991 (Rey, 1983). A third of over-65s are in fact over 75, and

Table 9.1: Italy: Population Characteristics from the 1981 Census

Region	% population <14yrs	% population >65yrs	% population >6yrs who are: graduates	illiterates	active population as % total	% active population in: agriculture	industry	comm. and serv.	unemployed %
North									
Piedmont-Val d'Aosta	18.1	15.1	2.4	0.9	43.7	8.3	49.2	42.5	8.8
Lombardy	19.3	12.3	2.7	0.7	43.7	4.0	51.4	44.6	7.5
Trentino-Alto Adige	22.0	12.1	2.3	0.3	41.2	11.4	31.8	56.8	7.9
Veneto	21.0	12.7	2.2	1.0	41.3	8.8	45.3	45.9	9.0
Friuli-Venezia-Giulia	17.7	16.7	2.2	0.6	40.2	5.2	39.7	55.1	7.5
Liguria	15.6	18.2	3.3	1.0	38.6	4.9	32.0	63.1	11.5
Centre									
Emilia-Romagna	17.3	15.9	2.8	1.4	45.3	12.9	40.4	46.7	7.3
Tuscany	17.7	16.7	2.8	2.1	41.9	6.7	43.8	49.5	9.1
Umbria	18.0	15.2	2.8	3.1	40.5	11.2	42.4	46.4	10.6
Marche	19.1	15.2	2.8	2.5	42.4	11.7	44.9	43.4	9.2
Latium	21.6	11.7	4.4	2.1	38.9	6.7	28.3	65.0	17.7
South									
Abruzzi	21.2	14.3	2.4	5.4	37.5	14.5	37.8	47.7	14.2
Molise	20.5	16.0	2.1	5.6	38.0	29.3	30.7	40.0	16.4
Campania	27.2	9.6	2.7	5.6	36.5	17.8	31.3	50.9	31.3
Apulia	26.7	10.6	2.2	5.7	36.5	25.5	28.9	45.6	23.8
Basilicata	24.7	12.2	1.8	8.7	37.8	27.6	32.0	40.4	23.4
Calabria	25.9	11.6	2.3	9.4	35.0	23.7	28.6	47.7	27.9
Sicily	24.8	12.0	2.7	6.5	32.9	19.8	29.4	50.8	25.8
Sardinia	25.8	10.8	2.3	4.9	35.4	13.4	32.1	54.5	23.2
Macro-regions									
North	19.1	14.1	2.6	0.9	42.9	7.4	45.8	46.8	8.2
Centre	19.7	14.1	3.6	2.8	40.5	7.8	37.3	54.9	13.0
South	25.7	11.2	2.5	6.3	35.5	20.4	30.6	49.0	26.0
Italy	21.6	13.0	2.7	3.0	39.8	11.2	39.8	49.0	14.8

Source: 12° Censimento Generale della Popolazione 25 Ottobre 1981, Dati sulle Caratteristiche Strutturali della Popolazione e delle Abitazioni (Campione al 2% dei Fogli di Famiglia), Dati Provvisori. Rome: ISTST, 1983, Tables 2, 3, 5, 6, 10, 13.

in 1981 12 per cent of Italian households had a member aged over 75. This spread of very old people poses important social questions as to their care and welfare: whether these should remain, as is traditional in Italy, within the family or whether public structures should play a bigger role in assistance. The sharp fall in under-14s (24.4 per cent in 1971, 21.6 per cent in 1981, an estimated 17.4 per cent in 1991) has obvious implications for the future structure of the labour market (Frey, 1983).

The next pair of columns in Table 9.1 concern education and literacy. Whilst illiteracy is 5–10 times higher in the south than in most northern regions, there is little difference with regard to the proportion of university graduates. With 4.4 per cent graduates, Latium stands out as an exception. This region contains Rome which not only has the largest university in the country but is also the major focus for the Italian intelligentsia and state bureaucracy, both of which groups contain high proportions of graduates.

The next five columns in Table 9.1 deal with employment characteristics. Northern regions have a generally higher proportion of their total populations economically active; in all northern and central regions it is above 38 per cent, whereas in all southern regions it is below that level. The two extremes are Emilia–Romagna (45.3 per cent) and Sicily (32.9 per cent). This regional dualism has been a permanent structural feature of the Italian labour market, reflecting the wider availability of a range of types of employment in the north and centre and the higher levels of underemployment and hidden unemployment in the south. Female activity rates are particularly low in the south, partly due to cultural sanctions against women working outside the home. Interestingly, the 1981 national activity rate, 39.8 per cent, marks an increase over the previous census and a reversal of a trend towards a steady decline which had been continuous since the first national census of 1861, when the labour force constituted 59.5 per cent of the population. In 1971 the figure was 34.7 per cent. Using annual data, Di Comite and Imbriani (1982) have shown that for the country as a whole the upturn in activity rates took place in 1971–73, but that the date was later for the male labour market (1977) and for the south (also 1977).

The decline in activity rates from north to south is matched by a corresponding rise in the unemployment figures, which include both those who, having been gainfully employed in the past, are registered unemployed and those who are in search of their first job. Unemployment rates in Campania (31.3 per cent) and Calabria (27.9 per cent) are four times those in some central and northern regions: Lombardy, Trentino, Friuli and Emilia-Romagna all have rates of 7–8 per cent. Overall, more than one in seven of the Italian work-force was out of work at the time of the 1981 census.

The national sectoral employment pattern shows that in 1981 nearly half the employed population were working in the tertiary sector (commerce, banking and insurance, services, transport and public administration); nearly 40 per cent in industry (including construction); and only a little over one tenth in agriculture (see Table 9.2). The long-term sectoral evolution of the Italian labour market since the war has seen a dramatic fall-off in agricultural employment. This flight from farming has been coupled by more or less parallel increases in industry (although only up until 1971) and services. The service sector has expanded with increasing momentum, whilst the industrial sector expanded explosively between 1951 and 1961 but then slowed down and finally lost ground. The decline in industrial employment is by no means regionally uniform; in fact, industrial employment has continued to increase in regions of central and north-eastern Italy (particularly in the belt which runs from Friuli through Veneto and Emilia-Romagna to Marche), but this has been outweighed by the industrial decline of the north-west (Piedmont, Lombardy, Liguria) and the shrinkage of industrial employment in some southern regions (see King, 1985b).

The main residues of farm employment are sited in the south where many regions have 20–30 per cent of their employment in agriculture. The level of tertiary employment is remarkably uniform over the country as a whole, most regions have 40–55 per cent. Only Liguria (63.1 per cent) and Latium (65.0 per cent) have

Table 9.2: Italy: Employment Structures 1951–81

| | Percentage of all employment | | | |
	1951	1961	1971	1981
Agriculture	42.2	29.3	17.6	11.2
Industry	32.0	40.7	44.6	39.8
Services	25.8	30.0	37.8	49.0

Source: Population censuses 1951, 1961, 1971, 1981

significantly higher levels, accounted for respectively by resort tourism and state bureaucracy. Industry is most important in the north, accounting for half the regional employment of Lombardy and Piedmont, and much less important in Latium and the south, where figures of around 30 per cent are normal.

Provincial Patterns of Population Change

Data at the level of Italy's 95 provinces provide an ideal mapping framework for a detailed spatial interpretation of the demographic changes shown up by the latest census. In order for the significance of these most recent trends to be fully grasped, the inter-censal decade 1971–81 needs to be set alongside the changes observed over the previous two inter-censal decades. Accordingly, Figures 9.1–3 record the provincial pattern of population change for the three successive decades 1951–61, 1961–71 and 1971–81. Comparison between these maps is facilitated by the fact that the same shading system is used throughout.

Figure 9.1 shows that the decade 1951–61 was a period of intense spatial contrast in the pattern of population losses and gains. Several northern provinces, in the process of rapid industrialisation and urbanisation, recorded high gains of population, including two above 25 per cent (Turin 27.3 per cent, Milan 26.0 per cent). Rome also grew rapidly, increasing its population by 29 per cent over the decade. Population losses occurred in two main areas: firstly, a block of about a dozen provinces corresponding to the rural parts of the central Po Valley from Cremona and Piacenza eastward to the delta and thence round to the north-eastern corner of Italy; secondly, an alignment of 15 provinces running down the Apennine backbone from Arezzo south to Potenza. Interestingly, the highest losses occurred not in the 'Deep South' but in provinces which were fairly close to fast-growth urban areas, such as Cuneo adjacent to Turin (−7.6 per cent), Rovigo (−22.4 per cent), Mantua (−8.8 per cent) and Cremona (−8.0 per cent) in the Po Plain, and Rieti (−9.4 per cent) and L'Aquila (−9.9 per cent) close to Rome.

Figure 9.2 (1961–71) shows a remarkably similar picture to Figure 9.1, indicating a continuation not only of the same basic spatial pattern but also of similar levels of change. Again, Turin, Milan (with its closely adjacent province of Varese) and Rome

Figure 9.1: Italy: Inter-censal Population Change by Province 1951–61

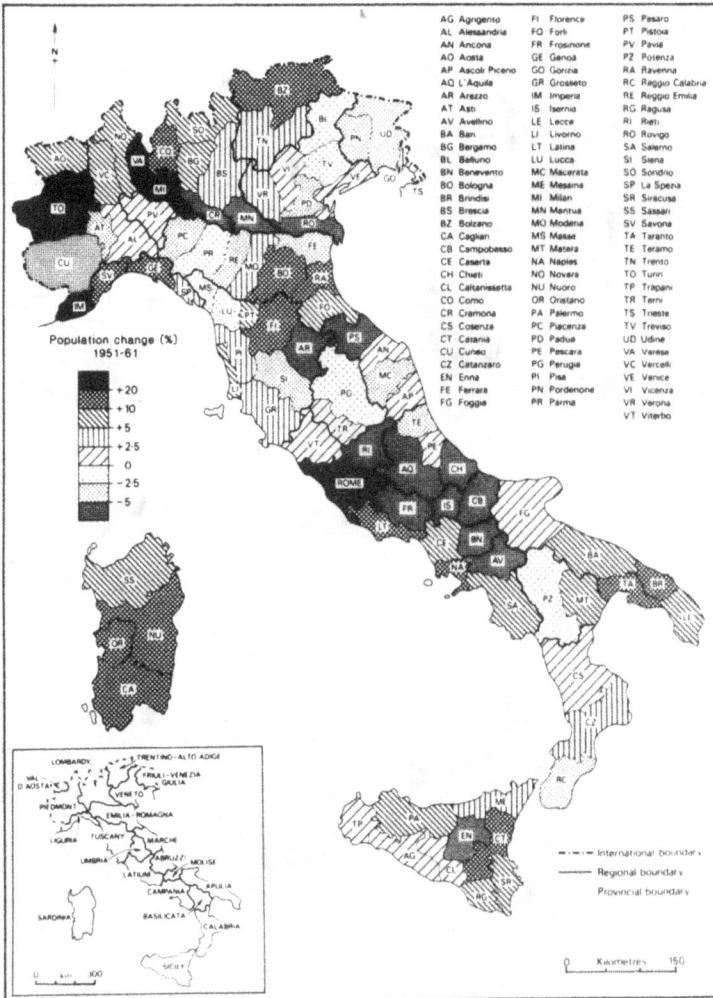

were the only provinces with a positive change of over 20 per cent. Again, the Po axis provinces from Piacenza and Cremona through to Ferrara and Rovigo lost heavily (but in 1961–71 there is, save for the depressed Alpine province of Belluno, no north-eastern continuation of this belt). And again the chain of depopulating Apennine provinces is clearly visible, but extending this time beyond Potenza right to the tip of the peninsula, crossing to

Figure 9.2: Italy: Inter-censal Population Change by Province 1961-71

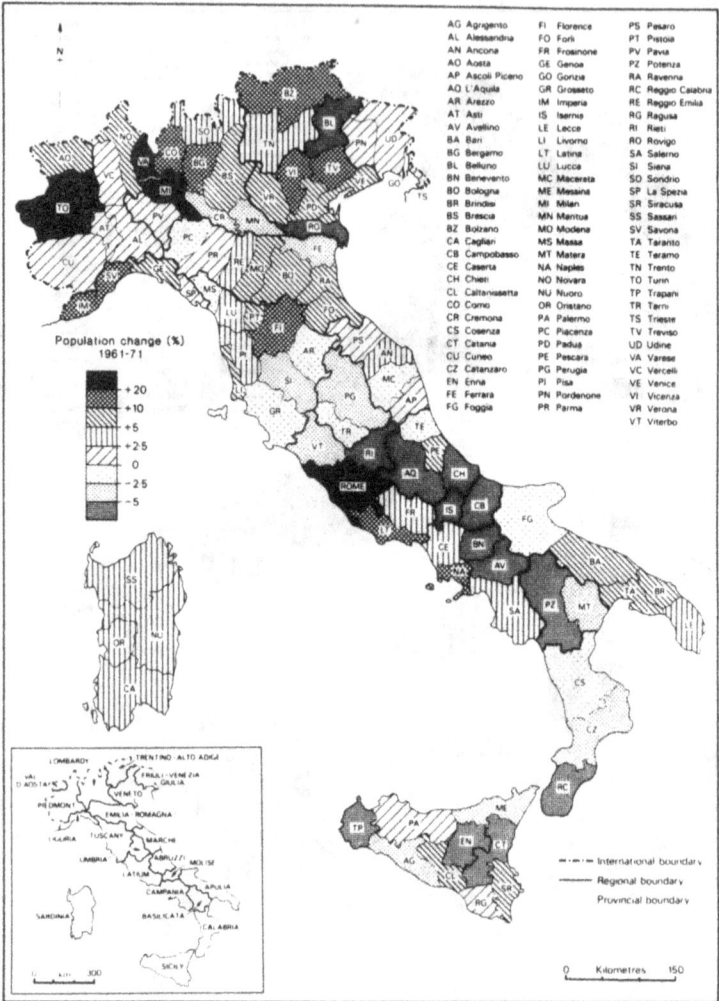

AG	Agrigento	FI	Florence	PS	Pesaro
AL	Alessandria	FO	Forlì	PT	Pistoia
AN	Ancona	FR	Frosinone	PV	Pavia
AO	Aosta	GE	Genoa	PZ	Potenza
AP	Ascoli Piceno	GO	Gorizia	RA	Ravenna
AQ	L'Aquila	GR	Grosseto	RC	Reggio Calabria
AR	Arezzo	IM	Imperia	RE	Reggio Emilia
AT	Asti	IS	Isernia	RG	Ragusa
AV	Avellino	LE	Lecce	RI	Rieti
BA	Bari	LI	Livorno	RO	Rovigo
BG	Bergamo	LT	Latina	SA	Salerno
BL	Belluno	LU	Lucca	SI	Siena
BN	Benevento	MC	Macerata	SO	Sondrio
BO	Bologna	ME	Messina	SP	La Spezia
BR	Brindisi	MI	Milan	SR	Siracusa
BS	Brescia	MN	Mantua	SS	Sassari
BZ	Bolzano	MO	Modena	SV	Savona
CA	Cagliari	MS	Massa	TA	Taranto
CB	Campobasso	MT	Matera	TE	Teramo
CE	Caserta	NA	Naples	TN	Trento
CH	Chieti	NO	Novara	TO	Turin
CL	Caltanissetta	NU	Nuoro	TP	Trapani
CO	Como	OR	Oristano	TR	Terni
CR	Cremona	PA	Palermo	TS	Trieste
CS	Cosenza	PC	Piacenza	TV	Treviso
CT	Catania	PD	Padua	UD	Udine
CU	Cuneo	PE	Pescara	VA	Varese
CZ	Catanzaro	PG	Perugia	VC	Vercelli
EN	Enna	PI	Pisa	VE	Venice
FE	Ferrara	PN	Pordenone	VI	Vicenza
FG	Foggia	PR	Parma	VR	Verona
				VT	Viterbo

embrace much of Sicily as well. So in 1961-71, compared to 1951-61, the area of population loss shrinks somewhat in the north (specifically in the north-east) but expands in the south to include the 'Deep South' regions of Calabria and Sicily. Two southern regions, Apulia and Sardinia, are unique in that they are strong population growth areas at both periods, 1951-61 and 1961-71.

Figure 9.3: Italy: Inter-censal Population Change by Province 1971-81

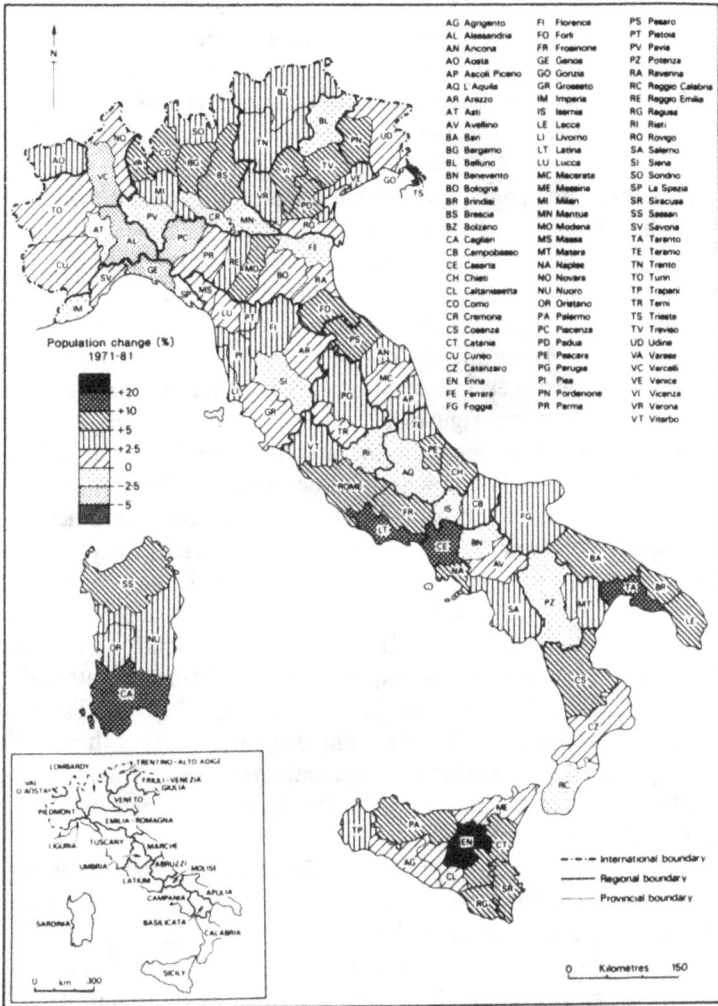

Source: 12° Censimento Generale della Popolazione 1981, vol. 1, Primi Risultati Provinciali

In contrast to the broad similarity between Figure 9.1 and 9.2, Figure 9.3, representing population change during 1971–81, shows radical changes in the evolution of the pattern. Firstly, the spatial contrasts become less intense. No provinces gained more than 20 per cent (in contrast to five provinces in 1951-61 and 4 in

1961–71), and fewer provinces gained between 10 and 20 per cent (4 in 1971–81, 10 in 1961–71, 15 in 1951–61). Likewise in 1971--81 losses were less dramatic: only two provinces lost more than 5 per cent, compared to 14 during 1961–71 and 15 during 1951–61. So there is a general evening out of spatial growth and decline rates, due largely to a fall-off in inter-regional migration since 1971.

Secondly, the geographical distribution of growth and decline in 1971–81 exhibits entirely new features. The 'Po River' provinces are still partially intact as an axis of decline, but the most remarkable feature in the north is the cluster of declining provinces (Vercelli, Asti, Alessandria, Genoa, Pavia) in the heart of the famous 'industrial triangle'. Trieste also loses heavily (−5.9 per cent). With the exception of Siena, all provinces of the northern Apennines which on Figures 9.1 and 9.2 were constant losers of population are now demographic growth areas. There is still an irregular axis of decline down the spine of the southern Apennines (Rieti, L'Aquila, Isernia, Benevento, Potenza), but it is much less extensive than formerly and much weaker losses (less than 2.5 per cent instead of over 5 per cent). In the islands, only Enna province continues to lose population. In fact the most dynamic growth provinces during 1971–81 are in the south. These are mostly provinces which have experienced a build-up of state-aided industry in the 1960s and 1970s: Latina, Caserta, Taranto, Cagliari. In northern Italy, the main provinces of growth now lie entirely east of the traditionally dynamic heartland of the western Po plain, in an area which at a previous stage (see especially Figure 9.1) was losing population.

Figures 9.4 and 9.5 break the 1971-81 population change pattern into its two constituents, natural change and migration. The spatial pattern of natural change is remarkably clear (Figure 9.4). The whole of peninsular Italy south of Tuscany and Emilia-Romagna (and including Sicily and Sardinia) is an area of natural increase with particularly high values occurring in Apulia, around Naples and in southern Sardinia. North of the transpeninsular dividing-line the story is one of natural decline or stagnation, with the exception of slight-to-moderate increases in some Alpine provinces, such as German-speaking Bolzano which has a long tradition of high birth rates. The sharpest natural declines are registered in a group of provinces which lie at the core of the industrial triangle — the same cluster

Figure 9.4: Italy: Natural Increase by Province 1971–81

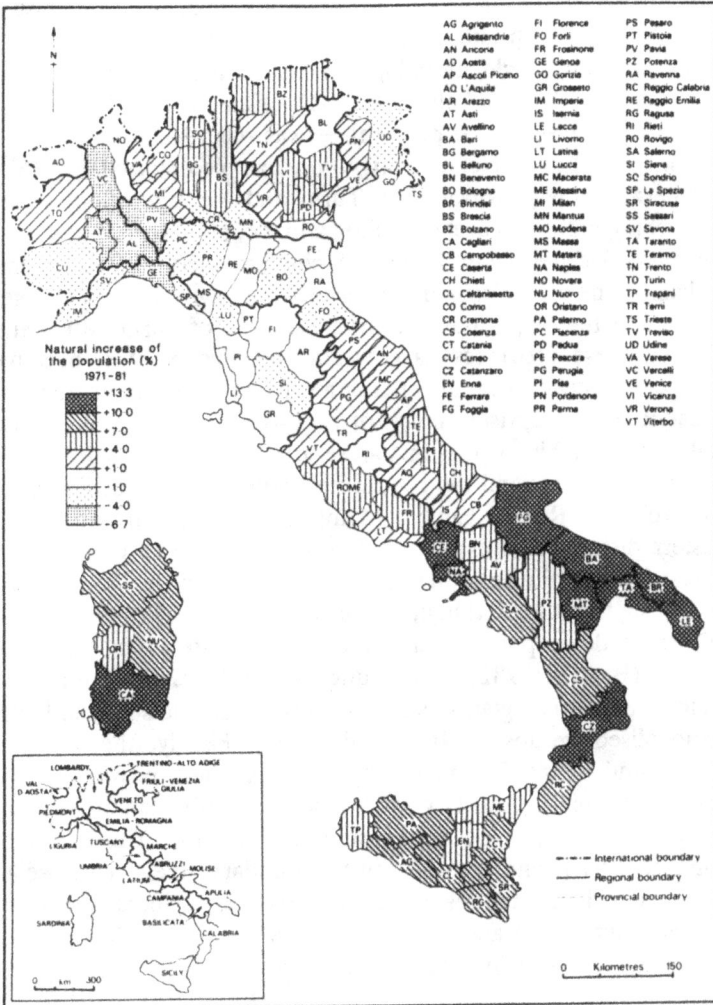

identified in the discussion of Figure 9.3.

Although inter-regional migration is much reduced compared with the hypermobility of the period 1951–71, net migratory losses (see Figure 9.5) are still widespread amongst the provinces of the south where natural increase is high — the classic demographic phenomenon of out-migration acting as a safety valve for excessive natural increase. Important qualitative changes have taken place in the character of the migration stream: the typical mover is no longer a male head of household seeking to establish a new life for himself and his family in the urban milieu; rather, he or she is young, single, more highly educated and more likely to be in possession of a marketable skill (Douglass, 1983). The biggest migratory loss — −12.6 per cent — was recorded in the Sicilian province of Enna. Net out-migration has also started to affect northern urban provinces like Turin and Venice, where once-flourishing industries are in decline; and it continues, as it has done for many decades, from the high Alpine provinces of Sondrio and Bolzano. The main destinations for internal migrants are no longer Rome and the three 'industrial triangle' cities of Turin, Milan and Genoa; these provinces have weakly positive or even negative balances. Instead, the main area of attraction for migrants now is a broader belt comprising much of northern and especially central Italy, reaching high values in Varese north of Milan, Pordenone in the far north-east and the central-northern provinces of Florence, Modena and Reggio Emilia. Many of these central and north-eastern districts have experienced over the last 10–15 years a rapid expansion of 'diffuse industrialisation', especially in the clothing, footwear, furniture and light engineering sectors. This new style of industrial development, sometimes referred to as the 'Emilian model' (Brusco, 1982), has sprung out of the crisis of the main Italian industrial giants such as Fiat, Montedison, and the nationalised groups (ENI, Italsider etc.). Finally, the cases of Latina and Frosinone are worthy of note. These provinces have attracted much industrial growth, and hence population, because of their strategic location just south of the *Cassa per il Mezzogiorno* (Fund for the south) boundary; they are close to Rome and the north, yet qualify for generous regional incentives. Latina's net in-migration during 1971–81 was equivalent to 12.4 per cent of the province's 1971 population.

Urban Growth and Decline

Any discussion of Italian urban demography is bedevilled by two statistical problems. One is the difficulty of establishing a meaningful threshold for the definition of 'urban' settlements, due basically to the existence of contrasting forms of urbanism in different parts

Figure 9.5: Italy: Net Migration by Province 1971–81

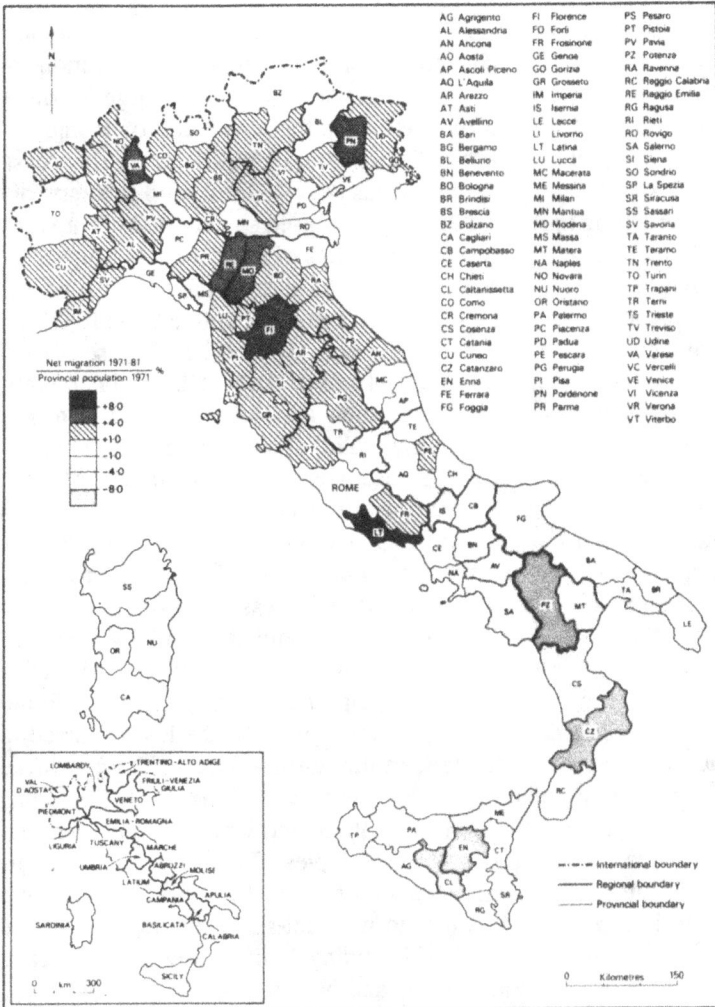

AG	Agrigento	FI	Florence	PS	Pesaro
AL	Alessandria	FO	Forlì	PT	Pistoa
AN	Ancona	FR	Frosinone	PV	Pavia
AO	Aosta	GE	Genoa	PZ	Potenza
AP	Ascoli Piceno	GO	Gorizia	RA	Ravenna
AQ	L'Aquila	GR	Grosseto	RC	Reggio Calabria
AR	Arezzo	IM	Imperia	RE	Reggio Emilia
AT	Asti	IS	Isernia	RG	Ragusa
AV	Avellino	LE	Lecce	RI	Rieti
BA	Bari	LI	Livorno	RO	Rovigo
BG	Bergamo	LT	Latina	SA	Salerno
BL	Belluno	LU	Lucca	SI	Siena
BN	Benevento	MC	Macerata	SO	Sondrio
BO	Bologna	ME	Messina	SP	La Spezia
BR	Brindisi	MI	Milan	SR	Siracusa
BS	Brescia	MN	Mantua	SS	Sassari
BZ	Bolzano	MO	Modena	SV	Savona
CA	Cagliari	MS	Massa	TA	Taranto
CB	Campobasso	MT	Matera	TE	Teramo
CE	Caserta	NA	Naples	TN	Trento
CH	Chieti	NO	Novara	TO	Turin
CL	Caltanissetta	NU	Nuoro	TP	Trapani
CO	Como	OR	Oristano	TR	Terni
CR	Cremona	PA	Palermo	TS	Trieste
CS	Cosenza	PC	Piacenza	TV	Treviso
CT	Catania	PD	Padua	UD	Udine
CU	Cuneo	PE	Pescara	VA	Varese
CZ	Catanzaro	PG	Perugia	VC	Vercelli
EN	Enna	PI	Pisa	VE	Venice
FE	Ferrara	PN	Pordenone	VI	Vicenza
FG	Foggia	PR	Parma	VR	Verona
				VT	Viterbo

of the country. If we take 20,000 as the lower limit for urban settlements, then we include dozens of southern 'agro-towns' which have 20,000–50,000 inhabitants yet which are basically 'rural dormitories' for a farming population. If we raise the limit to 50,000, then this excludes dozens of small towns in central and northern regions (particularly in Tuscany and Umbria) which are undeniably urban in form and character. The second problem is the fact that Italian population figures at the micro-level are available for units called communes (*communi*) which do not necessarily coincide with the boundaries of towns or urban agglomerations. The cases of Milan and Rome provide good illustrations of this problem. Rome Commune contains a very large territory (1508 km²) which includes not only the entire city of Rome but also surrounding country districts stretching as far as the coast. Milan Commune, by contrast, has only 182 km², and this territory has for a long time been entirely urbanised so that the built-up area of Milan has spread into the territories of adjacent communes.

An alternative approach, which at least in part gets round the first problem (but not the second) is to focus attention on Italy's 95 provincial capitals. These range in size from 18,794 (Isernia) to 2.83 millions (Rome), but only 13 have below 50,000 inhabitants. Provincial capitals, because of their administrative and historical importance, provide a fairly solid skeleton for Italy's urban geography. There are, for instance, only four towns of over 100,000 which are not provincial capitals (Prato, Rimini, Monza and Torre del Greco). The 1981 census shows that 18.46 million people — 32.8 per cent of the Italian total — live in the provincial capitals; this proportion represents a decrease over the 1971 figure (34.1 per cent). This loss of provincial capital population occurred in spite of the fact that only one-third of the capitals (32 out of 95) actually lost population. Once again, the explanation is to be found in the familiar north/south contrast. Most of the loss occurred in the bigger northern capitals. In the north, 23 out of 33 provincial capitals lost population; but in the whole of the south (including the adjacent central regions of Latium and Umbria) only three out of 41 provincial capitals shrank (Naples, Catania and Enna). The bigger inter-censal gains — all in the range 14–20 per cent — were made in a number of small- to medium-sized southern provincial towns (all under 100,000), including Latina, Frosinone, Isernia, Campobasso, Matera, Potenza and Nuoro.

Table 9.3 concentrates on the growth profiles of the eleven major cities between 1951 and 1981. The long time-span is essential to appreciate the significance of 1971–81 inter-censal change. All the cities in Table 9.3 contained at least 250,000 inhabitants in 1951 and at least 350,000 in 1971 (the twelfth city, Messina, is considerably smaller). In spite of the fact that Mussolini's laws discouraging rural-urban migration were not repealed until 1961, the decade 1951–61 was clearly the boom period for post-war

Table 9.3: Italy: Population of Major Cities 1951–81

	1951	1961	1971	1981	Per cent change 1951–61	Per cent change 1961–71	Per cent change 1971–81
Rome	1,651,754	2,188,160	2,781,993	2,830,569	+32.5	+27.1	+1.7
Milan	1,274,245	1,582,534	1,732,000	1,634,638	+24.2	+9.4	−6.0
Naples	1,010,550	1,182,815	1,226,594	1,210,503	+17.0	+3.7	−1.3
Turin	719,300	1,025,822	1,167,968	1,103,520	+42.6	+13.9	−5.5
Genoa	688,447	784,194	816,872	760,300	+13.9	+4.2	−6.9
Palermo	490,692	587,985	642,814	699,691	+19.8	+9.3	+8.8
Bologna	340,526	444,872	490,528	455,853	+30.6	+10.3	−7.1
Florence	374,625	436,516	457,803	453,293	+16.5	+4.9	−1.0
Catania	299,629	363,928	400,048	378,521	+21.5	+9.9	−5.4
Bari	268,183	312,023	357,274	370,781	+16.3	+14.5	+3.8
Venice	316,891	347,347	363,062	332,775	+9.6	+4.5	−8.3

Sources: Anuario Statistico Italiano, 1962 and 1982

Italian urban growth, especially in Rome and big northern industrial cities like Turin, Milan and Bologna. During the decade 1961–71 all eleven cities continued to grow, but at slower rates than 1951–61. Only Rome and Bari maintained most of their momentum.

During 1971–81, following a trend now well established in many European countries, most of the larger cities lost population. The greater proportional losses were recorded in northern cities: Turin, Milan, Genoa, Bologna and Venice all lost 5–9 per cent of their populations. In southern cities like Naples and Catania, the decline in total population is all the more significant given the high rate of natural increase still operating; Naples, for example, experienced a net loss of population of 16,091 in spite of a natural growth of 107,961 over the decade. The three cities of Table 9.3 which continued to grow during 1971–81, albeit at a reduced rate compared to earlier decades, are all important administrative centres, their expansion assured by the proliferation of tertiary employment, unaffected by northern industrial decline. Rome grows only slowly now, but Palermo, the Sicilian capital, and Bari, the regional and commercial capital of the southern Adriatic, still expand steadily.

All these data on city growth and decline are subject to the caveat about commune boundaries made above. There are no official figures for 'Greater Milan', 'Greater Turin' and so on. It is, however, possible to attempt a reconstruction of the approximate extent of urban agglomerations by adding in the populations of contiguous communes — detailed work with up-to-date maps is essential to do this exercise properly. If this is done, some rather different figures emerge. The Neapolitan agglomeration grew by 8 per cent during 1971–81, Milan and Florence increased by 3 per cent each, but Turin fell by 2 per cent (Reyne, 1983). The contiguous suburban communes of the big cities are themselves worthy of detailed study. A selection of these peri-urban communes (Table 9.4) shows consistent growth profiles: moderate to rapid growth during 1951–61, explosive expansion 1961–71, and then moderating growth or even decline during 1971–81.

This discussion points to the beginnings of counterurbanisation, at least in the northern part of the country. Further light is shed on this by Table 9.5, which gives the distribution of population amongst various commune size classes for 1971 and 1981. The results are quite interesting. Settlements below 5,000 inhabitants are losing population (21.4 per cent in 1971, 19.5 per cent in 1981); communes in the range 5,000–10,000 are stable, accounting for 13.7 per cent of Italian population at both dates; all classes between 10,000 and 250,000 are increasing their share (44.2 per cent in 1971, 47.2 per cent in 1981); whilst cities of over 250,000 are losing (from 20.7 per cent down to 19.5 per cent). The gains are particularly strong in the size class 50,000–100,000, a category

Table 9.4: Italy: Population of Selected Peri-Urban *Comuni* 1951–81

	1951	1961	1971	1981
Near Milan				
Bollate	11,932	24,073	42,770	42,159
Cinisello Balsamo	15,336	37,699	77,284	80,323
Sesto San Giovanni	45,027	71,457	92,053	94,738
Near Turin				
Moncalieri	26,039	34,857	56,115	61,740
Nichelino	7,257	14,907	44,837	44,218
Rivoli	13,833	20,253	47,280	49,136
Settimo Torinese	11,217	18,292	42,710	44,024
Near Florence				
Scandicci	15,115	18,218	47,441	53,974
Sesto Fiorentino	18,657	22,453	41,973	44,869

Source: Population censuses 1951, 1961, 1971, 1981

which corresponds to the many fast-growing southern provincial capitals noted above. The evidence from Table 9.5 indicates a process of counterurbanisation, with cities of over 250,000 declining in importance, with growth occurring down to the 10,000 threshold. However, the fact that communes of below 5,000 inhabitants are losing population shows there to be a continuing, if decelerating, phenomenon of rural depopulation. Much of this rural decline is likely to be in remote upland districts and indeed the 1981 census showed that mountain communes accounted for 13.5 per cent of the Italian population in 1981, compared to 14.3 per cent in 1971. The depopulation of mountainous regions has been a continuing phenomenon since the late nineteenth century.

With marked growth in the 10,000–20,000 category, Table 9.5 does indicate substantial population growth in larger villages and small towns. Just as different forms of urban change were seen to be in operation in different parts of the country, so recent rural dynamics are to be interpreted differently in different parts of Italy, reflecting the complexity of the current Italian demographic scene (Dematteis, 1981). In the north, small town and village growth is common around, but separate from, the major metropolises and in tourist areas in the Alps and along the popular resort coasts. In the north-east and centre, the processes of productive decentralisation and diffuse industrialisation are leading to population growth in mixed urban-rural districts in regions like Friuli,

Table 9.5: Italy: Distribution of Italian Population Amongst Size Classes of *Comuni* 1971 and 1981

Commune size	Percentages	
	1971	1981
Below 2,000	7.0	6.5
2,000–5,000	14.4	13.0
5,000–10,000	13.7	13.7
10,000–20,000	12.5	13.4
20,000–50,000	15.2	15.6
50,000–100,000	8.1	9.6
100,000–250,000	8.4	8.7
250,000–500,000	5.3	4.9
Over 500,000	15.5	14.7

Source: *12˚ Censimento Generale della Popolazione 1981*, vol. 1, Table 9

Marche and Umbria (regions which contain no major metropolises). In the south, rural repopulation is a function of the decline
in emigration combined with a high birth rate.

Emigration, Return Migration and Immigration

Data on migration are neither plentiful nor especially accurate in
Italy. The census is a poor source, and recourse is normally made
to annual statistical office publications. Using such sources, Figure
9.6 shows external migratory trends for the period 1946–82, both
for emigrants (*espatriati*) and returning Italian migrants
(*rimpatriati*). The annual outflow peaked at 387,123 in 1961,
since when a rapid decline set in, stabilising at around 1975 at a
level of about 90,000 emigrants per year. The return stream was
highest in the mid 1960s since when it too has fallen steadily,
though less rapidly than the outflow. Between 1973 and 1980
there was a net return, reaching a maximum of more than 30,000
in 1975. The most recent data (1981–82) indicate a renewed net
emigration, though of modest proportions.

Transformation of the Italian pattern of international labour
migration was not brought about simply by the 1974 oil crisis and
the ensuing recession. Figure 9.6 shows that annual departures
were already set on a downward trajectory in the 1960s and there
is no acceleration of this decline around the 1974 threshold —
indeed, the decline levels off after this date. Recent Italian emigration trends are to be interpreted less in terms of Western
Europe's fluctuating demands for migrant labour and more in
terms of the long-term evolution of Italian population movement
through a series of historical types including overseas emigration,
European emigration, internal migration and, ultimately, the
natural slackening-off of the country's migratory potential (King,
1985a).

Nor do annual returns suddenly jump in the mid-1970s; again,
the picture is one of stability or steady decline since the late 1960s.
As members of the European Community Italian migrant workers
could not be expelled from most receiving countries, and the social
pressures on them to leave have been less than those on, say, the
Turks in West Germany or the Algerians and Portuguese in
France. Surveys of recently-returned emigrants in southern Italy

Figure 9.6: Italy: Annual Emigration and Return Migration 1946–82

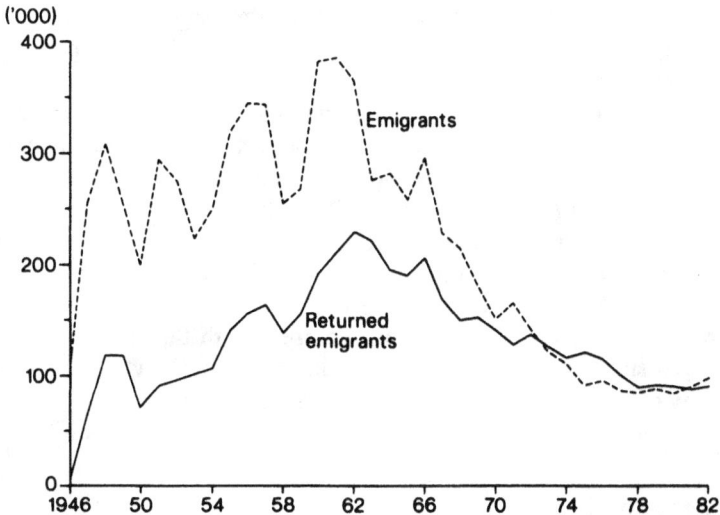

Sources: Anuario Statistico Italiano , various years

show that they rarely come back because of enforced unemployment; generally they return because of family circumstances and because it was always their intention so to do (King *et al.*, 1986).

Even more significant than return migration is the growing immigration of non-Italians. The origins of this trend may be dated to the late 1960s, when Yugoslav labour was used to plug labour shortages in some northern industries and North Africans started to play a role as fishing and farm labour in western Sicily. The 1970s and 1980s have seen considerable build-ups of illegal immigrants from Third World countries, notably Ethiopia and the Philippines. A number of official sources have published figures for the presence of foreigners in Italy, but they are all underestimates: the statistical office, ISTAT, gives 299,980 for 1980, the Ministry of the Interior gives 287,672 for 1981, and the Ministry of Foreign Affairs 383,765 for 1983. The fact, however, that around 70 per cent of these figures are made up of Europeans and North Americans indicates substantial failure to record Third World immigrants. Cagiano de Azevedo (1983) estimates at least half a million foreign workers in Italy, of whom a large proportion are in clandestine employment, including many domestic servants and illegally employed agricultural and industrial workers. Third World immigrants are prominent in all the large cities, notably Rome, Milan, Turin, Genoa, Naples and Bari. Many are badly exploited because of their illegal status.

The existence of so many foreign workers in a country traditionally of emigration and where there are 3.3 million unemployed may seem a paradox, but it can be explained by the rapid development of certain sections of the Italian economy in recent years and by wide wage differentials between Italy and the sending countries, differentials comparable to those which existed between Italy and industrial Europe in the 1950s and 1960s. Foreign immigrants do not, for the most part, compete with the Italian unemployed since most of the jobs they do are rejected by Italians and many of the native unemployed are graduates.

Conclusion

Although only a selection of topics has been dealt with here using the 1981 census as the main data source, this has been sufficient to demonstrate the arrival of a turning-point in Italian demography. A number of long-term trends are about to stop or have been clearly reversed. The following features may be distinguished in particular.

(i) Italy's long-term trend of steady population growth seems about to end: 'zero growth' is imminent.

(ii) The north-south demographic contrast now assumes different dimensions and characteristics. The demise of strong inter-regional migration streams means that the south is now a region of demographic growth instead of stagnation (birth rate still being higher than in the north), whereas the north is stagnant instead of growing rapidly through in-migration. Previous regional roles have thus been reversed.

(iii) By 1981 the decline in the active population, a constant trend since 1861, was reversed.

(iv) Similarly, the long-term increase in industrial employment was also reversed for the first time in Italian history.

(v) Although the statistical evidence is somewhat flawed, it appears that, at least in the larger cities of the north, urban growth has come to an end. In spite of Italy's late surge of urban-industrial growth — 50 years later than most other European countries — evidence for counterurbanisation is starting to appear. Rural repopulation is now affecting many parts of the country, including the south.

(vi) Italy is no longer a country of emigration but one of immigration.

It is clear that some kind of fundamental re-ordering of the Italian spatial economic system is under way. Golini (1983) has summarised this as the end of the industrialisation-urbanisation-migration triad. This means that many commonly-held images of the human geography of Italy — rapid industrialisation and urbanisation, buoyant population growth, dynamic internal migration and high emigration, rural depopulation and so on — are no longer valid.

References

Achenbach, H. (1983) 'Regionale Merkmale der natürliche Bevölkerungsdynamik in Italien', *Erdkunde, 37,* 175–86

Brusco, S. (1982) 'The Emilian model: productive decentralisation and social integration', *Cambridge Journal of Economics, 6,* 167–84

Cagiano de Azevedo, R. (1983) 'Breve analisi dei dati sulla presenza dei lavoratori stranieri in Italia' *Studi Emigrazione, 20,* 337–46

Cole, J.P. (1968) *Italy,* Chatto and Windus: London

Dagradi, P. (1980) 'Demographic trends', in M. Pinna and D. Ruocco (eds.) *Italy: A Geographical Survey,* Pacini, Pisa, pp. 181–90

Dematteis, G. (1982) 'Repeuplement et valorisation des espaces périphériques: le cas de l'Italie', *Revue Géographique des Pyrénées et du Sud-Ouest, 53,* 129–43

Di Comite, L. and Imbriani, C. (1982) 'Age structure of the population and labour market in Italy's Mezzogiorno', *Mezzogiorno d'Europa, 2,* 495–502

Douglass, W.A. (1983) 'Migration in Italy' in M. Kenny and D.I. Kertzer (eds.) *Urban Life in Mediterranean Europe,* University of Illinois Press, Urbana, pp. 162–202

Frey, L. (1983) 'Census development and labour market analyses', *Review of Economic Conditions in Italy, 37,* 223–47

Golini, A. (1983) 'Present relationships between migration and industrialization: the Italian case' in P.A. Morrison (ed.) *Population Movements,* Ordina, Liège, pp. 187–209

King, R.L. (1985a) 'Italian migration: the clotting of the haemorrhage', *Geography, 70,* 171–5

King, R.L. (1985b) *An Industrial Geography of Italy*, Croom Helm, Beckenham

King, R.L., Strachen, A.J. and Mortimer, J. (in press) 'Gastarbeiter go home: return migration and economic change in the Italian Mezzogiorno' in R.L. King (ed.) *Return Migration and Regional Economic Problems*, Croom Helm, Beckenham, pp. 38–68

Rey, G. (1983) 'Italy of censuses', *Review of Economic Conditions in Italy*, 37, 193–221

Reyne, G. (1983) L'évolution démographique récente de l'Italie d'après les résultats du recensement d'Octobre 1981', *Méditerranée*, 9, 19–25

Walker D.S. (1967) *A Geography of Italy* (2nd edn), Methuen, London

10 PORTUGAL

John Dewdney and Paul White

Introduction

Of all the countries of Western Europe it was arguably Portugal which underwent the most profound evolution during the 1970s. At the start of the decade the country was still a Fascist dictatorship with an extensive colonial interest existing alongside a highly traditionalist social and economic structure (de Figueiredo, 1975). By the end of the decade Portugal had undergone a peaceful *coup* leading to the establishment of democracy. She had decolonised almost all her overseas possessions, had produced powerful domestic political measures — such as land reform — to bring about change (Cabral, 1978), and had moved towards social change through the increased secularization of society.

Such political changes do not necessarily carry strong implications for population development — the democratisation of Spain during the same period is a case in point — but in Portugal, the demographic consequences flowing from events occurring in the wake of the *coup* of 25 April 1974 have been profound in the extreme. Principal amongst these was the decolonisation of Angola and Mozambique and the return flow into Portugal of hundreds of thousands of settlers from the African possessions. But on a more local scale, the initiation of new laws permitting divorce and remarriage have also been of considerable importance in both reflecting and fostering attitudinal changes in society towards the family.

Despite these 'revolutionary' developments it is also necessary to be aware of more long-term changes in population parameters for Portugal. Two of these are of particular significance: firstly the steady reduction in fertility that occurred throughout the decade; and secondly, the steady reduction in the numbers of Portugal's out-migrants during the years after the peak level was reached in 1970 (King, 1984), coupled with the steady increase of return movers to Portugal (leaving on one side the question of the returnees from the ex-colonies). Thus, whilst for Portugal the seventies were certainly the 'decade of return' (Lewis and

187

Williams, 1985a) it is necessary to see this return within the general demographic context of the country and its political history.

Population Change

During the inter-censal period from December 1960 to December 1970 the population of Portugal actually declined from 9.077 millions to 9.014 millions, a decline of 3.2 per cent. This was a remarkable feature in a country with, at the time, a fertility rate that was still well above the Western European norm (Poinard, 1972). The explanation lies in the massive level of out-migration that occurred during the decade, much of it illegal since the government actively restricted movement through refusal to issue exit permits, a procedure that resulted in large-scale clandestine emigration, especially to the labour-hungry countries of north-west Europe and predominantly to France. Figures established by Rocha Trindade (1979) including both legal and clandestine migrants give a total of almost exactly one million emigrants from Portugal during the period 1961–70, with the peak outflow occurring in 1970 at 173,000.

The results of the population census of March 1981 show a reversal in the previous decade's population decline. The total population had risen to 9.794 million, with an annual growth rate for the Portuguese mainland (excluding the Azores and Madeira) of 1.2 per cent per annum to contrast with the loss of 0.2 per cent per annum during the 1960s and the gain of 0.5 per cent per annum during the 1950s (Gaspar, 1983). The annual rate of population growth between 1970 and 1981 was the highest since the inter-censal decade 1931–40 (Monnier, 1980). The cause was the massive level of return migration to Portugal, since natural population increase during the decade was notably lower than at any other time in the post-war years.

The Portuguese mainland is divided into 18 *distritos* (Figure 10.1) and population is very unevenly distributed between these administrative units. In 1981, as for decades previously, the highest population densities occur along the western littoral (Figure 10.2) with the *distritos* of Lisbon and Oporto having the highest population concentrations. There are density gradients both from the Atlantic coast in the west to the Spanish frontier in

Figure 10.1: Portugal: Administrative Districts (*distritos*)

the east and, to a lesser extent, also from north to south. The eight *distritos* with the highest population densities, from Setúbal in the south to Viana do Castelo in the north, had a combined population in 1981 of 6.7 millions — over 70 per cent of the total for mainland Portugal. Lisbon and Oporto together account for 40 per cent of the total population. At the other extreme the six thinly populated *distritos* along the Spanish frontier, from Bragança in the north to Beja in the south, make up 48 per cent of the territory but have a combined population of only 1.1 million — 12 per cent of the total — at an overall density of only 26 per km^2.

In contrast with recent trends in most other European countries where counterurbanisation has been a feature of the 1970s (see Chapter 3), in Portugal the evolution of population growth has continued on more traditional lines, further accentuating existing spatial variations in population density. Figure 10.3 shows the

Figure 10.2: Portugal: Population Density 1981

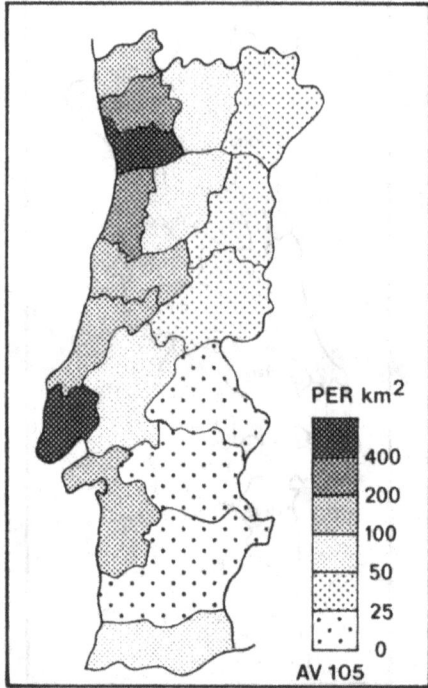

Source: Population census

pattern of population change over the period 1970–81. It is
immediately apparent that there is a strong contrast between rapid
growth in the western *distritos* and very slow growth — in five
cases actual decline — in the east. At this *distrito* level the pre-
dominance of the western littoral is very marked. The two *distritos*
of Lisbon and Setúbal, which together effectively cover the whole
Lisbon metropolitan area, accounted for 55 per cent of the total
inter-censal population growth of Portugal. However, within the
Lisbon *distrito* and also that of Oporto there is evidence of a lower
rate of growth within the city itself, with the highest rates of
increase occurring in the outer areas of the administrative unit.
Suburbanisation of population growth is occurring, and the highest
rate of increase occurred not in Lisbon itself but in Setúbal, across

Figure 10.3: Portugal: Regional Population Change 1970–81

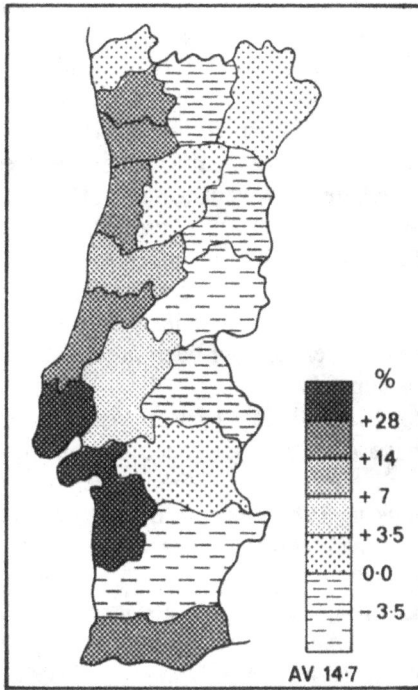

Source: Population census

the Tagus. The high rate of population growth in the Algarve is the result of tourist development in the area.

During the 1960s the government's chief economic concern was industrialisation, with little regard for the possible creation of patterns of regional imbalance. Since 1974 the new constitution has restored much economic control to the municipalities but, in practice, little has been achieved in terms of concerted new regional development policies (Gaspar, 1983). Nevertheless, there are signs of industrial growth in certain inland towns and smaller cities, particularly in the Tagus valley (the *distrito* of Santarém) and in individual places in the centre and north along good communications links (Lewis and Williams, 1985b). A certain process of decentralisation does, therefore, seem to be starting to occur.

Nevertheless the general features of Portugal's population growth between 1970 and 1981 echo in location the trends of earlier years. If the population totals of the *distritos* in 1940 are indexed at 100 and rates of change since then are calculated, the 18 *distritos* fall into three groups of six with only a very small number of doubtful cases (Figure 10.4).

Group I consists of the *distritos* of persistent growth, which are either those containing the major urban centres (Lisbon and Oporto) or immediately adjacent to them (Braga and Aveiro near Oporto; Setúbal, near Lisbon). These five have all experienced population growth since 1940 at well above the average of 29.1 per cent for mainland Portugal as a whole. Leiria, north of Lisbon, is also included in this group since its growth since 1940, although below the national average, has been greater than for *distritos* in the other two groups.

Group II comprises the six eastern *distritos* along the Spanish frontier. All have clearly experienced overall population decline since 1940, with the 1960s as the particularly critical decade. Population totals in 1981 were at 65–80 per cent of the 1940 levels, except in Evora and Bragança where there has been a slight recovery since 1970.

Group III is intermediate, both geographically and in terms of population growth. All six *distritos* had 1981 populations within 10 per cent of the 1940 figure. Viano do Castelo, Vila Real and Viseu, all in the rural north, have failed to recover from the decline of the 1960s. But in Coimbra and Santarém, both with some industrialisation in the 1970s, populations are back to the levels of 20 years ago. The special case of tourist development in Faro has already been referred to.

Natural Change

The 1970s saw Portugal's rate of natural increase cut back significantly as a result of a rapid fall in fertility. Between 1964 and 1970 the total fertility rate in Portugal fell from 3.17 to 2.62, and since then decline has continued, although with a certain standstill during the years 1974–6 (Monnier, 1980). By 1982 the rate had fallen to 2.02, whilst provisional figures for 1983 indicated a rate then of 1.96 (Monnier, 1985), indicating that Portugal had reached the point of long-term population decline as a result of

Figure 10.4: Portugal: Population Trends by *distrito* 1940–81

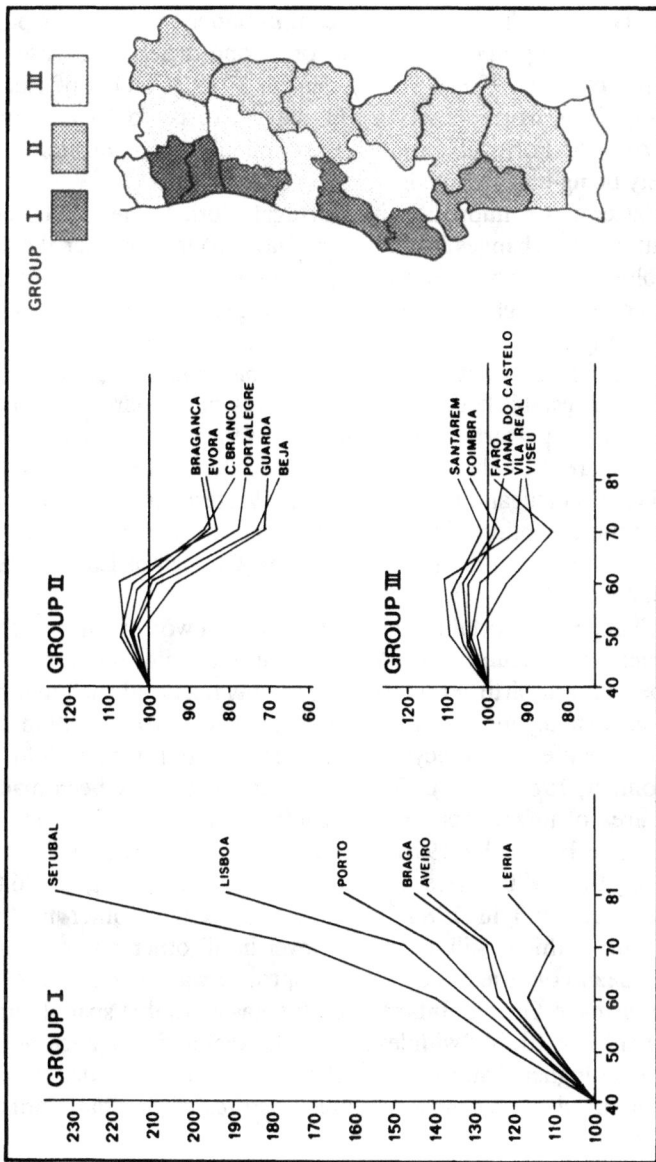

GROUP I

GROUP II

GROUP III

GROUP   I   II   III

SETUBAL
LISBOA
PORTO
BRAGA
AVEIRO
LEIRIA

BRAGANCA
EVORA
C.BRANCO
PORTALEGRE
GUARDA
BEJA

SANTAREM
COIMBRA
FARO
VIANA DO CASTELO
VILA REAL
VISEU

Source: Population censuses

non-replacement of the generations. According to this measure, fertility has declined by 38 per cent in under 20 years. As part of this trend the proportion of first- or second-order births rose from 59 per cent in 1970 to 76 per cent in 1979 (Council of Europe, 1983). It is worth pointing out that there is no legalisation of abortions in Portugal, although the criminal law on abortion is now rarely being implemented.

Patterns of nuptiality in Portugal during the 1970s were disturbed by changes in the divorce law brought in after the 1974 revolution: previously, only couples whose marriage had not been celebrated by a church ceremony could get divorced. The result of the changes was a high level of divorce in 1975 and 1976 along with high levels of remarriage to legitimise consensual unions that had been established whilst divorce was much harder to obtain. After these perturbations in the time-series settled down, it was still apparent at the end of the 1970s that marriage rates were higher in Portugal than in most other Western European countries (with the exception of Greece). Irregular unions and non-marriage are much less common than elsewhere (Council of Europe, 1983; Monnier, 1985).

Changes in mortality have been less noteworthy, and Portugal remains the country of Western Europe with the lowest life expectancy at birth. Progress has certainly occurred such that male life expectancy increased from 64.3 years in 1970 to 68.9 in 1981 whilst the life expectancy figure for females rose from 70.5 to 76.6 (Monnier, 1980, 1985). The greatest advances have been made in the area of infant mortality. In 1960 this stood at 77.5 per thousand live births; by 1970 the rate had only fallen to 55.5, but during the 1970s there was a notable improvement, to 26.0 in 1979 and 19.3 in 1983. Nevertheless, as with other mortality indicators, this is still above the level in all other major Western European countries; the nearest approach was 14.7 per thousand live births in Greece. Infant mortality has a notable spatial pattern to it (Figure 10.5A) with levels in Vila Real and Bragança over 50 per cent higher than the national average, and over twice the rates experienced in the most favoured *distritos* of Setúbal, Santarém and Leiria.

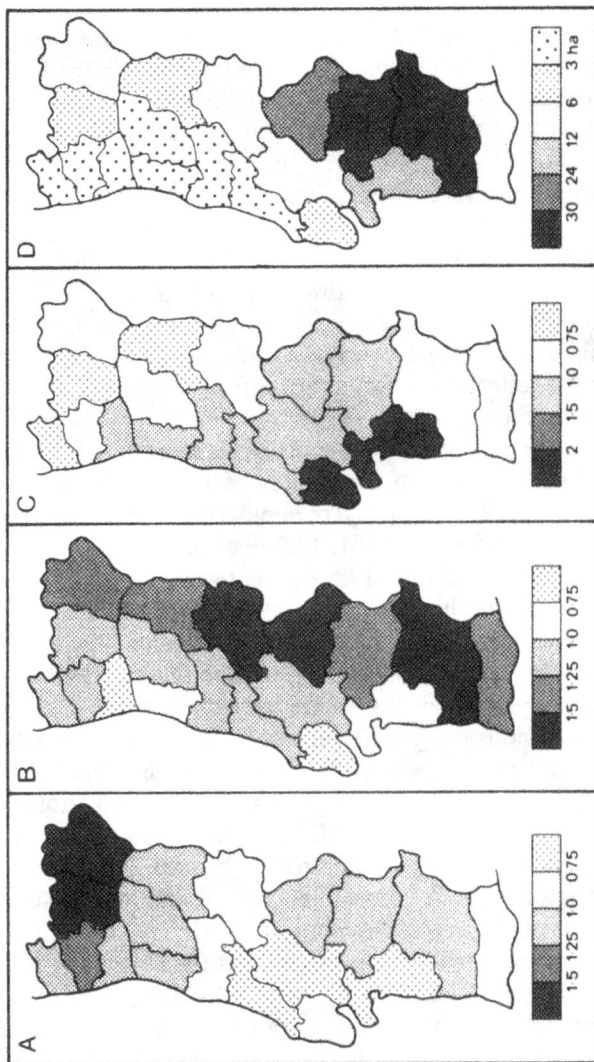

Figure 10.5: Portugal: Some Regional Indicators   A. Infant mortality 1981 (National average = 1.0)
B. Illiteracy 1981   C. Per capita GNP 1981   D. Average size of agricultural holdings 1968

Source: Anuario Estatistico   Source: Population census   Source: Anuario Estatistico   Source: Anuario Estatistico

Population Structure

The population structure of Portugal contains several distinctive features which reflect the importance of certain aspects of the controlling factors, such as migration. This is most clearly shown in the net structure of the population. For Portugal as a whole the sex ratio (males per hundred females) is low at 902, a figure that is explicable in terms of the high volume of male-dominated emigration over recent years. The ratio is at its lowest at a *distrito* level in Lisbon, at 846, a fact brought about in part by the tendency of females to migrate to Lisbon while males have gone abroad. Elsewhere certain *distritos* with high emigration (such as Guarda) have low sex ratios, as might be expected, but the relationship between these two variables is not a close one at the local level, the effects of the return of international migrants are important in complicating the pattern.

The age structure of the population is more regular but displays the effects of the high birth rates of the past by a population pyramid that is more truly pyramidal than that of many other European countries. In 1981, 17.2 per cent of the total population was aged 0–14 and only 14.6 per cent were over 60; but the signs of the fall in fertility during the 1970s were apparent in the fact that the age group with the greatest population was that of those aged 15–19. Successive age cohorts were smaller in size.

The areas of the most youthful age structures are those of recent urban and industrial growth such as the *distritos* of Oporto, Braga, Aveiro and Setúbal, whilst the oldest structures are found in the eastern agricultural *distritos* along the Spanish frontier. This distinction is clearly seen in the pattern of illiteracy rates (Figure 10.5B), which is largely controlled by age structure: here the lowest rates occur in Oporto and Lisbon and the highest in Beja, Portalegre and Castelo Branco.

The labour force and the employment market of Portugal were considerably affected by both the revolution of 1979 and the subsequent return movement of settlers from the colonies. The employment attributes of the return movers from Europe have also been notably non-random and have had a considerable impact (Lewis and Williams, 1986). If we concentrate on the years 1976–80, when both the revolution and return from Africa had taken place, it is apparent that the rate of increase in the registered labour force (at 8.7 per cent over the period) was somewhat above the increase in employment, which stood at 6.1 per cent. These rates of increase in the supply and demand of labour were exceptional in comparison with other Western European countries (Commission of the European Communities, 1984), and reflected Portugal's rapid rate of economic growth and industrialisation. In 1981 registered unemployment stood at only 8.4 per cent, with two-thirds of the unemployed being under 24 and two-thirds female. Female participation in the labour force is, however, low in comparison with that in many other countries, although it could be argued that there is much 'hidden' participation through family work in peasant agriculture. Over the period 1976–80 the most rapid increases in both labour force and employment occurred in the Lisbon area, but with the increase in the labour force far outstripping the increase in jobs: the result, therefore, was an unemployment rate there 60 per cent above the national average. In 1980 unemployment was lowest in the coastal central *distritos* (Leiria, Coimbra and Aveiro) and also in the Algarve. In the interior parts of southern Portugal (Beja, Evora and Portalegre) both the labour force and employment fell significantly between 1976 and 1980, in line with the continued polarisation of regional conditions in Portugal referred to earlier in this chapter.

In terms of employment sectors, recent years have seen a pronounced change in Portugal's economy (Table 10.1). The rate of change was considerably faster in the 1970s than in the preceding decade and involved a pronounced decline in the numbers employed in, and importance of, the agricultural sector coupled with increases in the significance of industry and of services. With the increase in the size of the labour force from 3.3 million in 1970 to 3.7 million in 1981, the numbers employed in agriculture declined by one-third whilst those in both industry and services increased by 50 per cent.

Table 10.1: Portugal: Sectoral Breakdown of Portuguese Employment (%) 1960–81

	1960	1970	1981
Agriculture and fisheries	45	33	18
Industry and construction	28	33	41
Services	27	34	41

Source: Population censuses

Strong regional contrasts exist in the evolution of occupation structures, and these are then reflected in the pattern of per capita Gross Domestic Product (Figure 10.5C) which highlights the wealth of the Lisbon area (Lisbon and Setúbal *distritos*) in comparison with the more rural parts of the country. Agriculture is still the principal activity in many parts of Portugal, employing as many as two-thirds of the work-force in the *distritos* of Vila Real and Bragança. As Figure 10.5D indicates, there has traditionally been a major north-south divide in the average size of agricultural holdings ranging from 1.5 ha in Viano do Castelo to just under 50 ha in Evora, a major factor in the north-south contrasts in population density discussed earlier. This pattern has, however, changed as a result of the land reform measures of the later 1970s.

Industrial employment is concentrated in the coastal regions, with the seven *distritos* of Braga, Oporto, Aveiro, Leiria, Lisbon, Santarém and Setúbal having, in total, 78 per cent of Portugal's industrial workers. The lowest values occur in the north-eastern interior, in Bragança and Vila Real. Service activities are particularly concentrated in Lisbon and in the tourist-oriented Algarve.

Portugal therefore stands in contrast to many other countries of Western Europe in which the 1970s saw the start of de-industrialisation. Industrial growth was the norm in Portugal, although by the end of the decade the indication was that the growth in industrial production was starting to slip below the rate of growth of the service economy (Gaspar, 1983).

Migration

In commenting on recent population trends, attention has already been drawn to the overwhelming significance of migration in the demographic evolution of Portugal, and particularly the phenomenon of the reversal of migration streams that occurred during the 1970s. Unfortunately, data on migration both within Portugal and between Portugal and other countries are far from being as complete and as accurate as might be desired, such that data sets often can only be estimated from data held on Portuguese arrivals and departures by other countries (Rocha Trindade, 1979). An obvious deficiency is the lack of any direct measure of the number of return migrants, a matter of particular significance in the case of the relatively short-distance movements between Portugal and the rest of Western Europe that have been so important in recent years. Clues are available from the 1981 census, which records, for those in the country at that time, the place of residence in 1973; but such data ignore repeated in- and out-movements undertaken by many Portuguese migrants. Working by the residuals method (taking known vital rates and population census totals into account), it would appear that Portugal suffered a net loss of the order of one million during the 1960s and a net gain of just under 500,000 during the 1970s.

The record of emigration from Portugal is far from being a complete one. The number of legal emigrants from the country totalled 1.1 million between 1960 and 1982 (see Figure 10.6B). For those migrants who left the country without the necessary exit papers, it is possible to estimate totals from the records kept by other countries of the 'regularisations' or arrivals of Portuguese citizens in their territories. These estimates yield a total number of 'clandestine' emigrants between 1960 and 1982 of some 617,000 individuals, equivalent to 57 per cent of the number of legal migrants and thus to 36 per cent of all emigrants. In addition it is necessary to remember that these figures exclude movements to Portugal's colonies (principally Angola and Mozambique) which, prior to 1975 and independence, were considered to be part of Portugal. At least 300,000 of such moves probably took place between 1960 and 1974.

This yields a total of around two million out-movements from Portugal during the period since 1960, a remarkable increase in the rate of such movements in comparison with earlier periods in the country's history. The years before 1960 saw emigration at about 20,000 per annum, or one-fifth the average rate that has occurred in more recent years. It is very clear, however, that emigration peaked in 1970 and has been steadily reducing ever since: there were about 1.25 million departures between 1964 and 1973 but only about 300,000 during the ensuing decade from 1974 to 1983.

It is also clear (see Table 10.2) that the destinations of emigrants have been changing in recent years, which show that the Portuguese have been involved in a number of different international flows. The data in Table 10.2 cover only about 54 per cent of all exits, and ignore the 15 per cent of exits that, between 1960 and 1974, went to Portugal's overseas territories in Africa;

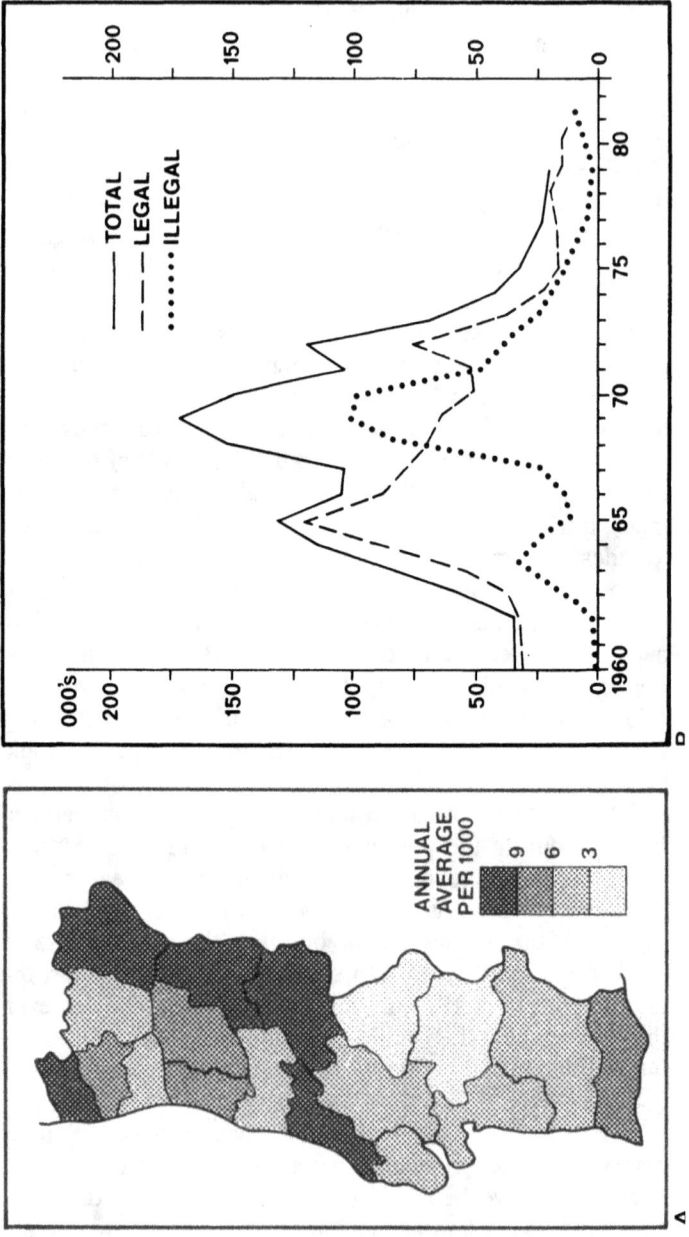

Figure 10.6: Portugal: Patterns of Emigration 1960–82
A. Emigration rates 1960–74   B. Estimated legal and illegal emigration 1960–82

Table 10.2: Portugal: Destinations of Portuguese Legal Emigrants
1960-82

| | Percentages | | | |
	1960-9	1970-4	1975-9	1980-2
France	50.9	27.6	10.0	9.0
West Germany	7.3	29.2	1.8	0.3
Benelux	0.9	2.6	1.8	1.9
United Kingdom	0.6	0.8	1.5	0.4
Switzerland	0.2	1.1	0.7	0.3
USA	10.3	14.9	40.2	24.9
Canada	7.8	13.4	16.6	15.6
Australia	2.4	0.7	1.0	1.6
South Africa	0.3	0.8	1.7	7.1
Brazil	11.3	1.9	3.5	1.4
Venezuela	5.8	5.8	15.1	18.0

Source: Secratariado Nacional da Emigracao, annual data

this movement came to an abrupt end in 1975.

Long-distance, predominantly transatlantic, movements have traditionally been of importance, and it is arguable that the later 1970s saw a return to earlier patterns in this respect after the interlude of intra-European migration of the years 1960–74 (Lewis and Williams, 1985a). Movement to Brazil — a long-established flow — has died out, but that to Venezuela has taken its place. In the most recent years South Africa has become a notable destination, possibly reflecting the diversion of migration that earlier would have gone to Angola or Mozambique. Movement to Canada has also increased significantly.

In retrospect the massive movement of Portuguese into northwest Europe in the years 1960–74 appear as a short-term phenomenon, but one of the greatest importance. During these years Portugal supplied about 740,000 workers to the economies of the rest of Europe, or 20 per cent of her own labour force. The number of Portuguese migrant workers was exceeded only by those from Italy (960,000) and Turkey (813,000), in both cases countries with home populations over five times that of Portugal's. Prior to 1960, moves from Portugal to the rest of Europe were very few in number; but within a year or two the out-movement in that direction was increasing enormously as emigration fever developed in the country and as expectations and strategies of migration became part of the socialisation processes at work in society at large (Brettell, 1979; Rocha Trindade, 1977). The cut-back of movement to Europe during the 1970s was as sharp as the increase had been in the early 1960s, with the reduction starting immediately after the peak year for emigration in 1970.

The regional impact of emigration from 1960 to 1974 is illus-trated in Figure 10.6A, which shows annual average rates of out-movement. Urban-rural, north-south and east-west gradients are all visible. Emigration rates were lowest from the most urbanised *distritos* of Oporto, Lisbon and Setúbal, and highest in the rural, less developed east. At the same time, rates were generally higher in the more densely populated rural areas of the north than in the less densely populated south, although it has also been suggested that variations in rural family structures from north to south may have importance as a control (Rocha Trindade, 1977). These regional patterns of emigrant origin have remained broadly the same in the most recent period, although with emigration from Bragança in the north-east having dropped significantly and with a tendency towards higher rates along the coast (Lewis and Williams, 1985a). However, it must be remembered that emi-gration levels are now very low in comparison with those of even a decade ago.

As has already been indicated, the number of returnees to Portugal in recent years can not be accurately established. It has been estimated that the return flow, dominantly from north-west Europe, averaged over 30,000 per annum during the later 1970s and early 1980s (Lewis and Williams, 1985b). Sample studies have suggested that the majority of the *regressados* (returning European migrants) go back to their *distrito* of origin, but it is also clear that whilst the initial return is most often to the place of original resi-dence this is often followed by a move to a nearby urban centre with better economic prospects so that returnees are a force for urbanisation (Lewis and Williams, in press). However, this aspect of urban drift appears to be less strong among returnees in Portugal than in certain other southern European countries such as Spain or Greece. The progressive return of the *regressados* is potentially of great economic significance for Portugal. Many of the migrants originally left the country with the expectation of improving their circumstances on return (Brettell, 1979; Mendosa, 1982), whilst the government expected the return flow of foreign currency earnings and newly-skilled labour would be of consider-able economic benefit. However, recent sample studies have suggested that the benefits of return are most strongly felt at the level of individual families and that the spread effects to the rest of the economy and society are relatively limited. Migrants returning to poor agricultural areas, whence most of them departed initially, have little real choice except either retiring completely to live off their savings or going back into an impoverished agriculture. It is only by going to the expanding urban centres that any real impact is possible (Lewis and Williams, 1985b; 1986).

The most notable events affecting migration and the Portuguese scene during the 1970s were those surrounding the decolonisation of Angola and Mozambique. Mozambique achieved independence in June 1975, and Angola reached the same state five months later in November. The political situation in Angola was extremely unstable because of civil war, and between May 1975 and Independence Day 400,000 white and mixed-race Angolans left the country in circumstances reminiscent of the French departure from Algeria in 1962. Although aircraft from the United States, the United Kingdom, France and West Germany helped in the airlift, all the *retornados* were repatriated to Portugal. By May 1976 approximately 650,000 refugee returnees had arrived in Portugal, a country with which some had very few ties. Further movement over the next few months brought the total near to 800,000, representing an 8 per cent increase in Portugal's resident population and placing a serious strain on the country's resources. Although Venezuela offered remigration destinations for the *retornados* (accounting for the increased level of movement to that country seen in Table 10.2), Portugal was otherwise left to deal with the problems created with no recourse to offers of settlement from elsewhere. A special government organisation, funded in part from foreign and United Nations aid, was set up to provide housing, employment and social services for the *retornados*, and a special census was taken in 1976 which recorded the whereabouts of some 450,000. About half were settled at that time in the urbanised *distritos* of Oporto, Lisbon and Setúbal, whilst other concentrations existed in holiday areas such as Faro and Aveiro where holiday accommodation was made available for them. In the urban centres the need for housing for the *retornados* added to the already grave problems of temporary housing, shanty towns and *bairros clandestinos* (illegal housing) and led in part to the higher than average unemployment levels — especially in Lisbon — already referred to.

The *retornados* moving straight to the city *distritos* were often those who had no direct connections with any particular part of Portugal. Those with close connections returned to their ancestral areas such that it was in the poorest inland areas of the north and east, traditionally most susceptible to emigration, that *retornados* formed the highest proportion of the population in 1976 — 11.3 per cent of the population of Bragança *distrito* and 8.9 per cent in Guarda. However, these destinations often proved to be only temporary, so that during the following years there was a considerable redistribution of the *retornados* towards the urban *distritos* and especially to Lisbon and Setúbal (Lewis and Williams, 1985a).

It can therefore be seen that both the *regressados* from Western Europe and the *retornados* from Africa have tended to migrate not just internationally but also within Portugal, adding fuel to large-scale urbanisation which has seen the proportion of Portugal's population living in urban settlements almost double from 23 per cent in 1960 to 40 per cent in 1981 (Gaspar, 1983). It is for this reason that internal movement has been left to last in the discussion of recent migration.

Table 10.3 compares the data available from the 1981 census on residences in 1973, whether elsewhere within Portugal or abroad (including the Portuguese overseas provinces). In total 7.7 per cent of those enumerated in 1981 had lived elsewhere in Portugal in 1973, whilst 8.2 per cent had lived outside the country. Movement within Portugal between 1973 and 1981 was slightly biased towards female over-representation, whilst transitions from abroad to a Portuguese residence were notably male-dominated. It must be borne in mind that the data only refer to transitions between points in time, and it is certain that a high proportion of those indicated as being abroad in 1973 also made an internal move within Portugal during the ensuing eight years.

At a regional level, only in six *distritos* were recent movers wholly within Portugal more numerous in 1981 than were those who had come from abroad (basically *regressados* and *retornados*). Three of these *distritos* (Beja, Evora and Portalegre) were in the Allentejo region of the south, which had participated little in emigration in the first place (Figure 10.6A) and which therefore received few locally-connected returnees. The other three *distritos* dominated by internal migrants were all urban centres — Lisbon, Oporto and Setúbal — whilst in Santarém,

Table 10.3: Portugal: Place of Residence in 1973 by Place of
Residence in 1981

| | Residence in 1973 | | | | | |
| Present residence | Different municipality within Portugal | | | Abroad (including overseas provinces) | | |
1981	Total %	Male %	Female %	Total %	Male %	Female %
Mainland Portugal	7.7	7.6	7.8	8.2	9.2	7.4
Urbanised distritos						
Lisbon	12.6	12.2	12.9	10.5	11.2	9.8
Setúbal	13.1	12.7	13.5	10.2	10.7	9.7
Oporto	7.0	6.9	7.1	5.7	6.4	5.0
Growth areas						
Leiria	4.8	4.7	4.9	9.6	10.8	8.4
Faro	7.5	7.5	7.5	10.0	10.6	9.4
Rural north-east						
Bragança	4.8	4.6	5.0	13.7	15.3	12.2
Guarda	4.4	4.6	4.3	12.0	13.6	10.6
Vila Real	5.4	5.3	5.5	8.8	10.0	7.8
Rural south-centre						
Portalegre	6.8	6.9	6.8	3.7	4.1	3.2
Beja	3.8	4.1	3.5	5.5	7.1	4.1

Source: Recenceamento Geral da Populacao e Habitacao, 1981, Table 6.15

internal movers and recent returnees were in equal proportion. It
should, however, be noted that both Lisbon and Setúbal were also
very attractive destinations for returnees, often on an internal
move subsequent to their arrival back in Portugal, such that in
both *distritos* 23 per cent of their resident populations in 1981 had
been living elsewhere in 1973, producing the rapid rate of population increase in the Lisbon metropolitan area during the 1970s
(Golini and Gesano, 1983).

In contrast to these features of movement to the capital and its
surroundings, Oporto proved much less attractive to migrants. The
decentralising economic growth areas, represented in Table 10.3
by Leiria and by tourist-influenced Faro, witnessed the arrival of
migrants initially from abroad as being of much greater importance
than those only from Portugal. The rural north-east, the traditional
origin area for much international movement, showed the effect of
the return in the presence of up to three times as many international returnees as domestic migrants. Finally, it was in the rural

parts of southern Portugal that in-movement of all sorts was at the lowest levels: less than 10 per cent of the 1981 inhabitants of Beja had lived elsewhere in 1973.

In total it seems clear from these data (and no other data exist on internal movement in Portugal) that purely internal migration during the 1970s was highly focused on the Lisbon area, and that females were over-represented in such moves. But such purely internal moves were coupled with an even larger redistributional effect resulting from return movement from abroad which produced different patterns, highlighting the rural areas from which the migrants had originally gone but also showing some important concentration on Lisbon and on other growth areas in the Portuguese economy.

Conclusions

The political events of the 1970s will never be repeatable for Portugal: decolonisation was a 'once and for all' experience. It is nevertheless conceivable that the country could in the future witness another mass return movement: a wary eye is being kept on the 600,000 persons of Portuguese origin now living in South Africa who might seek to return to Portugal in the event of certain political developments occurring in their adoptive country (Gaspar, 1983).

However, in the near future the prospects are for much greater demographic stability than Portugal experienced during the 1970s. The fertility rate is now such that future natural growth will be slow or non-existent. The initiation of economic decentralisation within the country may reduce the concentration of migration and population growth in the Lisbon area. The *retornados* movement is now complete, although return from Western Europe continues at a significant level. Emigration has settled to a consistent figure after the peaks of the last 20 years. The 1980s are therefore likely to see trends as different from those of the past 20 years as were the latter from those of earlier periods.

Acknowledgements

The authors would like to thank Jim Lewis and Allan Williams for their advice during the preparation of this chapter.

References

Brettell, C.B. (1979) '"Emigrar para voltar": a Portuguese ideology of return migration', *Papers in Anthropology*, *20*, 1–20

Cabral, M.V. (1978) 'Agrarian structures and recent rural movements in Portugal', *Journal of Peasant Studies*, *5*, 411–45

Commission of the European Communities (1984) *The Regions of Europe*, Commission of the EEC, Brussels

Council of Europe (1983) *Recent Demographic Developments in the Member States of the Council of Europe*, Council of Europe, Strasbourg

De Figueiredo, A. (1975) *Portugal: Fifty Years of Dictatorship*, Penguin, Harmondsworth

Gaspar, J. (1983) 'Le Portugal: évolution démographique récente', *Mediterranée*, *50*, 3–9

Golini, A. and Gesano, G. (1983) *Structure and Composition of the Population of Urban Areas. 1. Southern Europe*, Council of Europe, Strasbourg

King, R. (1984) 'Population mobility: emigration, return migration and internal migration' in A. Williams (ed.) *Southern Europe Transformed*, Harper & Row, London pp. 145–78

Lewis, J. and Williams, A. (1985a) 'Portugal: the decade of return', *Geography*, *70*, 178–82

Lewis, J. and Williams, A. (1985b) *Returned Emigrants and Regional Development in Portugal* (occasional publication no. 20), Department of Geography, University of Durham

Lewis, J. and Williams A. (1986) 'The economic impact of returned European migrants and *retornados* in central Portugal' in R. King (ed.) *Return Migration and Regional Economic Problems*, Croom Helm, Beckenham, pp. 100-28

Mendosa, E.L. (1982) 'Benefits of migration as a personal strategy in Nazaré, Portugal', *International Migration Review*, *16*, 635–645

Monnier, A. (1980) 'L'Italie, L'Espagne et le Portugal: situation démographique', *Population*, *35*, 927–57

Monnier, A. (1985) 'La conjoncture démographique: l'Europe et les pays développés d'outremer', *Population*, *40*, 749-63

Poinard, M. (1972) 'La stagnation de la population portugaise 1960–70', *Revue Géographique des Pyrénées et du Sud-Ouest*, *43*, 427–44

Rocha Trindade, M.R. (1977) 'Structure sociale et familiale d'origine dans l'émigration au Portugal', *Ethnologie Française*, *7*, 277–84

Rocha Trindade, M.B. (1979) 'Portugal', in R.E. Krane (ed.) *International Labour Migration in Europe*, Praeger, New York

11 GREAT BRITAIN

Anthony Champion

Introduction

The census of population held on the night of 5/6 April 1981 was Britain's nineteenth full enumeration, the exercise having been repeated every ten years since the first in 1801 with the exception of the wartime year of 1941. Because it provides the only nation-wide count of population for small areas, the census serves an important function in Britain and — along with the accuracy checks resulting from a Post-Enumeration Survey — forms the datum for local as well as national population estimates. Moreover, though data on individuals are not released for 100 years, the cross-tabulations and small-area statistics allow a wealth of information about associations between demographic, economic and social characteristics (Rhind, 1983).

At the same time, the census suffers from a number of short-comings. In particular, the examination of trends over time is made difficult by alterations in definitions, modifications in the range and nature of questions, and changes in the geographical frame-work of reporting units (Dewdney, 1985). Perhaps the most fundamental of the changes brought by the 1981 census was that relating to the concept of population used for the majority of tabulations, which switched from 'persons present' to 'usual residents' (OPCS, 1983). Secondly, the census for England, Wales and Scotland continued to avoid a number of more contentious topics such as income, religion and race. Appendix 11.1 lists the coverage of specific topics in the 1981 census.

This chapter outlines the main characteristics of the population of Great Britain (i.e. excluding Northern Ireland) as revealed by the 1981 census and, where possible, indicates trends since the previous census. Attention is focused primarily on overall population change, its components and its geographical patterns. The chapter also deals with age structure and dependency rates, labour force characteristics, household size and composition, and minority populations as indicated by language, birthplace and ethnic origin. The results are amplified by reference to complementary sources where appropriate, the most useful being registers of births and deaths, the International Passenger Survey, the Labour Force Survey and the General Household Survey.

Population Change and its Components

The National Picture

The published figure for the number of people present in Great Britain on census night in 1981 was 54,285,422. In relation to the area of just over 22.8 million hectares, this means an overall population density of 2.38 persons per hectare. Of the total persons present at the 1981 census, some 26.3 million — or 48.5 per cent were males, yielding a ratio of 1061 females per 1000 males. The 1981 census population was 306,884 or 0.57 per cent, larger than the comparable figure at the previous census held on 25/26 April 1971. This level of inter-censal change compares with 5.25 per cent for 1961–71 and 4.97 per cent for 1951–61 and indeed is the smallest on record, contrasting with decennial averages of 4–5 per cent since 1911 and 10–18 per cent before that.

The mid-year data for Britain confirm the substantial fall in growth rate between the 1960s and 1970s. During the early 1960s population increase averaged 357,000 a year, and the rate was still relatively high for 1966–71 at 240,000 a year. The increase between 1971 and 1976, by contrast, was only 295,000 in total, an average addition of only 59,000 a year; while for 1976–80 the annual increase fell further to only 23,000. The full 1961–83 series for England and Wales (Figure 11.1) shows that the annual increment was of the order of 300,000 and over up to 1967, then fell substantially and in 1973/74 levelled out at around zero population change where it remained for five years before showing a slight recovery. The latter, however, has only barely been maintained since 1980.

Components of Population Change

According to the National Summary Report for the 1981 census, the overall inter-censal population increase of 0.57 per cent was generated entirely by a surplus of births over deaths, which provided a natural increase of 1.15 per cent for the ten-year period. The effect of the latter was offset by a negative 'balance' equivalent to 0.59 per cent of the 1971 population, comprising the net effects

Figure 11.1: Great Britain: Annual Population Change Mid-1961 to Mid-1983, England and Wales

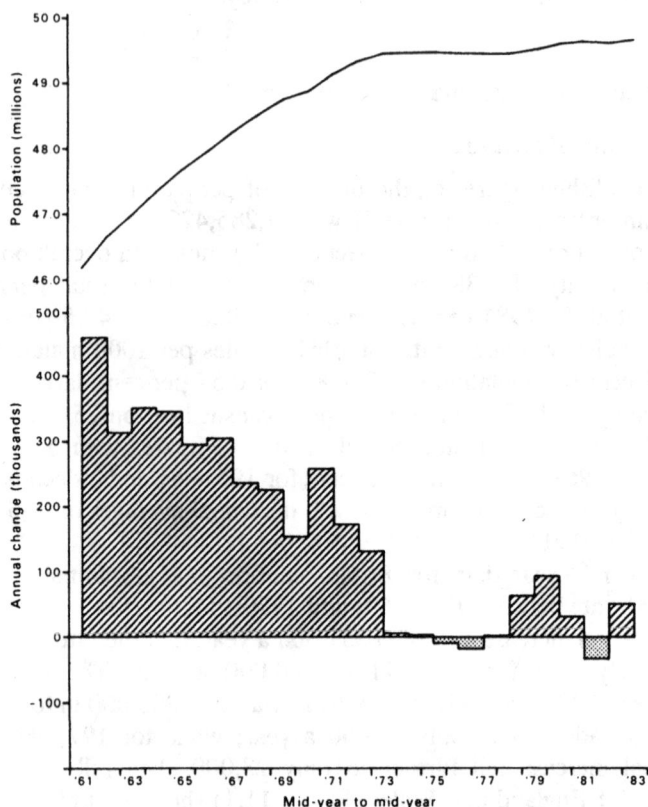

Source: *OPCS Monitors,* 84-1 and 84-3

of international migration and other causes such as differences in the accuracy of the enumeration and the movement of the armed forces.

Table 11.1 gives an annual breakdown of the components of change between mid-year estimates, distinguishing births and deaths on the basis of the Registrar-General's records and also giving a separate estimate of the net migration component derived from the International Passenger Survey. The most conspicuous change has been the fall in the number of births (OPCS, 1982).

From an average of 954,000 a year in Great Britain in the first half of the 1960s, births had dropped to barely two-thirds of this level by 1976–77. From 1978–79 the figure has stabilised in the range 692–716,000. By contrast, the number of deaths increased somewhat between the 1960s and 1970s, but over the past ten years it has oscillated within a similarly narrow range of 640–664,000. As a result the level of natural change fell dramatically from an annual average surplus of births over deaths of well over 300,000 in the early 1960s to a slight birth deficit in the mid 1970s. Since then there has been a return to natural increase, but only at a rate of between one-tenth and one-fifth of that in the early 1960s.

Net migration between Britain and the rest of the world (including Northern Ireland) has shown less variability over time than has natural increase, but as the latter has diminished in size so the migration component has exerted a greater influence on whether the British population increases or decreases in size each year. Also more crucial in this respect now are the movement of armed forces and the accounting adjustments, both subsumed in 'other changes' (Table 11.1). The migration component was virtually in balance during the first half of the 1960s, in 1971–72 and towards the end of the 1970s, but otherwise it has been negative, reaching its highest levels in 1973–75 and 1980–82.

As regards the scale and nature of international migration, the International Passenger Survey data show clearly the important role of the gross outflows of British citizens in producing the more recent peaks in overall net migration loss in 1973–75 and 1980–82. Generally, however, the outflow of British citizens has been lower since 1971 than during the 1960s, while their gross inflow has been much more consistent over time. The net loss of British citizens was thus greater in the 1960s than subsequently. Meanwhile, the trade in non-UK citizens has produced gains for the United Kingdom throughout the period, with the main change being the relatively smaller size of the gross inflow in the 1970s compared to the 1960s. In summary, the estimates for 1971–83 indicate a net migrational loss from the United Kingdom of 465,000 people, composed of a net loss of 953,000 British citizens and a net gain of 488,000 others.

Table 11.1: Great Britain: Components of Population Change (thousands)

Mid-year to mid-year	Population at start of period	Components of change (mid-year to mid-year)				
		Births	Deaths	Natural increase	Net migration	Other changes[b]
1961/66[a]	51,380	954	617	+337	−1	+21
1966/71[a]	53,167	904	628	+276	−50	+15
1971/72	54,369	832	644	+188	−39	+20
1972/73	54,537	778	654	+124	-	+9
1973/74	54,671	724	647	+77	−72	+9
1974/75	54,685	694	654	+40	−69	+20
1975/76	54,676	663	664	−1	−22	+11
1976/77	54,664	630	643	−14	−24	+10
1977/78	54,636	639	648	−9	−34	+29
1978/79	54,621	692	656	+36	+4	+13
1979/80	54,675	716	642	+74	+4	+3
1980/81	54,756	713	640	+73	−74	+28
1981/82	54,784	695	653	+42	−82	+24
1982/83	54,768	695	644	+51	−19	+4
1983/84	54,804					

Note: a. Components of change shown as annual averages
b. Changes in numbers of armed forces plus adjustment to reconcile differences between estimated population change and the figures for natural change and net civilian migration
Source: Population Trends

Geographical Patterns of Population Change

The main dimension of post-war population change at the broad regional level of ten British Standard Regions (including Wales and Scotland) has traditionally been the drift from north to south, but the finer spatial scale of the county (or, in Scotland, local government 'region') has increasingly drawn attention to differences in population change between more urban and more rural areas (Champion, 1976; Lawton, 1977). The results of the 1981 census reveal that the 'urban-rural shift' has recently grown so extensively both in numerical scale and in geographical spread that it has become as significant an element in broader regional patterns as the 'north-south drift' (Champion, 1981; OPCS, 1981a, 1981b; Randolph and Robert, 1981).

Table 11.2 shows the key features of population change for the 1971–81 inter-censal period on the basis of the ten Standard Regions. The most rapid rate of population growth was recorded by East Anglia, followed by the south-west and East Midlands. Lower growth rates were registered by Wales and the West Midlands, while for Yorkshire and Humberside the figure remained virtually static. Finally, the south-east, north-west, northern region and Scotland experienced population declines of up to 3 per cent for the ten-year period.

Natural change and migration both played a part in producing these regional differences in performance, but it appears to have been the latter which exercised the greater influence. While the rate of natural change for the decade ranged from 2.0 per cent to −0.7 per cent, a percentage point difference of 2.7, the equivalent range for migration (and other causes) was 13.4 percentage points spanning a high of 10.1 per cent and a low of −3.3 per cent (Table 11.2). In terms of regional incidence, the rapid growth of East Anglia resulted from the combination of the nation's highest rates of both natural increase and net in-migration, whereas for the south-west a high level of in-migration was partly offset by its being the only region to register natural decrease over the decade. The population decline sustained by the north-west and the northern region as a whole was produced by a combination of substantial net out-migration and below-average natural increase, but in the cases of Scotland and particularly south-east England it was the large negative migration balances that were solely to blame for their below-average performance.

It is also clear from Table 11.2 that the 1971–81 regional performance presents some immediate contrasts with the trends of the 1960s. Most noticeable is the fact that whereas four of the ten regions saw population decline between 1971 and 1981 no region experienced an overall loss of population over the previous ten-year period. Moreover, the most dramatic changes in fortune are found to have taken place in the two regions which are traditionally associated with relatively rapid economic growth and the 'north-south drift': both the south-east and the West Midlands are affected by a downward shift of nearly 7 percentage points in their overall growth rates between the two decades. By contrast Wales, East Anglia, the northern region and Scotland, though experiencing some reduction in growth rate, nevertheless all achieved a strong performance relative to the national average shift of −4.7.

Table 11.2: Great Britain: Population Change by Region 1961–81
(per cent persons present)

Regions	1971 to 81 change			1961 to 71 Change Total	1961 to 71/71 to 81 shift		
	NC	NM/O	Total		Total	NC	NM/O
Northern	0.5	−1.7	−1.2	0.7	−1.9	−4.9	3.0
Yorkshire & Humberside	0.8	−0.7	0.1	3.7	−3.6	−5.0	1.4
East Midlands	2.0	3.1	5.1	9.4	−4.3	−4.9	0.6
East Anglia	2.0	10.1	12.1	13.6	−1.5	−3.8	2.3
South-east	1.6	−2.4	−0.8	5.9	−6.7	−4.8	−1.9
South-west	−0.7	7.3	6.6	10.6	−4.0	−4.7	0.7
West Midlands	2.6	−1.9	0.8	7.4	−6.6	−5.8	−0.8
North-west	0.5	−3.3	−2.8	2.6	−5.4	−4.8	−0.6
Wales	0.1	2.1	2.2	3.3	−1.1	−3.6	2.5
Scotland	1.2	−3.0	−1.9	1.0	−2.8	−5.5	2.7
Great Britain	1.2	−0.6	0.6	5.3	−4.7	−4.9	0.2

Source: Census 1981 National Report Great Britain, Part 1, Table 3; and analysis by
component provided by OPCS and Registrar-General Scotland

The south west and East Midlands retained their positions as the second- and third-fastest growing regions after East Anglia, with negative shifts marginally below the national average, but the north-west suffered worse than average and replaced the northern region as the least dynamic in the 1970s (Table 11.2).

The direct explanations for these shifts between the 1960s and 1970s can be identified by reference to the components of population change, also shown in Table 11.2. The general pattern of slower population growth can be traced, not surprisingly, to the reduction in natural change rates, resulting almost entirely from the fall in birth rate mentioned above. The downward shift in natural change is relatively consistent across the regions at around 4.7–5.0 percentage points, except for the West Midlands and Scotland where the natural increase had previously been well above average, Wales where the level had previously been very low, and East Anglia where the reduction was ameliorated by the continuing high level of in-migration of young families. It is very largely the trend in migration balance which is responsible for the altered ranking of regional performances, with a 2–3 percentage point increase in migration balance from the 1960s to 1970s for Wales, the northern region, Scotland and East Anglia in contrast to the négative shifts found for the north-west, West Midlands and south-east (Table 11.2).

The importance of the migration component appears even greater at the more refined spatial scale of the county and Scottish 'region', both in explaining geographical differences in population growth in the 1970s and in accounting for changes in relative performance since the previous decade. As shown in Figure 11.2 (A and B), high overall levels of population decrease and net out-migration in the 1970s occur in association in all the major urban concentrations including Greater London, West Midlands County, Greater Manchester, Merseyside, Tyne and Wear, and Strathclyde; while the main areas of rapid population growth and net in-migration tend to lie just beyond the traditional suburban counties, particularly in south-eastern England where they form a broad arc around the north and west of the Home Counties but also in the counties to the west of the West Midlands conurbation. In terms of trends from the 1960s to the 1970s (Figure 11.2, C and D), the migration component broadly differentiates the main axial belt of more urbanised counties in England from the rest of England and Wales, which generally experienced an improvement in net migration balance and a shift in overall population change that was either positive or less negative than the national shift.

Counterurbanisation

The greater-than-average deceleration in population growth which affected most of the more urbanised parts of Britain between the 1960s and 1970s — observed not merely at the subregional level but also reflected at the broader regional scale — suggests that widespread and powerful counterurbanisation forces were at work during this period. The experience of the major cities certainly supports this conclusion, for these suffered population losses of 10–20 per cent during the 1970s, though in some cases these rates were not much worse than in the 1960s. Meanwhile, many of the smaller urban centres and districts in the less heavily populated parts of the country registered faster population growth between 1971 and 1981 than in the previous decade, with the positive shift in net migration balance more than offsetting the decline in natural increase (Champion, 1981; Randolph and Robert, 1981).

Various attempts have been made to identify the scale and

Figure 11.2: Great Britain: Population and Migration: Inter-censal Changes 1971–81 and Shifts 1961–81 by Counties (England and Wales) and Regions (Scotland)

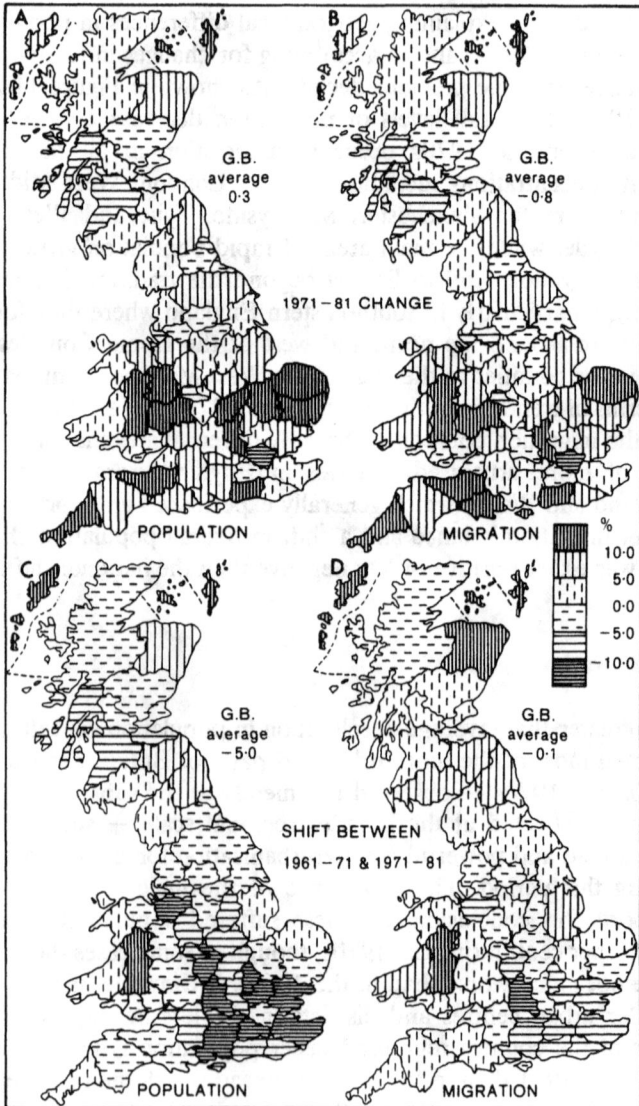

nature of counterurban tendencies on a more universal and rigorous basis. *The 1981 Census Preliminary Report for England and Wales* (OPCS, 1981b) classified the post-1974 local government districts broadly by size, urban status and function. The results revealed that Greater London as a whole and the principal cities of the metropolitan counties have declined in population by 10 per cent on average over the decade, while the highest growth rates had been recorded by 'districts that include new towns' and by 'remoter, largely rural districts'. Particularly significant is the fact that this last group was the only one of the eleven categories in the classification to have increased its growth rate since the 1960s, moving against the national trend of a fall of 5 percentage points. The *Preliminary Report for Towns* (OPCS, 1981c) also demonstrated the shift to rural areas, with a 1971–81 growth rate for the latter of 9.7 per cent as opposed to the −1.9 per cent for towns, but the approach used in that analysis did not reveal so clearly the dynamism of truly rural Britain in the 1970s because the pre-1974 rural districts which it used had grown by as much as 17.9 per cent in 1961–71 as a result of their inclusion of much of fast-growing suburban England.

The 'functional regions' framework, developed at Newcastle University, provides a more satisfactory geographical basis for studying 1971–81 urban and regional trends than either the pre-1974 or current local authority areas, because it defines places on the basis of a consistent set of 'city–region' criteria (Champion *et al.*, 1983). The results show that, if the 281 Local Labour Market Areas are grouped into five categories on the basis of population size and urban status, there is a very regular urban-rural progression in terms of 1971–81 population growth rates (Figure 11.3). Moreover, if the LLMAs are grouped according to whether they form part of the wider metropolitan regions dominated by the country's largest cities or are relatively independent of their influence, it is the latter category which proved most dynamic in the 1970s. While the sub-dominant group of functional regions increased their populations by 3.9 per cent in contrast to the dominant group's overall decline of 6.2 per cent, the freestanding cities and their regions achieved a 5.8 per cent growth rate (Table 11.3). The shift from the metropolitan regions to freestanding Britain was even more impressive in absolute terms, because the sub-dominants were able to absorb barely two-fifths of the 1.3 million people lost by the dominants so that the freestanding category took up the 820,000 loss from metropolitan Britain as well as accounting for the whole national increase — a total increase of over 1.1 million people (Table 11.3). Unfortunately the absence of comparable figures for 1961 precludes an examination of longer-term trends on this geographical basis.

Age Distribution and Dependency Rates

Though the national population was virtually stationary in size during the 1970s, its age structure was changing as dramatically as its geographical distribution. The most impressive feature was the growth of the elderly population (Craig, 1983). Between 1971 and 1981 the number of people of pensionable age (65 years for men, 60 years for women) grew from 8.8 to 9.7 million, an increase of

Figure 11.3: Great Britain: Population Change 1971–81 (by Local Labour Market Areas) Grouped by Urban Status

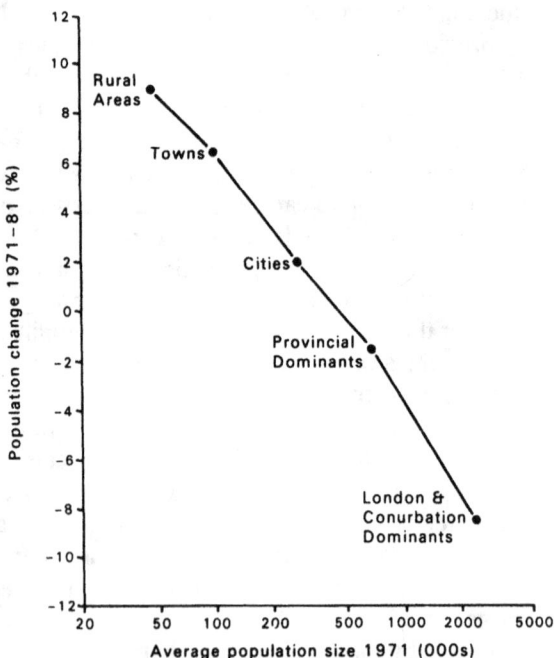

Table 11.3: Great Britain: Population Distribution and Change by
Type of Functional Region 1971 and 1981

Type of functional region	1971 000s	1971 % share	1981 000s	1981 % share	1971–81 change 000s	1971–81 change % change
All dominants	21512	39.9	20175	37.2	−1337	−6.2
of which 6 largest[a]	(14844)	(27.5)	(13586)	(25.0)	(−1258)	(−8.5)
Sub-dominants	13305	24.6	13820	25.5	+515	+3.9
Metropolitan regions	34816	64.5	33995	62.6	−821	−2.4
Freestanding	19161	35.5	20279	37.4	+1118	+5.8
All regions	53977	100.0	54274	100.0	+296	+0.5

Note: a. London, Birmingham, Glasgow, Manchester, Newcastle upon Tyne and
Liverpool. Numbers may not sum to given total because of rounding

882,500 or 10 per cent over the 1971 level. The number of those
aged 75 and over grew by 24 per cent from 2.54 to 3.15 million.
This growth results from the ageing of the large birth cohorts
dating from the early years of this century and, coming at the same
time as the dramatic fall in the birth rate since 1964, has contributed to a marked increase in the mean age of the British population. Between 1971 and 1981 the elderly's share of the total
population increased from 16.3 to 17.9 per cent, while that of
children aged 0–15 has fallen from 25.4 to 22.2 per cent. Meanwhile, the legacy of the more rapid birth rates recorded in the later
1950s and early 1960s is reflected in the increase in the size of the
school-leaving cohorts during the 1970s, as can be seen from
Figure 11.4.

Past patterns of migration, together with the lesser influence of
differential birth rates, have left their mark on the geographical
distribution of population by age group. In 1981 young adults (16–
24 years old) were found most notably in the major cities, in the
more mature new towns, and in industrial north-east England and
central Scotland. The intermediate working-age group (25–44
years old) had the highest degree of spatial clustering of all the
groups, with the top quintile of areas concentrated in a massive
and compact zone to the north and west of London, with the few
remaining areas adopting similar locations round the other major
English cities. With the older age groups, the emphasis switches to
parts of Britain suffering from long-term unemployment problems
and to those proving attractive as retirement areas. Older working-
age people (from 45 to retirement age) are disproportionately

Figure 11.4: Great Britain: Age Structure 1971 and 1981 (by one-year age groups)

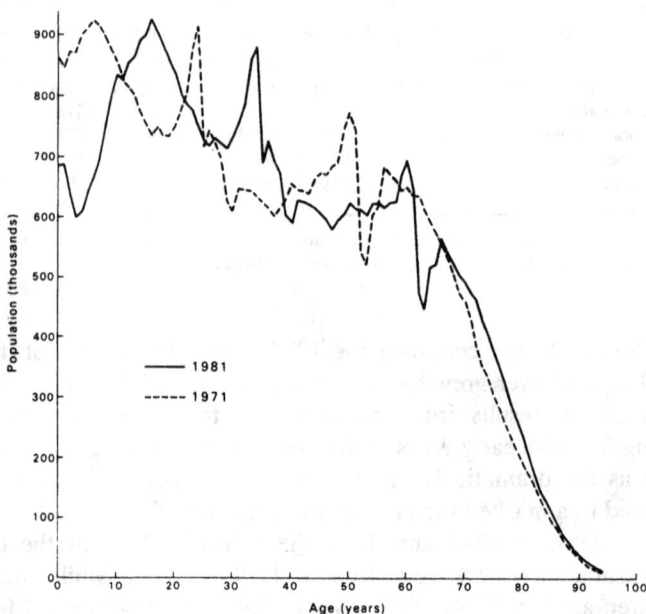

represented in western Wales, northern England and the Scottish Borders, while the top quintile for those of pensionable age is dominated by East Anglia, the south coast, the south-west peninsula and western Wales (Champion, 1984).

The overall impression conveyed by the age-group patterns in 1981 is one of relatively youthful populations in the more urbanised parts of Britain, particularly in central and southern England, and older populations in the industrial and rural peripheries of the nation. This picture is very largely confirmed by the 1981 pattern of dependency ratios, which increase with some regularity outwards from a broad zone embracing much of the south-east and Midlands where there are relatively few dependants per hundred of working age (Figure 11.5). More detailed analysis suggests that this distinctive type of core-periphery pattern was largely inherited from before 1971, for though recent trends have reinforced the low dependency rates north and west of London

Figure 11.5: Great Britain: Dependants per Hundred Persons of
Working Age 1981 (by Local Labour Market Areas)

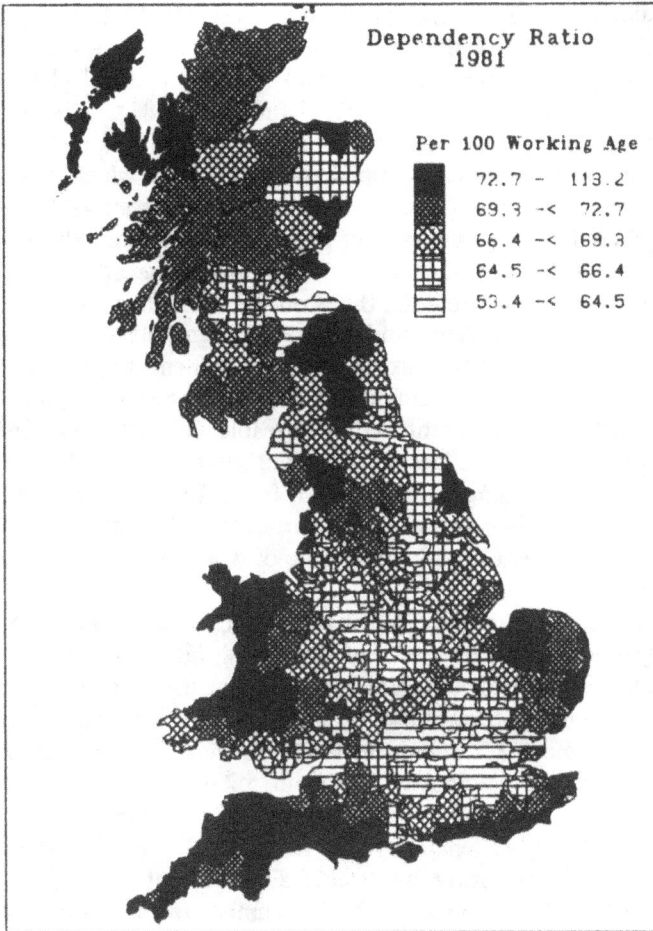

Souce: CURDS Functional Regions Factsheet 14

and the relatively elderly profiles of some more rural areas, many
of the more peripheral areas with substantial urban centres saw an
influx of younger working-age families with children during the
1970s (see Warnes and Law, 1984).

Labour-Force Characteristics

The main labour-force characteristics of Britain's working-age population for 1981 are summarised in Table 11.4, along with rough indications of the changes since 1971 — rough, because of the change in population base from 'persons present' (1971) to 'usual residents present/absent' definition (1981). The overall economic activity rate for males of working age was recorded at 90.4 per cent in 1981, a distinct fall from 1971 which was only partly due to the increase in the proportion classed as students. The overall employment rate for males had fallen from 88 per cent to below 80 per cent during the decade, mainly because of the 5.5 percentage point increase in those out of work but also fuelled by the increase in students and others economically inactive (presumably mainly those taking early retirement as well as the permanently sick). For females the trends between 1971 and 1981 are substantially different, with a sizeable fall in the proportion economically inactive despite both the surge in student numbers and the discouraging unemployment trend. Increases in both full-time and part-time employment, particularly the latter, served to increase the overall employment rate of working-age women from 52.8 to 56.2 per cent.

The increase in unemployment is the single most dramatic change in the characteristics of the British labour force over the decade. For males and females together, the number of economically active people out of work rose by 1.19 million from 1971 to almost 2.5 million at the 1981 census, representing an increase in unemployment rate from 5.2 to 9.8 per cent. This increase was partly due to the net effects of larger working-age cohorts and higher female activity rates, which served to swell the size of the labour force by around 270,000, but the bulk of the increase resulted from a fall in the number of occupied jobs by over 900,000 (these figures again are subject to some problems because of the differences in base population).

The geographical pattern of unemployment in 1981 (Figure 11.6) contains a strong regional dimension, with the almost complete absence of above-average unemployment rates south of the Severn/Wash line. With the exception of the blackspot of Corby, the only places there with a rate above 10 per cent were a few coastal areas including King's Lynn, Great Yarmouth, Clacton, Thanet and some in the far south-west, all presumably suffering

Table 11.4: Great Britain: Labour-Force Characteristics 1971 and 1981

	Males aged 16–64		Females aged 16–59	
	1971 (EP)	1981 (UR)	1971 (EP)	1981 (UR)
Working-age population (thousands)	16,435	16,774	15,049	15,384
% Economically inactive	7.0	9.6	44.6	39.1
Students	4.2	5.3	3.9	5.6
Others	2.8	4.3	40.7	33.5
% Economically active	93.0	90.4	55.4	60.9
Out of employment	5.0	10.5	2.6	4.7
In employment	88.0	79.9	52.8	56.2
Full-time	N/A	79.0	34.0	35.3
Part-time	N/A	0.9	18.7	20.9

Note: EP–Enumerated population; UR–Usual residents (present/absent base)
Source: OPCS Monitor Census 1981, Great Britain, National and Regional Summary (CEN81 CM 57)

from the out-of-season problems of the tourist industry. Further north, too, traditional holiday-making areas on both east and west coasts show up as areas of above-average unemployment, but these are overshadowed by the major unemployment blackspots of the conurbations and old industrial areas (Figure 11.6). In terms both of 1981 rates and changes since 1971, the most severely affected group comprised the steel closure areas, but the endemic loss of manufacturing jobs had widespread effects and helped to produce a widening of the unemployment gap between north and south during the decade, with the West Midlands being placed firmly within the fomer after several decades of relative prosperity.

Household Structure

The study of household characteristics is fraught with definitional problems, relating not just to the population base but also to the definitions of a household and of the size and nature of the housing unit which it occupies. In particular, the description of a housing unit (including room count) in Scotland differs from practice in England and Wales; while a new definition of a household was used in the 1981 census which probably resulted in a reduction of almost 94,000 households in England alone. Moreover, besides the change in overall population base, differences in treatment of students between the two censuses mean a fall of

Figure 11.6: Great Britain: Residence-based Unemployment Rates
1981 (by Local Labour Market Areas)

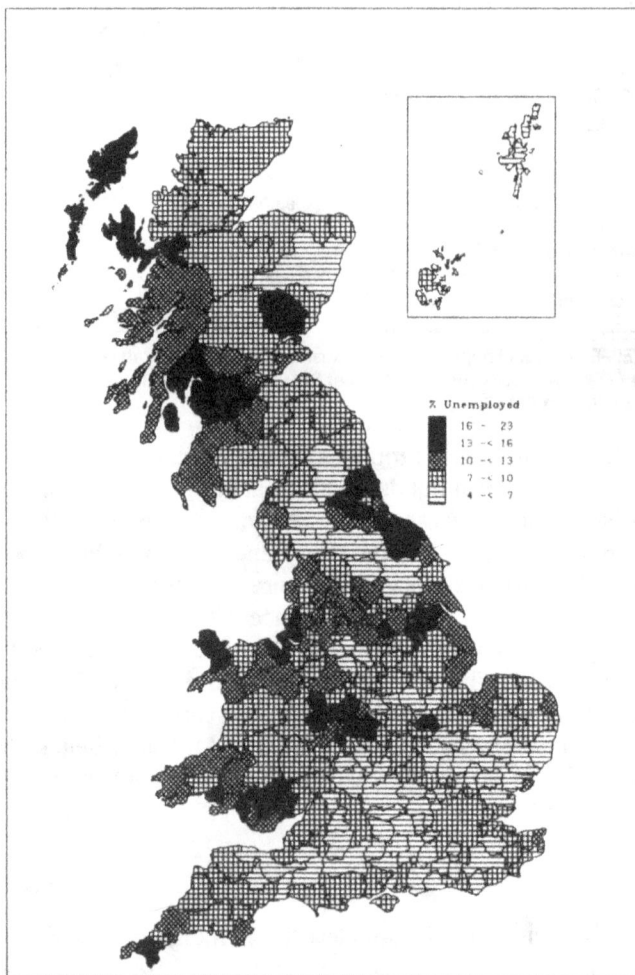

Source: CURDS Functional Regions Factsheet 7

140,000 in the numbers recorded outside private households at
schools and colleges. This section therefore ignores all reference to
density measures and focuses on household size and composition;
but even here trends between 1971 and 1981 must be treated with
caution.

One of the main features of household change between 1971

and 1981 was the fall in average household size. The 1981 census enumerated a total of nearly 19.5 million households in Britain, accommodating around 52.8 million people. This yields an average size of 2.71 persons per household. A direct comparison with 1971 census data shows that over the decade the number of households had increased by 1.3 million or around 7 per cent, while the household population had grown by 0.8 per cent, barely one-tenth as much. In 1971 the average household size had been 2.88 persons, indicating a fall of 6 per cent or — in other words — an increase of 6 per cent in the occupied housing stock without allowing for the effect of overall population growth.

The direct reasons for the reduction in average household size are a fall in the number of very large households and a very marked increase in the number of households comprising only one person. The underlying causes can be traced to lower rates of fertility, the increasing number of elderly, the rising level of divorce or separation, and other forms of household fission including young single people living away from home. According to the General Household Survey, barely a third (35 per cent) of all households in 1981 contained any children under 16 years old, compared with 39 per cent in 1971; while the proportion of one-person households grew from 17 to 22 per cent, with the figure for those aged 60 and over rising from 12 to 15 per cent and with that for other adults up from 5 to 7 per cent.

In geographical terms average household size varies considerably across Britain, generally in line with age structure. By far the smallest household sizes in 1981 were to be found in the traditional retirement areas such as the coastal ones of Eastbourne, Clacton, Worthing, Hastings, Brighton, Torquay and Thanet, all with 2.45 or fewer persons per household. At the other extreme came a number of places with 2.93 or more persons per household: either those experiencing recent in-migration, such as certain new towns, or high-fertility industrial zones such as Merseyside, Teeside and Clydeside. Between 1971 and 1981 all places in Britain, as defined at the Local Labour Market Area level, recorded some decline in average household size, but the fall was generally greater in Britain's largest cities and smallest in free-standing urban regions and rural areas.

Minority Populations

In Britain the last few years have witnessed an upsurge of interest in minority groups — a term which is often used very widely, almost to the extent of including in some guise everyone except the two-parent two-child British-born white family occupying a separate dwelling and with at least the male head of household in employment (even though this stereotype has never formed the majority and is becoming less common). 'Minority groups' can thus include non-whites, those born overseas, single-parent families, households sharing accommodation or essential facilities, the elderly, and the unemployed. For present purposes, however, attention is concentrated on cultural and ethnic minorities.

The 1981 census provides data on the strength of the Welsh language in Wales and Gaelic in Scotland — both indicators of the survival of the original British (Celtic) culture. It found that some 504,000 people living in Wales were able to speak Welsh, around 19 per cent of the whole population. The proportion was highest in the more rural western areas, being 61 per cent in Gwynedd and 46 per cent in Dyfed. The ability of the population of Wales to speak Welsh has fallen at each census date since at least 1921, when it was 37 per cent, with a particularly large drop from 26 to 21 per cent between 1961 and 1971 but with some stabilisation in the last inter-censal period. Considerably fewer people speak Gaelic in Scotland — barely 80,000 or 1.6 per cent — though the proportion is as high as 80 per cent in the Western Isles, 54 per cent in Skye and Lochalsh, and 10 per cent in the Highlands region as a whole. Even in 1921, barely 3 per cent of the Scottish population could speak Gaelic.

The 1981 census is far less helpful in identifying the racial origins of the British population, because questions directly about ethnicity have traditionally been avoided on the grounds of sensitivity and the effects which this would have on the overall response rate. The 1971 census attempted to get round this omission by asking for the parents' birthplace as well as the individual's birthplace, but only the latter was requested in 1981. According to the latter, 3.36 million of Britain's usual residents (present/absent base) had been born outside the United Kingdom some 6.3 per cent of the total. The largest single national group was from the Irish Republic, involving 607,000 or 1.1 per cent. Those born in the New Commonwealth and Pakistan amounted to just over 1.5 million, or 2.8 per cent of Britain's total population, with the largest contributions being from India, the Caribbean, Pakistan and East Africa (Table 11.5).

The fraction of the British population born in the New Commonwealth and Pakistan (NCWP) appears to have risen substantially since 1971, when it was 2.1 per cent. Numerical comparisons are, however, complicated by differences in population base between the two censuses. Moreover, both 1971 and 1981 figures exclude those born to NCWP parents after their move to Britain. The only measure of the total number of people of NCWP extraction that can be derived from the 1981 census relates to the numbers living in private households headed by a person born in the NCWP: nearly 2.2 million or about 4.1 per cent of Britain's household population in 1981.

An alternative source — the Labour Force Survey — provides much more useful information on ethnic origin and correlates it with place of birth. The grossed-up results suggest that 94.8 per cent of Great Britain's 1981 population was white, 2.0 per cent was Indian, Pakistani or Bangladeshi, and 1.0 per cent was West Indian or Guyanese. Of the last two groups, 32 and 47 per cent

Table 11.5: Great Britain: Usually Resident Population 1981 by Country of Birth

Country of birth	Thousand	% total population	% total born outside UK
United Kingdom	50,197	93.7	—
Irish Republic	607	1.1	18.1
Old Commonwealth	153	0.3	4.6
New Commonwealth & Pakistan	1,513	2.8	45.0
India	392	0.7	11.7
Pakistan	188	0.4	5.6
Bangladesh	49	0.1	1.5
Far East	137	0.3	4.1
Mediterranean	130	0.3	3.9
East Africa	197	0.4	5.9
Caribbean	295	0.6	5.8
Other EEC countries	374	0.7	11.1
Other countries in Europe	251	0.5	7.5
Other foreign countries	461	0.9	13.7
Total	53,557	100.0	—
Total from outside UK	3,360	—	100.0

Source: Census 1981, Great Britain, National Summary Part II, Table 51

respectively had been born in the United Kingdom. Note, however, that the overall figures can be questioned because of a relatively large and probably biased 'not stated' figure. Mid-year estimates based on the best available data indicate that the population of NCWP ethnic origin totalled 2,184,000 in mid-1981, 4.0 per cent of the total British population. The comparable figures for mid-1971 were 1,371,000 and 2.5 per cent, giving an increase of around 60 per cent for the decade in contrast to the overall British population change of less than 1 per cent. Of the total increase of 813,000 over the decade, it is calculated that natural increase contributed 448,000 (502,000 births and only 53,000 deaths) compared to 363,000 extra due to net immigration.

The census gives the most reliable indication of the localised distribution of this minority group, though subject to all the definitional limitations. The pattern of NCWP-born persons in 1981 was highly skewed towards a few major cities in the main axial belt of England (Figure 11.7). In 1981 only 34 of Britain's 281 Local Labour Market Areas had a location quotient of more than 1.0, that is had more than the national average proportion of 2.83 per cent. London and Leicester had almost three times this level, while Bradford, Slough, Birmingham and Smethwick had over twice the national average. These six places accounted for 55 per cent of all NCWP-born people enumerated by the 1981 census.

Conclusions

The 1981 census of population has therefore confirmed the existence of a number of trends which other sources were indicating during the 1970s and early 1980s, such as the slowdown in the rate of overall population growth, the increase in the proportion of the elderly, the continued fall in the average size of household and the massive rise in unemployment. At the same time, it has the advantages of providing more accurate information than is normally available from the other sources and giving a great deal more geographical detail. In this latter respect, particularly notable are the acceleration of population growth rates for smaller cities and more rural areas at considerable distances from the major urban centres, the distinctiveness of industrial conurbations outside southern England in terms of their high unemployment

Figure 11.7: Great Britain: New Commonwealth and Pakistan
Immigrants 1981 (by Local Labour Market Area)

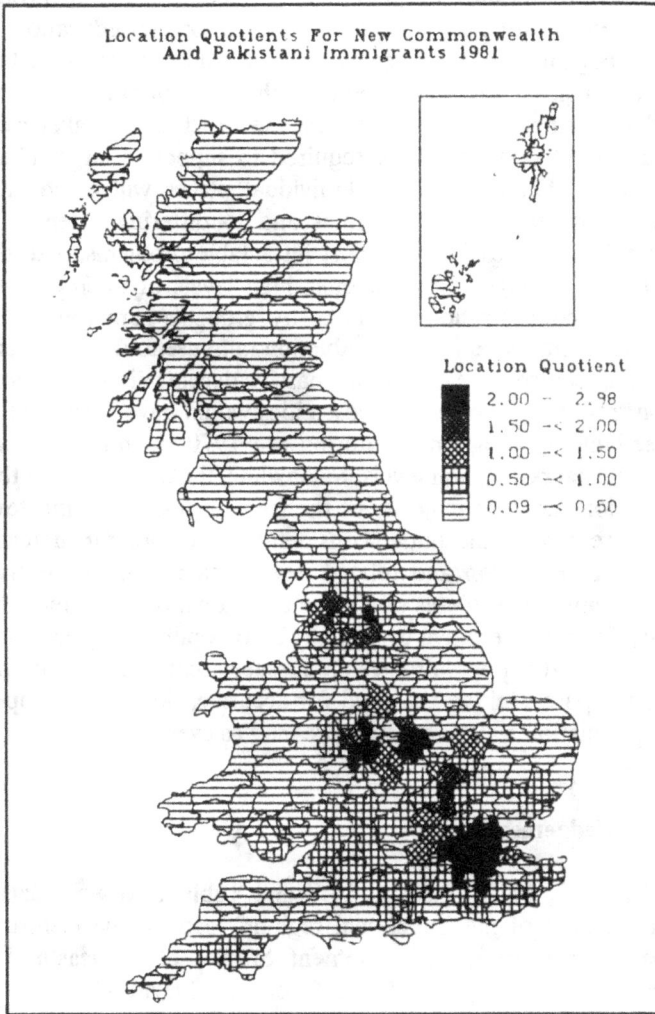

Location Quotients For New Commonwealth And Pakistani Immigrants 1981

Location Quotient
2.00 – 2.98
1.50 –< 2.00
1.00 –< 1.50
0.50 –< 1.00
0.09 –< 0.50

Source: CURDS Functional Regions Factsheet 12

rates, and the continued concentration in a few large cities of those
born in the New Commonwealth and Pakistan.

Both the nationwide trends and the more localised contrasts
hold important implications for Britain's future and are the source

of major concern amongst the nation's policy-makers. At the national level, attention is focused principally on the decline in number of births since the mid 1960s, which have already brought lower demand for places in primary and secondary education and is now beginning to affect entry rates into the labour force. Over the next half-century the ageing of the baby-boom cohorts will produce further problems, not least the fact that a smaller work-force than at present will be required to support a larger elderly population (Ermisch, 1983). Individual places will come under these pressures at different times and to differing extents. The main urban centres face the most intractable problems, with their net loss of younger families, their high levels of unemployment and their concentrations of minority groups (Cameron, 1980). Whether their above-average reduction in household size is merely the effect or also the cause of the massive decentralisation of population from the major cities, these cities would have required huge house-building programmes during the 1970s in order to retain their original population levels. Meanwhile, the outer parts of these city regions and the majority of the freestanding cities and towns elsewhere have come under considerable pressure for increasing housing construction and related development, which are giving rise to planning problems of a more traditional nature (Herington, 1984). Despite the move to virtually zero population growth since the early 1970s, population-related issues seem as important now as in the past, making the need for accurate, detailed and up-to-date population statistics just as pressing as ever.

Acknowledgements

Figures 11.3, 11.5, 11.6 and 11.7 and Table 11.6 were derived with the help of the 'functional regions' team at the Centre for Urban and Regional Development Studies at Newcastle University, which comprises Mike Coombes, David Owen, Anne Green, Andy Gillespie, Martin Charlton, Stan Openshaw, David Ellin, John Goddard and Tony Champion. Tony Champion was responsible for the various analyses, except for Figure 11.6 (Mike Coombes) and Figure 11.7 (David Ellin). The 'functional regions' maps were drawn using GIMMS. The other illustrations are based on official sources: the 1981 census, unless stated otherwise. Eric Quenet drew Figures 11.1, 11.3 and 11.4, and Olive Teasdale

Figure 11.2. Figure 11.2 is reproduced from J.B. Goddard and A.G. Champion (eds) *The Urban and Regional Transformation of Britain*, Methuen, 1983, by permission of the publishers.

References

Cameron G.C. (ed.) (1980) *The Future of the British Conurbations*, Longman, London

Champion, A.G. (1976) 'Evolving patterns of population distribution in England and Wales 1951–71', *Transactions, Institute of British Geographers*, NS 1, 401–20

Champion, A.G. (1981) 'Urban-rural contrasts in Britain's population change 1961–71' in A. Findlay (ed.), *Recent National Population Change*, IBG, London, pp. 5–21

Champion, A.G. (1984) 'Age structure 1981', *Functional Regions Factsheet, 10*, Centre for Urban and Regional Development Studies, Newcastle upon Tyne

Champion, A.G., Coombes, M.G. and Openshaw, S. (1983) 'A new definition of cities', *Town and Country Planning, 52*, 305–8

Craig, J. (1983) 'The growth of the elderly population', *Population Trends, 25*, 21–9

Dewdney, J. (1985) *The UK Census of 1981* (Catmog Series, 43) Geobooks, Norwich

Ermisch, J.F. (1983) *The Political Economy of Demographic Change*, Heinemann, London

Herington, J. (1984) *The Outer City*, Harper & Row, London

Lawton, R. (1977) 'People and work' in J.W. House (ed.), *The UK Space*, Weidenfeld & Nicolson, London, pp. 109–213

OPCS (1981a) 'The first results of the 1981 Census of England and Wales', *Population Trends, 25*, 21–9

OPCS (1981b) *Census 1981, Preliminary Report, England and Wales*, HMSO, London

OPCS (1981c) *Census 1981, Preliminary Report for Towns*, England and Wales, HMSO, London

OPCS (1982) 'Recent population growth and the effect of the decline in births', *Population Trends, 27*, 18–24

OPCS (1983) 'Population definitions', *Population Trends, 33*, 21–25

Randolph, W. and Robert, S. (1981) 'Population redistribution in Great Britain', *Town and Country Planning, 50*, 227–31

Rhind, D. (ed.) (1983), *A Census User's Handbook*, Methuen, London

Warnes, A.M. and Law, C.M. (1984) 'The elderly population of Great Britain: locational trends and policy implications', *Transactions, Institute of British Geographers*, NS 9, 37–59

Appendix 11.1: Census Coverage 1981

As in previous British censuses, the questions were divided into those to which the answers were easy to process and those to which the answers were most difficult and expensive to process, with the former available at the 100 per cent level and the latter generally restricted to a 10 per cent sample. The 100-per-cent items were, for *persons*: date of birth (age), sex, marital status, whereabouts on census night, usual address, usual address one year ago, country of birth, Welsh language (for forms in Wales), Gaelic language (for forms in Scotland), economic activity last week, and employment status; and for *households*: nature of accommodation and sharing, number of rooms, tenure, amenities, and availability of cars and vans. The 10 per cent items were: relationship (household/family composition), name and business of employer (industry), occupation, address of place of work, means of daily journey to work, and higher qualifications. The questions were substantially the same for all three constituent countries of Great Britain, except for the Welsh and Gaelic language questions noted above and except for a different set of questions and definitions for the household section in the Scottish form.

It should not be assumed that the census provides a completely accurate statement of Britain's population and its characteristics. While the 10 per cent data are naturally affected by sampling error, inaccuracies also arise in both 10 per cent and 100 per cent data because of enumeration problems and poor form-filling. An extensive post-enumeration survey in England and Wales suggested that as many as 296,000 people may have been overlooked by the census while another 83,000 may have been double-counted, making an estimated net under-enumeration of 214,000 or 0.45 per cent. The post enumeration survey also found a high gross error rate for several questions, amounting to 29 per cent for number of rooms, 8 per cent for economic position, 10 per cent for employment status, and 9 per cent for means of travel to work — though the net error rate was considerably lower because certain of the individual errors tended, in aggregate, to cancel one another out. Errors are also likely to have occurred in the subsequent coding and processing stages, and indeed it is known that the overall count for England and Wales has been artificially inflated by the figure of some 100,000 persons as a result of the miscoding of certain 'absent' persons as present.

12 THE COURSE OF FUTURE CHANGE IN EUROPEAN POPULATIONS

Allan Findlay and Paul White

Introduction

Discussion in this volume has been concentrated on demographic developments in certain Western European countries during the 1970s, with that time period extended to the early 1980s for those countries, such as France, where the census was taken late and those, such as Denmark and West Germany, where annual data are particularly useful. Looking back on the period considered, it is easy to characterise it as one of considerable change. Put in its simplest terms, over much of Western Europe natural population increase has halted, internal migration patterns have been reversed, and international flows have been transformed in composition.

In practice many of these changes can be shown to have their roots in developments during the 1960s; for example, it was in 1964 that the more sensitive of the measures of population fertility started to show a downward trend from the predominantly elevated fertility levels that had up to then characterised the post-war period. However, it was during the 1970s that demographic 'innovators' — whether in terms of family limitation, urban-to-rural residential movement or return flow from northern to southern Europe — ceased to be pioneers and were joined by large numbers of other people. The initial changes of the 1960s became patterns of transformation of the 1970s. And those transformations have considerable implications for the future population geography of Western Europe and, through the role of demography, for economic, social and political futures as a whole. This chapter will consider whether change in the most significant population parameters is likely to continue over the next 20–30 years in the ways that have been established in the recent past. First, however, it is useful to summarise some of the main recent trends as shown in the earlier chapters of this book.

Fertility has declined everywhere since the early 1960s and is now at or below replacement level in most Western European countries. By the early 1980s total period fertility rates estimating likely completed family sizes were below the critical 2.1 replacement value everywhere except in Eire (3.2), Spain (2.6), Portugal (2.5) and Greece (2.3). The lowest rates of all were in West Germany (1.4), Denmark (1.4) and Luxembourg (1.5). Figures of net reproduction rates tell a similar story (Council for Europe, 1983). Mortality rates have generally also been falling, though not as rapidly as the decline in fertility. The results have been reductions in rates of population increase. Except in the more peripheral areas of the continent, the population total of Western Europe is now largely static.

Changes in fertility are closely tied up with changes in household structures and size, changes in the role of women in the economy and the family, and changes in attitudes to the traditional norms of demographic behaviour. Everywhere except in the poorest regions there has been a strong movement of women into the labour force, and it is notable that such movement has been concentrated in the employment sectors that hold the greatest long-term prospect of growth — tertiary and quaternary employment in particular. In many countries — albeit only to a very limited extent in southern Europe and in Eire — recent years have seen a marked decline in the importance of marriage as an institution though this tendency can easily be over-emphasised (Calot and Blayo, 1982): the evidence is that many of the unmarried unions now occurring are as stable as married ones (Nilsson, 1985; Anon., 1983). The greatest significance of this trend may in fact lie in its demonstration of the continuation of long-term processes of secularisation which are doubtless partly responsible for the reduction in fertility.

Over much of Western Europe, the last 15 years or so have seen the aggregate effects of a process of counterurbanisation. The 1980—82 census round gives general verification of the counterurbanisation trends which were first recorded in the early 1970s. Spatial patterns of population growth, whether in northern Italy, central France or southern Germany, all show a trend towards decentralisation from the biggest, oldest and most industrial conurbations, with real growth occurring in smaller urban centres at lower levels in the settlement hierarchy. It is important here to note the significance of low overall population growth. In the past, internal migration within Western European countries has largely redistributed population growth. Now, in a situation of overall population stability, internal migration flows rob some regions to give to others. The phenomenon of population decline in the big cities has become almost universal in northern Europe as a result of this population redistribution (Drewe, 1983; White, 1984). Chapter 3 revealed an apparent halt to counterurbanisation in the Scandinavian states in the early 1980s. The 1980s census round also indicates the wide spectrum of mobility trends evident in Europe, with net urbanisation still occurring in the Iberian states. Overall inter-regional mobility has been reduced over recent years in several countries (Stillwell, 1985; Drewe, 1985; Courgeau and Pumain, 1984); whether this is a result of the expected influences of the final stages of Zelinsky's (1971) mobility transition (increased information flow replacing flows of people) or whether this has been brought about by economic stagnation is a point for debate.

On an international comparative scale, it is apparent that counterurbanisation has been much less operative in southern Europe simply because there population growth has continued to occur such that out-moves from city regions are still to some extent balanced by new arrivals, whereas in northern Europe the flow of those new arrivals has been cut back. Such an interpretation would certainly be analogous to the conclusions of those researching in rural environments, where population growth has been seen to be highly localised and the result of new inflows rather than the stopping of traditional outflows (Grafton, 1982). In the debate on counterurbanisation, it is also too easy to accept regional level data and to forget that at the level of individual settlements absolute population decline is still common in rural areas.

The final set of recent trends concerns international movement. Here, once again, a distinction is needed between southern and northern Europe. Despite the existence of large-scale return migration flows it could not be said, as with counterurbanisation, that net movements have been reversed. Rather, international labour moves have tended towards a position of balance resulting from international exchanges of population rather than population flows with a net redistributional effect. The returnees have been balanced by new flows of dependants and by newly-developing flows of high-level labour (Salt, 1984). The most significant demographic implication of change during the 1970s might thus be seen as the transformation of the composition of international flows.

The Next 20 Years

The task of predicting the future course of population change is one that is rarely attempted on any large scale; the work presided over by Maurice Kirk for the Council of Europe (Kirk, 1981) is a notable exception. Most national planning or census agencies make population projections on the basis of existing trends, some of these involving plausible assumptions about future changes in some of the vital rates involved (see Chapter 8 for a discussion of this topic for West Germany). The greatest uncertainty and differences of opinion surround projections of fertility rates, while greater agreement exists concerning the future course of mortality rates. In many ways qualitative forecasts of population composition are as necessary as quantitative projections of size, even though the former are much more difficult to produce and defend. In seeking to outline possible population trends much of what follows in this chapter is therefore inherently speculative and hesitant.

Certain things can, however, be said with some confidence. For example, the labour forces of West European countries for the year 2000 have already been born and, given the low likelihood of large-scale international migration, are already living in the countries where they will be seeking employment. Since projections of the further age distribution of those already born are subject to only a very limited range resulting from minor variations in mortality rates, the number of persons moving into the elderly age categories in countries such as the United Kingdom can also be estimated relatively accurately, with all the implications this has for pension schemes and other forms of social provision (Hubbard, 1983). Across Europe as a whole the proportion of the population aged over 65 years is projected at between 17 and 18 per cent by the year 2000, but might exceed 40 per cent by the year 2050 according to Bourgeois-Pichat (1981).

Projections of absolute population sizes for the next 15 years must make assumptions about fertility levels, a task which is far from easy even although it is almost impossible to imagine a rapid return to higher fertility across the continent as a whole. Even if the most draconian pro-natalist policies were introduced — which in itself seems unlikely — Eastern European experience suggests that little real change in fertility practices would occur (Frejka, 1983).

Table 12.1 provides certain data on population projections for the year 2000 as derived by the European Community's statistical service, Eurostat. Varying assumptions about the level of fertility are, of course, crucial. For example, Norwegian government statisticians have made three projections for the year 2025. If fertility rose to replacement level (total fertility rate of 2.1) by 1992, the total population of Norway in 2025 would be 4.9 million; if fertility stayed at its 1981 level (TFR = 1.7), the 2025 population would be 4.4 million; if fertility continued to fall to the lowest levels so far recorded in Western Europe (1.4), then the final population would be 4.1 million (Council of Europe, 1983). The variation in these projections is of the order of 20 per cent.

Despite the massive efforts of demographers there is still inadequate understanding of the causal links in the chain from external factors to decisions on family size; nor is there any real agreement on what those external factors might be. It is therefore impossible to model the economic and social circumstances that might give rise to increased fertility levels, although surveys have suggested that recent reductions in fertility have markedly reduced the numbers of unwanted children born (Leridon, 1985) so that in the future it may prove possible to model fertility more satisfactorily as a result of this elimination of the chance element.

In practice it is therefore most plausible to assume continuing

Table 12.1: Projected West European Populations 2000

	Population 1981 (millions)	Projected population 2000 (millions)	Per cent change 1981–2000
Belgium	9.8	9.9	+1.0
Denmark	5.1	4.9	−3.9
Eire	3.5	4.1	+17.1
France	53.8	58.5	+8.7
West Germany	61.7	59.1	−4.2
Greece	9.7	10.4	+7.4
Italy	56.6	57.9	+2.3
Netherlands	14.2	15.6	+9.9
Portugal	9.9	11.5	+16.2
Spain	37.5	43.3	+15.5
United Kingdom	56.0	57.9	+3.4

Source: Eurostat, 1985

low fertility levels in the short and medium terms, and this assumption strongly influences the projections shown in Table 12.1, except in countries such as Eire, Portugal and Spain where fertility is still high and might be expected to fall steadily over the coming years. The projections of Table 12.1 all depend on assumptions of mortality remaining as at present or ameliorating only slightly. Trends in levels of disease-specific mortality have, however, always varied greatly from disease to disease: in France, for example, mortality from cardiovascular disease has recently been declining but that from various types of cancer has been stable (Vallin, 1983). If, for example, a cure for certain types of cancer were found in the near future, assumptions of stable mortality rates would have to be revised.

Lower fertility rates imply smaller household sizes and the continuation into the future of this reduction; however, this does not imply a similar reduction in housing demand — instead, the reverse may be the case. Low fertility is associated with an increasing rate of female participation in the labour force. The future of this trend will inevitably depend on both macro- and micro-scale developments in the employment situation. If, as is possible, the best employment opportunities continue to develop in conjunction with economic and industrial deconcentration, then female activity rates may continue to rise in rural regions to the levels that have traditionally applied in urban areas. In the process of de-industrialisation in these urban centres recent experience in Britain and France has shown that it is often male jobs that are lost whilst replacement jobs, encouraged by governmental initiatives, are often most attractive to a female work-force: thus unemployed steel workers stay at home while their wives take part-time jobs in the tertiary sector. Such a scenario implies the continuation of low fertility, the diffusion of low-fertility behaviour into more rural areas — rural-urban fertility differentials seem to be still of importance in both France and Italy, for example — and perhaps more profound changes in social norms, household formation and patterns of nuptiality.

One of the most profound unknowns in the projection of fertility and thus of total population concerns the behaviour of immigrant populations. The projection quoted in Chapter 8 for West Germany is based on the assumption that immigrant fertility will fall steadily over the period considered. This is not, however, the only plausible assumption. It might be equally plausible, for example, to expect the fertility levels of Islamic minorities (amongst whom there is greatest adherence to traditional norms for female and familial behaviour) to remain elevated. Both Woods (1977) and Coleman (1983) have shown the existence and significance of fertility differentials between ethnic groups in the United Kingdom, and Coleman has shown how, during the years 1971–6, whilst total fertility of the UK population fell by 25 per cent there was no change at all in the fertility of those from the Indian subcontinent whilst the fertility of the West Indian population fell by 43 per cent to within striking distance of white fertility. Ethnically differentiated fertility also exists in France (see Chapter 7). Those who expect immigrant fertility to fall to the levels shown by the indigenous population can draw their support from recent experience in Vienna (Lichtenberger, 1984, p. 427), or from Switzerland, where the proportion of births to foreigners halved from 32 per cent in 1973 to 17 per cent in 1982, although this in part reflected the maturation process in the age structure of the immigrant community (White, 1985). In neither the case of Vienna nor that of Switzerland, however, were significant numbers of Islamic immigrants involved.

One further set of assumptions that has to be made for population projections concerns levels of international migration. Certainly such migration is now strictly controlled by most countries but, paradoxically, at the same time the progressive enlargement of the European Community is creating a much larger free-market labour area. Although Spanish entry into this free market has now been deferred until 1994 (instead of occurring with that country's accession to Community membership in 1986), the potential of international migration for altering the population balances of a twelve-member European Community is none the less great. In particular, it is quite plausible to see Eire exporting a significant proportion of the high level of population growth it is projected to experience between 1981 and 2000, conditional upon renewed economic growth providing a market for such labour.

However, such renewed growth could well involve a further development of a trend that is already becoming noticeable in the early 1970s: the diffusion of the industrial economy to peripheral areas with, in particular, the aim of utilising the regional labour reserves that exist in southern Europe (Hudson, 1983; Paine, 1979). Such a development would add further to the new spatial division of labour at an international scale and would also enhance the progressive de-industrialisation of the old core economies, creating further local economic and population deconcentration away from the decaying industrial cities. The nature of renewed growth would, of course, be of the greatest importance. If the fifth Kondratieff cycle — of long-period economic growth — is based on microprocessor industries, Hall's (1981) assertion that 'tomorrow's industries are not going to be born in yesterday's regions' may well be proved correct, implying economic growth in 'green-field' regions away from the old cores. And where new industries do locate within or close to old industrial heartlands there is no guarantee that they will bring regional population growth in their wake. Thus despite the publicity given to the 'Silicon Glen' concentration of microprocessor industries in central Scotland, the Scottish electronics industry actually reduced its labour requirement between 1970 and 1984 by 10,000 as a result of increased automation: increased profits and turnover do not necessarily mean more jobs.

The future growth of high technology industry and quaternary activities is likely to create more demands for interchanges of high-level personnel, often facilitated by mobile career structures within multinational corporations, with the benefiting regions being those already marked out as the beneficiaries of the counterurbanisation trends of the 1970s; these trends themselves might be expected to be further enhanced in the future.

If the most likely areas of population growth in the future are likely to be accessible rural regions receiving high-level migrants from both internal and international sources, what will happen to the populations of the declining areas of old economic concentration? Over much of Western Europe the simple answer is polarisation, with gentrification on the one hand and marginalisation on the other. Such a process has been clearly defined by Merlin (in press) in the case of Paris, whilst elements of it have been outlined by Van Amersfoort and De Klerk (in press) for Amsterdam. Over much of Western Europe there is still a dominant cultural norm that stresses the high degree of desirability of residence in the inner city (White, 1984): the result is a rapid rate of gentrification, with property renovation, urban renewal and the replacement of working-class populations with the new middle class employed in quaternary activities still concentrated in the cities (head offices of large corporations, the media, financial organisations and government). The working class and the more economically marginal elements in society — including immigrants, the old, students and the young adults — become concentrated in limited areas which are constantly under the threat of 'improvement' schemes, or in purpose-built social housing estates designed specifically to rehouse those least able to compete on the gentrifying open market.

Crucial to the future of such polarisation will be the behaviour of second-generation immigrants. Polarisation would imply the development of further immigrant segregation, and it has been one conclusion of recent work, for example from Borris *et al.* (1977) in Stuttgart, that intra-urban migration of foreigners leads to greater concentration, although alternative explanations for such a process may exist (Gans, in press). Certainly the importance of migrant selectivity, both in intra-urban and urban-regional migration, will be immense, and it is quite plausible to suggest that there may be selective in-migration of vulnerable groups to deprived areas of cities, accentuating concentrations further (Drewe, 1983).

The appropriateness of this suggestion of polarisation to the countries of southern Europe and to the United Kingdom is more doubtful. In southern Europe, the processes have been identified as being in operation (Golini and Gesano, 1983) but with immigrants as a marginal group being of very little significance. In the United Kingdom, in contrast, the gentrification process, although certainly occurring in parts of London and elsewhere, is of much less importance than on the European mainland: this is the result of the Anglo-Saxon tendency to place a much higher value on peripheral locations than on inner-city residence and access (Claval, 1981).

On a macro-scale, it can be suggested that the next 20 years or so will see not only a redrawing of the map of economic activities in Western Europe through economic decentralisation but also the creation of new regional patterns of demographic segregation. We are already familiar with the existence of developing segregation amongst the old and, given the much enhanced role that the old will play in total populations in the future, this is a phenomenon of considerable importance (Warnes and Law, 1984). In future there may be further demographic segregation, with the cities housing the young adult and the old alongside the new middle class but with very few children. It is the suburban — and, more specifically, counterurbanising — regions that will accommodate those in the family stage of the life cycle and which will produce the only areas of natural growth. Increasing regional differentiation of population by age cohort may therefore be expected to emerge, with some life-cycle increments occurring on a national core-periphery basis rather than merely within the city as happened in the past.

Finally in this set of predictions and forecasts, it is useful to return to a more certain set of statements which link population developments to economy, society and policy. Declining, stable or slow-growth populations at national or regional levels involve significant changes in age-structures. As certain material in the earlier part of this book (for example, Chapters 5 and 8) has stressed, this will have strong implications at the opposite ends of the age range — both for the provision of education and for the care of the elderly. At present public opinion in most Western European countries (with the probable exception of France) seems to be largely unaware of the need for resource redistribution that this will entail. A more useful feature of age-structure change is that the size of the cohorts of young adults entering the labour force will steadily diminish, and in some countries, such as West Germany, there will be periods when withdrawals from the labour force through retirement will exceed new entrants (Chesnais, 1982). This might serve to reduce high levels of structural unemployment, although such an optimistic prediction assumes a higher level of geographical and occupational mobility than has customarily occurred in recent years. On the other hand, the increase in female participation rates might serve to eliminate this feature of labour force stabilisation: for example, at present it is the case that one cause of international variations in unemployment rates is variation in the level of female activity from country to country — the United Kingdom, with a high unemployment rate, has a female activity rate that is above that in several other countries of lower unemployment.

In total the course of population change over the next two or three decades may be expected both to produce and reflect certain profound spatial reorientations of human activity at a variety of scales. On a continental scale, the political balance in the European Community will be altered by the much more rapid population growth of the Mediterranean countries. At a national level, some regions will grow much faster than others and this will produce enhanced demographic segregation: such regions may well be 'new' ones which do not have an industrial legacy. And at more local levels, population changes within regions may well create new patterns of demographic distributions distinguishing areas of growth and decline in both population and economic terms.

Unanswered Questions: A Research Agenda for the Future

Population geographers have taken a great interest in a broad set of themes in Western European population change over recent years. As with all studies of real-world phenomena, the themes considered in great detail have in part been dependent on data availability. Chapters 1 and 2 of this volume showed how there were marked variations in data availability from country to country. Unfortunately, difficulties over data are likely to continue to constrain the types of research questions that will be asked in the near future. In the longer term, there are a number of important topics which must be tackled by survey research if census data do not permit more comprehensive analysis.

The first essential research topic will be continued investigation of the nature of the inter-relationships between fertility and household structures, nuptiality, family units and the labour force. Within this topic considerable stress is needed on the role of women. It is no longer — if it ever was — sufficient to classify households or families by the occupation of the male wage-earner. With two-career households, an increased frequency of divorce and lower nuptiality the use of more disaggregated approaches to the population under study is important. To the population geographer the feature that is going to be of greatest interest and importance is the degree to which changes in this bundle of household-fertility-employment variables will be spatially differentiated, reflecting the location of new employment opportunities or reflecting the local balances between sub-groups. As has been argued above, regional variations in, for example, levels of female economic activity may be dynamic in character during a period of change in the economic basis of national life in many countries.

The second essential research topic for the future relates to the spatial pattern of demographic change *per se* and the components of that change. This, of course, is a research field with a solid recent basis to build on; yet it is arguable that in future a fuller and more rigorous analysis will be needed of the causal relationships affecting population change, particularly in relation to economic influences. These relationships are, of course, two-way so that the rate and type of population change occurring in a region — and in particular the population composition involved — are among the determining factors for future economic changes (Watts, in press). In an era when economic growth, stagnation and decline are likely to affect the individual regional economies of Western Europe in new ways, the economic-demographic systems involved require detailed investigation, including consideration of the feedback processes that are operative. A start has been made (Batey and Madden, 1983), but much more work is needed.

A third research field which may at the outset appear to be more simply descriptive will be the monitoring of changing population distributions, with particular attention being paid to subgroups of the total, defined in a variety of ways using variables such as sex, age, economic activity, ethnicity and so on. In a period of changed differentiation in economic basis, population distributions will be a reflection of the extent and effects of such change, and will, in part, be an index of it.

The fourth research field relates to the driving mechanism of regional demographic differentiation, namely the migration process. Arguably the distinction between inter-regional and international migration, at least within the European Community, will be downgraded in significance, but one aspect of all movement on which much more detailed information is needed is the question of migrant selectivity. It has been a considerable drawback in recent work on, for example, counterurbanisation that insufficient attention has been paid to the characteristics of the migrants involved; in part, this has been the result of poor data sources and a lack of cross-classifications of movers against other variables. This is a gap in research methodology and objectives that needs filling. Another migration research topic of the utmost importance is the analysis of the influence of organisation structures on mobility. With the ever-increasing importance of multi-plant firms and multinational organisations, migration must increasingly be studied within the major economic units within which job moves occur between regions and nations.

Finally, there is the vital question of the futue demographic behaviour of minority groups, such as those created through recent international migration. As has been suggested in the previous sections, two aspects are of the greatest significance: that of fertility behaviour and that of migration. In large part what is needed is an assessment of the extent of what might be called 'demographic assimilation': whether second and subsequent generations behave in ways that reproduce the behaviour of individuals or groups of similar age or status amongst the rest of the population.

Inevitably, the availability of data will be a problem for certain of these topics, whilst for others refinements of existing research methods and models will be needed. New social norms and practices in the household and family arena require new definitions and the consideration of disaggregated data. Whether specific surveys can fill this gap is a problematic issue. Accurate description of disaggregated population distributions requires census-type data that are only available on an infrequent basis. Data on migrant selectivity — virtually entirely lacking in some countries — are nowhere as plentiful, accurate or detailed as might be wished. The identification of minority populations, often a sensitive political matter, is becoming increasingly difficult in many countries, where neither birthplace nor nationality data are satisfactory surrogates for information on ethnicity. The modelling of economic-demographic processes requires copious amounts of continuously-recorded data which in practice are often incomplete.

In overcoming many of these problems population geographers will have to investigate new data sources or methods of research. More use could be made, in many countries, of survey data, whilst the monitoring of population change might encourage co-operation with institutional data-holders such as educational or social services agencies. Certain questions, particularly those involving minority groups, may be best approached by developing humanistic methods of participation and interpretation.

The next 20 years of Western Europe's population evolution are certain to be extremely interesting ones, and the role of population geographers in exploring, describing, analysing, interpreting, explaining and predicting the changes that occur will be of major significance.

References

Anon. (1983) 'Douzième rapport sur la situation démographique de la France', *Population*, *38*, 665–705

Batey, P.W.J. and Madden, M. (1983) 'The modelling of demographic economic change within the context of regional decline', *Socio-Economic Planning Sciences*, *17*, 315-28

Bourgeois-Pichat, J. (1981) 'Recent demographic change in Western Europe: an assessment', *Population and Development Review*, 7, 19–42

Borris, M. *et al.* (1977) *Les Etrangers à Stuttgart*, Editions du CNRS, Paris

Calot, G. and Blayo, C. (1982) 'The recent course of fertility in Western Europe', *Population Studies*, *36*, 349–72

Chesnais, J-C. (1982) 'La baisse de la natalité et ses conséquences pour la planification sectorielle dans les pays capitalistes développés', *Population*, *37*, 1133–58

Claval, P. (1981) *La Logique des Villes: Essai d'Urbanologie*, Litec, Paris

Coleman, D. (1983) 'The demography of ethnic minorities', in K. Kirkwood *et al.* (eds.) *Biosocial Aspects of Ethnic Minorities*, Journal of Biosocial Science Supplement no. 8, 43–87

Council of Europe (1983) *Recent Demographic Developments in the Member States of the Council of Europe*, Council of Europe, Strasbourg

Courgeau, D. and Pumain, D. (1984) 'Baisse de la mobilité residentielle', *Populations et Sociétés*, *179*

Drewe, P. (1983) *Structure and Composition of the Population of Urban Areas 2: Northern and Central Europe*, Council of Europe, Strasbourg

Drewe, P. (1985) 'Model migration schedules in the Netherlands', in G.A. Van der Knaap and P.E. White (eds.) *Contemporary Studies of Migration*, Geo Books, Norwich, pp. 79–89

Eurostat (1985) *Demographic Statistics*, Statistical Office of the European Communities, Luxembourg

Frejka, T. (1983) 'Induced abortion and fertility: a quarter century of experience in Eastern Europe', *Population and Development Review*, 9, 494–520

Gans, P. (in press) 'Intraurban mobility of Turkish families in Kiel' in G. Glebe and J. O'Loughlin, (eds.) *Foreign Minorities in Continental European Cities*, Steiner, Wiesbaden

Golini, A. and Gesano, G. (1983) *Structure and Composition of the Population of Urban Areas 1: Southern Europe*, Council of Europe, Strasbourg

Grafton, D.J. (1982) 'Net migration, outmigration and remote rural areas', *Area*, *14*, 313–18

Hall, P. (1981) 'The geography of the fifth Kondratieff cycle', *New Society*, 55, 535–7

Hubbard, D. (1983) *Population Trends in Great Britain: Their Policy Implications*, Simon Population Trust, London

Hudson, R. (1983) 'Regional labour reserves and industrialisation in the EEC', *Area*, 15, 223–30

Kirk, M. (1981) *Demographic and Social Change in Europe: 1975–2000*, Liverpool University Press, Liverpool

Leridon, H. (1985) 'La baisse de la fécondité depuis 1965: moins d'enfants désirés et moins de grossesses non désirés', *Population*, 40, 507–25

Lichtenberger, E. (1984) *Gastarbeiter: Leben in Zwei Gesellschaften*, Böhlau, Vienna

Merlin, P. (in press) 'Housing policies in the inner city and the development of ghettos of marginal groups: the example of Paris' in G. Heinritz and E. Lichtenberger (eds.), *The Crisis of the City and the Take-Off of Suburbia*, Münchner Geographische Hefte, Munich

Nilsson, T. (1985) 'Les Ménages en Suède, 1960–1980', *Population*, 40, 223–47

Paine, S. (1979) 'Replacement of the West European migrant labour system by investment in the European periphery', in Seers, D., Schaffer, B. and M-L Kiljunen (eds.), *Underdeveloped Europe: Studies in Core-Periphery Relations*, Harvester, Hassocks, pp. 65–96

Salt, J. (1984) 'High-level manpower movements in north-west Europe and the role of careers', *International Migration Review, 17,* 633–52

Stillwell, J.C.H. (1985) 'Migration between metropolitan and non-metropolitan regions in the UK' in G.A. Van der Knaap and P.E. White, (eds.), *Contemporary Studies in Migration,* Geo Books, Norwich, pp. 7–25

Vallin, J. (1983) 'Tendances récentes de la mortalité française', *Population, 38,* 77–105

Van Amersfoort, J.M.M. and De Klerk, L. (in press) 'The dynamics of immigrant settlement: Turks and Moroccans in Amsterdam, 1973–1982' in G. Glebe and J. O'Loughlin (eds.) *Foreign Minorities in Continental European Cities,* Steiner, Wiesbaden

Warnes, A.M. and Law, C.M. (1984) 'The elderly population of Great Britain: location trends and policy implications', *Transactions, Institute of British Geographers, 9,* 37–59

Watts, H.D. (in press) *Industrial Geography,* Longman, London

White, P.E. (1984) *The West European City: A Social Geography,* Longman, London

White, P.E. (1985) 'Switzerland: from migrant rotation to migrant communities', *Geography, 70,* 168–71

Woods, R.I. (1977) 'A note on the future demographic structure of the coloured population of Birmingham, England', *Journal of Biosocial Science, 9,* 239–50

Zelinsky, W. (1971) 'The hypothesis of the mobility transition', *Geographical Review, 61,* 219–49

NOTES ON CONTRIBUTORS

Jürgen Bähr, Geographical Institute, University of Kiel, Federal Republic of Germany

Tony Champion, Department of Geography, University of Newcastle upon Tyne, England

Yvonne Court, Department of Geography, Portsmouth Polytechnic, England

John Coward, Department of Environmental Studies, University of Ulster at Coleraine, Northern Ireland

John Dewdney, Department of Geography, University of Durham, England

Anthony Fielding, School of Social Sciences, University of Sussex, Brighton, England

Allan Findlay, Department of Geography, University of Glasgow, Scotland

Paul Gans, Geographical Institute, University of Kiel, Federal Republic of Germany

Ray Hall, Department of Geography and Earth Science, Queen Mary College, University of London, England

Russell King, Department of Geography, University of Leicester, England

Philip Ogden, Department of Geography, Queen Mary College, University of London, England

Paul White, Department of Geography, University of Sheffield, England

Hilary Winchester, Department of Geographical Sciences, Plymouth Polytechnic, England

INDEX

age and sex structure 9, 82, 105-6, 121-2, 136-7, 146-7, 164-5, 166-7, 196, 219-21, 236, 242
ageing 26-7, 82-3, 86, 218-19, 230, 242
Amsterdam 240
Angola 59, 187, 203
Austria, census 3, 4, 7, 10, 11, 12, 13
  counterurbanisation 40, 41, 43
  deindustrialisation 57
  economic growth 52, 53
  guestworker system 66, 75, 77
  internal migration 12, 13, 39, 43
  international migration 66, 69, 71, 72, 75-6
  refugees 58
  unemployment 55
  see also Vienna

Belgium, census 3, 4, 7, 8, 11, 13
  counterurbanisation 40-2, 43-4
  deindustrialisation 57
  economic growth 52, 53
  female activity rate 31
  households 20, 22, 28
  internal migration 14, 43-4
  international migration 50, 67-8, 71, 75-6
  population projection 237
  racial tension 61
  registration data 14, 50
  unemployment 55
  see also Brussels
birthplace data 7, 8, 12
Brussels 28

census underenumeration 5-7, 134-5, 232
censuses 1-16, 19, 20, 102-4, 112, 119, 134, 143, 208, 231-2
cohabitation 20, 21, 29, 32, 94-5, 145
  see also divorce, marriage
core and periphery 52, 54, 57, 58, 77, 239
counterurbanisation 35-49, 93-4, 111, 112-13, 129, 130, 132-3, 140, 180-1, 215-19, 234-5

decolonisation 59-60, 187, 203

deindustrialisation 57, 77, 238, 240
Denmark, age and sex structure 82-3
  census data 1, 3, 4, 7-8, 10, 11, 13, 19
  cohabitation 94-5
  counterurbanisation 40-1, 42, 44, 93-4
  deindustrialisation 57
  economic growth 53, 87
  employment structure 98-100
  female activity rate 31, 84, 95-8, 99
  fertility 81, 83-5, 234
  households 22, 23, 94-5, 96
  immigrants 88-9
  immigration policies 63, 65, 87
  internal migration 14, 44, 90-4
  international migration 63, 67, 71, 86-9
  labour force 95-8
  mortality 85-7
  population decline 81-3
  population projection 237
  racial tension 61
  registration data 14, 50, 94, 95
  unemployment 55-6
divorce 29, 128-9

economic growth 52-4, 56-7, 58, 77, 156, 239-40, 244
educational attainment 167-8
Eire, age structure 105-7
  census 3, 6, 7, 9, 10, 11, 13, 39, 102-4, 112
  counterurbanisation 40-1, 44-5, 111, 112-13
  economic growth 52-4, 77, 105
  employment 30, 114-15
  female activity rate 31, 115
  fertility 24, 25, 104, 107, 234, 238
  households 22, 23, 25, 26, 27, 30, 32, 115-16
  industrialisation 57, 109
  internal migration 39, 44-5, 109-10
  international migration 63, 69, 74, 105, 107, 239
  marriage 234
  minorities 116-17

natural increase 107-8, 110
net migration 109-11
population growth 104-7, 110,
   117
population projection 237
regional variations 107-11,
   113-14, 115
return migration 105
survey data 114
unemployment 55-6, 114-15
urbanisation 112-13
employment 10-11, 70, 95-100, 114,
   115, 142, 149-51, 167-70, 197-8,
   238, 242, 243
England and Wales, age structure 106
   census 232
   immigrants 5-6
   see also Great Britain, Northern
      Ireland, United Kingdom
ethnic minorities 74-5, 226-9
   see also immigrants
ethnicity, data on 8
European Community 2, 3, 19, 63,
   239

families 20, 24-7, 166
   extended 30
   reunification by migration 70-1,
      74-5
   see also households
female activity rates 30, 95-8, 115,
   123-5, 168, 222, 234, 238, 242
fertility 24-5, 30-1, 32, 83-5, 104,
   107, 120-1, 144-6, 164, 192-4,
   233-4, 236, 237-9, 243
Finland, census 3, 4, 7-8, 10, 11, 13,
   19-20, 21
   economic growth 53-4, 56
   female activity rate 30-1
   households 19-28 *passim*, 34
   industrialisation 57
   international migration 63, 69-70,
      71
   registration data 14
   unemployment 55, 56
France, age and sex structure 121-2,
   136-7
   census 2, 3, 6, 7, 10, 11, 13,
      19-20, 35, 119, 134-5
   counterurbanisation 35, 36-9, 40,
      41, 129, 130, 132-4, 140, 234
   deindustrialisation 57
   divorce 128-9
   economic growth 52-4, 56

employment 238
female activity rate 30-1, 123-5
fertility 25, 120-1, 238, 239
households 19-29 *passim*, 33,
   126-9, 136
immigrants 6, 60, 62, 134-9, 239
immigration policies 60, 61, 63,
   65, 66
internal migration 36-9, 130-1,
   134
international migration 51, 61-2,
   65, 69, 71, 72, 139, 140
labour force 122-5, 126, 129, 137
mortality 120, 238
population growth 120, 129-31
population policy 139-40
population projection 237
racial tension 60, 61, 65
reference persons 21, 126-7
refugees 58-9
regional variations 38, 121,
   129-31, 138
registration data 14
unemployment 55-6, 125-6
urban populations 28-9, 37-8
   see also Paris
free labour movement 63, 64, 239

Germany, Federal Republic of, age
   structure 146-7
   census, absence of 1, 3, 7, 9, 16,
      143
   cohabitation 145
   counterurbanisation 40-2, 48-9,
      234
   deindustrialisation 57
   economic growth 52-3, 156
   employment structure 142,
      149-51
   female activity rate 31
   fertility 25, 144-6, 234
   households 22, 23, 25, 26, 27,
      142, 150-2
   immigrants 61, 62, 142, 145-6,
      153, 159-61
   immigration policies 63-4, 158-9
   internal migration 40-2, 48-9,
      153-4, 156-7
   international migration 59, 67-9,
      71, 72-3, 77, 156, 158-9
   labour force 148-9, 242
   population growth and decline
      142-4, 153-5
   population projections 146-7, 237

reference persons 21
refugees 59
regional variations 143, 152-5,
    159
registration data 12, 14, 50
unemployment 55-6, 148-9
Great Britain, age and sex structure
    219-21
ageing population 28, 218-19, 230
census 4, 7, 8, 9, 10, 11, 13, 19,
    208, 231-2
counterurbanisation 215-19
employment 238
ethnic minorities 226-9
female activity rate 30-1, 222
fertility 24
households 20, 21, 22, 23, 24, 26,
    27, 28, 30, 34, 223-5
immigrants 8
internal migration 213-15, 216
international migration 105, 211
labour force 222-3
language groups 226
population growth 209-15
regional variations 213-15, 222-3,
    225
survey data 14, 19, 20, 209, 227
unemployment 222-4
see also England and Wales,
    Northern Ireland, United
    Kingdom
Greece, census 3, 4, 7, 10, 11, 13
economic growth 52-4
female activity rate 31
fertility 234
households 22, 28
industrialisation 57
international migration 50, 69-70,
    71, 72, 74, 75
population projection 237
households 10, 18-32, 94-5, 115-16,
    126-9, 136, 142, 150-2, 165-6,
    223-5, 243
head of 5, 18, 19, 20, 32; *see also*
    reference persons
size 18, 21-30, 32, 94, 95, 116,
    127-8, 150-2, 225

Iceland 1
immigrants 5-6, 58-9, 60-1, 62-3, 65,
    66, 70-2, 75-6, 88, 89, 134-9,
    142, 145-6, 153, 159-61, 183,
    238-9, 241, 244-5
see also ethnic minorities

immigration policy 63-6, 72, 78, 87,
    158-9
income data 7-9, 10
Ireland *see* Eire, Northern Ireland
Italy, age and sex structure 164-5,
    166-7
ageing 27, 28, 168
census 2, 3, 4-5, 6, 7, 10, 11, 13,
    19
counterurbanisation 180-1, 234
economic growth 52-3
education 167-8
employment 10, 11, 30, 167-70
family structures 27, 166
female activity rate 31, 168
fertility 25, 164, 238
households 19-28 *passim*, 30, 33,
    165-6
immigrants 183
industrial growth 57
internal migration 40-2, 45-6,
    175-7
international migration 64, 66, 69,
    71, 74, 75, 78, 164, 182, 201
labour force 167-8
population growth 164-5, 170-5
population projection 237
regional variations 25, 45-6,
    163-4, 165, 166-77, 184
registration data 12-14
return migration 182-3
rural depopulation 181, 182
unemployment 55-6, 168-9
urban growth and decline 177-81

Kondratieff cycles 240

labour force 10, 51, 95-100, 122-5,
    126, 129, 137, 148-9, 167-8,
    196-7, 222-3, 236
language data 8, 117, 226
Luxembourg 3, 8, 31, 52, 53, 55, 56,
    57, 67-8, 77, 234

marriage 29, 194, 234
    see also cohabitation
micro-states 2, 63
migration, high-level manpower 71-2,
    75, 240
    internal 11-13, 14, 38, 90-4, 109,
        130-1, 134, 153-4, 156-7,
        175-7, 204-6, 213-15, 216,
        233, 234-5, 244
    international 50-2, 57-79, 86-9,

105, 139, 140, 156, 158-9,
  164, 182-3, 188, 196,
  198-204, 211, 233, 235, 239,
  244
intra-urban 241
net 35-7, 39, 40, 41-2, 43-9,
  69-70, 71-2, 75, 86-7, 109-11,
  175-7, 235
return 56, 62, 69, 71, 72, 74, 77,
  78, 88, 105, 182-3, 187, 196,
  202-3, 235
mortality 32, 85-7, 120, 194, 238
Mozambique 59, 187, 203

nationality data 7, 8-9
Netherlands, census, absence of 1, 3,
  9
  counterurbanisation 40-1, 42
  deindustrialisation 57
  economic growth 52-3
  female activity rate 31
  fertility 25
  households 19, 20, 22-9 *passim*
  immigration policy 59, 65
  internal migration 46
  international migration 67-8,
    70-1, 72, 75
  population projection 237
  registration data 12, 14
  Surinam 59-60, 62
  terrorism 61
  unemployment 55
  see also Amsterdam
Northern Ireland 6-7, 11, 13, 105,
  110
  see also United Kingdom
Norway, census 1, 3, 4, 7-8, 10, 11,
  13
  economic growth 52-4, 57, 66
  immigration policy 63, 64, 65-6
  industrialisation 57
  internal migration 14, 40, 41, 46
  international migration 50, 67-8
  population projection 237
  registration data 14, 50
  unemployment 55

Paris 62, 132-3, 240
population growth and decline 81-2,
  104-8, 110-11, 120-1, 129-31,
  142-4, 153-5, 164-5, 170-5,
  188-90, 192-3, 209-15, 233, 234,
  243-4
population policy 139-40

population projections 81, 146-7,
  236-7
Portugal, age and sex structure 196
  census 3, 7, 10, 11, 13
  decolonisation 187, 203
  economic growth 53-4, 77
  employment structure 197-8
  fertility 192-4, 234, 238
  households 22
  industrialisation 57, 191, 198
  internal migration 39, 40, 41,
    46-7, 204-6
  international migration 6, 62, 69,
    72, 73, 75, 188, 196, 198-204
  labour force 196-7
  marriage 194
  mortality 194
  population growth and decline
    188-90, 192-3
  population projection 237
  regional variations 189-90, 192-3,
    195, 198, 202
  return migration 8, 59, 69, 187,
    196, 202-4, 206
  unemployment 197
  urbanisation 204, 205
racial tension 60, 61, 65
reference persons 20-1, 126-7
  see also households, head of
refugees 58-9
regional variations 107-11, 113-14,
  115, 121, 129-31, 143, 152-5,
  159, 163-4, 165, 166-77, 184,
  189-90, 192-3, 195, 198, 202,
  213-15, 222-3, 225, 241-2
registration data 1, 9, 12-14, 50, 94,
  95, 245
religion, data on 7, 9, 116-17
repatriation schemes 64, 65, 66
rural depopulation 39, 181, 182

socio-economic classes, data on 10,
  123
Spain, census 1, 3, 5, 7, 10, 11, 13
  economic growth 52-4, 56
  fertility 234, 238
  households 22, 23, 28
  industrialisation 57
  internal migration 39, 40, 41, 47
  international migration 6, 50, 69,
    72, 74, 75-6, 78, 239
  population projection 237
  unemployment 55-6
  urbanisation 40, 41, 47

Stuttgart 241
Surinam 59-60, 62, 67, 70
surveys 10, 14-16, 19, 20, 114, 209,
   227, 243, 245
Sweden, census 1, 3, 4, 7, 10, 11, 13,
   19
   cohabitation 21
   counterurbanisation 40, 41, 42
   deindustrialisation 57
   economic growth 53-4
   female activity rate 30
   households 19, 20, 22, 23, 24, 25,
      26
   immigration policy 63, 65
   internal migration 14, 40, 41, 47
   international migration 67-8,
      71-2, 75-6
   racial tension 61
   reference persons 20
   registration data 14
   unemployment 55-6, 61
Switzerland, census 3, 4, 6, 7, 10, 11,
   13, 19
   deindustrialisation 57
   economic growth 52-4
   fertility 239
   households 19-26 *passim*
   immigrants 6, 60, 239
   immigration policy 64, 66, 69
   internal migration 39, 40, 41, 42,
      47-8
   international migration 56, 60, 66,
      69, 71, 72, 75-6, 77
   refugees 58, 59
   unemployment 56, 66

unemployment 54-6, 58, 61, 66, 78,
   114-15, 125-6, 148-9, 197,
   222-4, 242
United Kingdom
   ageing 236
   census 1, 3
   counterurbanisation 40-1, 48
   deindustrialisation 57
   economic growth 52-4
   female activity rate 242
   immigrants 62, 239
   immigration policy 61, 63, 65, 66
   internal migration 39, 40-1, 48
   international migration 67-8, 71,
      72, 74
   population projection 237
   refugees 58, 59
   unemployment 55

urban change 241
   see also England and Wales, Great
      Britain, Northern Ireland
urban change 240-1
urban growth and decline 28-9, 37-8,
   177-81
urbanisation 40, 41, 42, 47, 112-13,
   204, 205, 235

Vienna 62-3, 239

West Germany *see* Germany, Federal
   Republic of

For Product Safety Concerns and Information please contact our EU
representative GPSR@taylorandfrancis.com
Taylor & Francis Verlag GmbH, Kaufingerstraße 24, 80331 München, Germany